Christmas from the Back Side

Christmas from the Back Side

J. ELLSWORTH KALAS

Abingdon Press
NASHVILLE

CHRISTMAS FROM THE BACK SIDE

This book is printed on acid-free, elemental-chlorine–free paper.

Library of Congress Cataloging-in-Publication Data

Kalas, J. Ellsworth, 1923-
Christmas from the back side / J. Ellsworth Kalas.
p. cm.
ISBN 0-687-02706-3 (pbk. : alk. paper)
1. Jesus Christ—Nativity. 2. Christmas. I. Title.

BT315.2.K27 2003
263'.915—dc21

2003007334

Study Guide prepared by John D. Schroeder.

03 04 05 06 07 08 09 10 11 12—10 9 8 7 6 5

MANUFACTURED IN THE UNITED STATES OF AMERICA

To Albin Whitworth,
whose musical genius has blessed untold thousands,
at Christmas, and in every season;
and to Katie and Albin, together,
because there is always room in their inn

CONTENTS

INTRODUCTION

Of course, all of us know the Christmas story. Or do we?

We hear so many conversations during the Advent and Christmas seasons that should make us wonder what Christmas means to the average person in the shopping mall or at the neighborhood Christmas party. "Getting together with friends," one person says. "That's what Christmas is all about." Another says, "Seeing the whole family again. That's what Christmas is all about." Or someone with altruistic vision ventures, "Peace on earth. That's what Christmas is all about."

Mind you, these are all nice ideas, and I applaud them. But they're hardly "what Christmas is all about." There's much more to the Christmas story. *Infinitely* more. But of course as a reader of this book, you aren't "the average person in the shopping mall or at the neighborhood Christmas party." Christmas means enough to you that you're reading a religious book about Christmas, and you may very well be part of a church study group or class. So I venture you know that the basic Christmas story is found in two places in the New Testament: in the first and second chapters of Matthew, and in the first and second chapters of Luke.

But I'd like by this little book to enlarge the familiar borders of the Christmas story. I'd like for us to visit Christmas together from the back side—sometimes by way of a new look at some of the familiar stories, and sometimes by reminding ourselves that the roots of the Christmas story are much deeper than we often realize. And also, we should keep in mind that although the story dates to around two thousand years ago, it is in truth even older than that.

You're getting this book from someone who loves the Christmas story. I've celebrated Christmas through days of war and through the Great Depression, through times with full family and times of family diminished, through times of abundance and times of severe restriction. But always it has been Christmas! The reality of God's love as shown in the gift of Jesus Christ has blessed my life through all of my years, thanks to a home and church that introduced me early to the magnificent story of God's love in Jesus Christ. I wish such a blessing for you, and I pray that its wonder will only increase as the years go by.

J. Ellsworth Kalas

CHAPTER 1

The Scandal of Christmas

GENESIS 3:1-10: Now the serpent was more crafty than any other wild animal that the LORD God had made. He said to the woman, "Did God say, 'You shall not eat from any tree in the garden'?" The woman said to the serpent, "We may eat of the fruit of the trees in the garden; but God said, 'You shall not eat of the fruit of the tree that is in the middle of the garden, nor shall you touch it, or you shall die.' " But the serpent said to the woman, "You will not die; for God knows that when you eat of it your eyes will be opened, and you will be like God, knowing good and evil." So when the woman saw that the tree was good for food, and that it was a delight to the eyes, and that the tree was to be desired to make one wise, she took of its fruit and ate; and she also gave some to her husband, who was with her, and he ate. Then the eyes of both were opened, and they knew that they were naked; and they sewed fig leaves together and made loincloths for themselves.

They heard the sound of the LORD God walking in the garden at the time of the evening breeze, and the man and his wife hid themselves from the presence of the LORD God among the trees of the garden. But the LORD God called to the man, and said to him, "Where are you?" He said, "I heard the sound of you in the garden, and I was afraid, because I was naked; and I hid myself."

Christmas from the Back Side

I'm quite sure my title has offended you. Believe me, I mean no offense nor do I intend to shock. I suppose that sometimes the preacher in me has used a title to shock, but not this time. In truth, my only aim is to give you an honest title. I'm about to say something that needs to be said at Christmastime, something that is not often mentioned.

Christmas began with a scandal. It's easy to avoid this scandal, because the occasion of Christmas itself is bathed in so much loveliness. Think of the pictures, whether graphic or verbal. There's a Baby; what could be lovelier? And a star; of course, that has a heavenward pull. And there are angels singing, and wise men on a quest. The manger itself, if truth be told, was not a pretty place, but our artists through the ages have kindly hidden its distasteful elements in mystical shadows. And besides, in our increasingly urban age, a manger speaks of a simpler, quieter world, so that even its crudeness adds to the mystique of loveliness.

But the church calendar has prepared us for the Christmas scandal, and as a result, so has some of the music related to that calendar. I'm speaking of Advent, the season celebrated in the church since the sixth century. In liturgical churches, the color of Advent is purple, symbolic of repentance. It is in that mood of repentance that earnest Christians over scores of generations have prepared themselves for the celebration of our Lord's coming by reminding themselves of our great need for a Savior. We modern and postmodern Christians don't easily get into that mood. At Christmas, we're planning festivities, and the music around us encourages it. Not just "I Saw Mommy Kissing Santa Claus" and "Jingle Bell Rock," but the festive church music. You may hear "Joy to the World" and "Silent Night" in a shopping mall, but you'll probably not hear "Come, Thou Long-Expected Jesus," or "O Come, O Come, Emmanuel."

That's because we don't face up to the Christmas scandal.

And if we don't comprehend the scandal, we're not likely to get the full, magnificent impact of Christmas. It may well be that one of the reasons so many people have to deal with depression at the Christmas season is because in our cultural patterns, Christmas is so tied to fun, celebration, childhood memories, and a sense of belonging; and because we have so little grounding in the theology of Christmas, we can be quite bereft when these elements are missing. As a result, we're easily susceptible in the Christmas season to feelings of melancholy, loneliness, or depression.

So here's the hard fact. There wouldn't be a Christmas, wouldn't be a need for Christmas, if it weren't for our scandal. Note that I said *our* scandal. Stay with me, and I'll try to tell you what I mean. And if you'll stay with me, I promise to bring you out to a Christmas that has very substantial foundations—the kind of foundations, that is, upon which we can build a thoroughly celebrative Christmas.

There are many ways to tell the story, but the book of Genesis tells it best. In a peculiar, painful sense, it is the Christmas story, though you may be offended to hear me say so.

Genesis tells us that once there was this couple—let's call them Adam and Eve, since that's what the Bible calls them. In truth, we could just as well call them John and Mary, or Lance and Amber, because we know them well. Anyway, they had everything going for them, living as they were in a garden of exquisite beauty and perfection. But they turned their lives into a shambles by disobeying God.

There's a word for what happened to them, and for what they did. It's called *sin,* and that's where the scandal comes in. The human race became a race of sinners.

Now, let me be very clear about this, because most postmodern folks aren't very good at understanding sin; but for that matter, we humans never have been. If we think of sin (and a great many don't; they find the word distasteful and therefore judge it to be outmoded and inappropriate), we generally think of rather lurid, back-street matters. "Sin" brings to mind pictures of drug addiction, pornography shops, criminal conduct, or cheap adulteries. There's some truth in these images, but just enough truth to distract us from the larger, more compelling facts.

This is because sin is a problem all of us have to deal with. It's a fact of life for *all* of our lives. You see, the basic sin is *disobeying God.* The ways in which we disobey God may be crude or sophisticated, naïve or knowing, but the root issue is the same. To be specific, it's the issue of *self;* and the reason it's so complicated is that we have to *live* with self, and self is so familiar that it doesn't really frighten us. S*elf* is also complicated because we need a right view of self in order to survive. But if that view becomes distorted, or all-consuming, it destroys us. I think only the saints know how to live effectively with this issue called self, and I suspect they'd tell you that they have to keep alert to the issue every hour, else they'll be seduced into troublesome ways.

So there we have it. Sin is our problem, and it's related to that human essential called self. Every generation has found ways to excuse its sins, but our generation has raised this skill to a particularly high level. We have euphemisms for sin that take away its sting. We identify sin as a personality disorder, a genetic predisposition, a problem in our genetic code, a pattern of antisocial conduct. Or, at a simpler, everyday level, our synonym for sin is *mistake.* Do you realize how often we hear persons guilty of everything, from corporate fraud to child abuse or murder, offer explanation by saying, "I made a terrible *mistake*"? We find it very hard to describe our conduct for what it is. That is, we hate to admit that we are *sinners*—or, to put it another way, to confess that we're part of a scandal. The human scandal.

Incidentally, isn't it interesting that we sometimes identify newspapers as "scandal sheets"? Why? Because they tell us about some of the particular acts of sin that are going on in our world. Mind you, they rarely get at our deeper problem, nor do they often compel us to face some of the hidden sins that affect the lives of even model citizens. But it is quite true that when the newspapers report on the world in which we live—a world of war, poverty, rape, murder, fraud, slander—we call them *scandal* sheets. And the term is well chosen, because this is what we're dealing with—the scandal of our human condition.

But let me bring the matter closer to home, because probably not many of us feel very scandalous at this moment. We may well have some chapters in our lives that we wish we could forget, and certainly some thoughts that we'd rather were not broadcast in the late-night news. But because I've used such a strong word, *scandal,* we may think sin relates more to others than to ourselves. So hear me. When we live below our best potential, when we're mediocre when we ought to be fine, cheap when we ought to be noble, shoddy when we should be upright—this is sin. When we're anything less than *godly,* it's because we're involved in this scandal called sin.

Now what makes our human scandal even worse is the way we deal with it. I refer us once again to the story in Genesis 3 because the experience related there sounds so much like our own. By their sin, Adam and Eve felt guilty before God. Good sense would suggest that they therefore should have sought God's forgiveness, in order to get back on the right track. Instead, the Bible tells us, they "hid themselves from the presence of the LORD God among the trees of the garden" (Genesis 3:8). The trees of the garden ought to have been instruments for revealing God to them, and for giving them still another reason to appreciate God's blessings. Instead, Adam and Eve used these lovely instruments as a way of hiding from God.

And so do we. Almost any wondrous thing in this world of ours can be turned into a means of holding God at a distance. We absorb ourselves with "the trees of the garden"—family, work, civic activities, sports, politics, music—all of them good things, some of them very good. But we can so easily use these good things the way Adam and Eve used the trees of the garden, to hide ourselves from God—or perhaps more correctly, to distract ourselves from God. All of us know that people flee from God through alcohol, drugs, gambling, pornography, but we aren't as quick to recognize that we may use the good things of life (yes, even some of the best things in life) to hide us from God and from God's demands.

Well, this is a scandal. God has provided a wonderful potential for our human race, and we squander it. Then, to make it worse, we flee from God, and we use God's own gifts of loveliness to hide ourselves from him.

And that's why we need Christmas. Christmas didn't come to our human race because we worked ourselves up to it, or because we evolved to a state of deserving such a favor; Christmas came because we're a scandalous lot. Christmas is, indeed, a Gift, the ultimate Gift, because it is a Gift undeserved and unjustified.

But we try, generally, to avoid these crucial facts about the Christmas story. That's why we don't really "get" Advent. When we sing, in a true Advent hymn, "from our sins and fears release us, let us find our rest in thee," we're inclined to sing it in a detached sort of way, not really applying it to ourselves. Who wants to be told that Christmas happened because there was a scandal, and that we are the obvious inheritors and perpetuators of that scandal?

So let me point out a peculiar and fascinating thing. The *secular* Christmas stories we love best are remarkably true to this original Christmas story, in their own special way. Perhaps the classic Christmas story of the Western world is Charles Dickens's *Christmas Carol*. It's the story, you'll probably remember, of a mean man, Scrooge. See how Dickens describes him: "Oh! But he was a tight-fisted hand at the grindstone, Scrooge! a squeezing, wrenching, grasping, scraping, clutching, covetous old sinner!"

Did you get that? Dickens called Scrooge a *sinner!* And so he was. Scrooge was the quintessential sinner, though he broke no laws and was quite safe from prison. But he was a miserable human being who was all wrapped up in himself (that word, *self,* again!), and who seemed almost to enjoy making other people miserable.

And do you remember how the story ends? Scrooge is converted! Dickens doesn't use that theological term, but that's what happened. So as the story ends, Dickens sums it up this way: "It was always said of [Scrooge], that he knew how to keep Christmas well, if any man alive possessed the knowledge." The man who violated Christmas worst became the man who kept it best. What a conversion!

These days one of the most popular secular Christmas stories comes to us from Dr. Seuss, *How the Grinch Stole Christmas.* Dr. Seuss doesn't get around to Dickens, in calling the Grinch a sinner, but he surely describes him as such—so much so that the term "Grinch" now competes with the name "Scrooge" as the epitome of everything that is bad. But as many of us know, at the end of the story, the Grinch is completely changed (*converted,* though Dr. Seuss wouldn't use such a word), so that every "Who down in Who-ville" has the greatest Christmas ever.

I'm trying to say that our secular Christmas stories can't help saying what the original Christmas story has always said. We human beings have a scandal to deal with, whether our name is Scrooge, Grinch, Adam, Eve, Sally, or Bob. We all need to be converted—to be born again. And that's why we have Christmas.

And of course that's also why we change the style of the words, and often also the melody, when we move from Advent music to the songs of Christmas. Advent songs are so often cast in a minor key, and with slow, deliberate timing. They're the songs of longing and of waiting.

But Christmas music is an entirely different matter. Mind you, it may be quiet and pensive, as is "Silent Night" or "O Little Town of Bethlehem," but if so it is a tranquil quietness; the mood is peace, not longing. And more often than not, the words and music are light and celebrative. Sometimes, in fact, almost raucous, as in one of my favorites:

God rest ye merry, gentlemen, let nothing you dismay,
Remember Christ our Savior was born on Christmas Day;
To save us all from Satan's power when we were gone astray.
O tidings of comfort and joy, comfort and joy;
O tidings of comfort and joy.

Now there's a song to be sung by people of scandal—people who need to be saved from Satan's power, and who realize it, and who now have found the way. This is the good news that turns our scandal into laughter. Tidings, indeed, of comfort and joy! The power of the scandal has been broken. The Savior Christ has come.

CHAPTER 2

Three Votes for an Early Christmas

ISAIAH 9:2-7: The people who walked in darkness / have seen a great light; / those who lived in a land of deep darkness— / on them light has shined. / You have multiplied the nation, / you have increased its joy; / they rejoice before you / as with joy at the harvest, / as people exult when dividing plunder. / For the yoke of their burden, / and the bar across their shoulders, / the rod of their oppressor, / you have broken as on the day of Midian. / For all the boots of the tramping warriors / and all the garments rolled in blood / shall be burned as fuel for the fire. / For a child has been born for us, / a son given to us; / authority rests upon his shoulders; / and he is named / Wonderful Counselor, Mighty God, / Everlasting Father, Prince of Peace. / His authority shall grow continually, / and there shall be endless peace / for the throne of David and his kingdom. / He will establish and uphold it / with justice and with righteousness / from this time onward and forevermore. / The zeal of the LORD of hosts will do this.

MICAH 5:2-5*a*: But you, O Bethlehem of Ephrathah, / who are one of the little clans of Judah, / from you shall come forth for me / one who is to rule in Israel, / whose origin is from of old, / from ancient days. / Therefore he shall give them up until the time / when she who is in labor has brought forth; / then the rest of his kindred shall return / to the people of Israel. / And he shall stand and feed his flock in the strength of the LORD, / in the majesty of the name of the LORD his God. / And they shall live secure, for now he shall be great / to the ends of the earth; / and he shall be the one of peace.

JOB 9:25-33: "My days are swifter than a runner; / they flee away, they see no good. / They go by like skiffs of reed, / like an eagle swooping on the prey. / If I say, 'I will forget my complaint; / I will put off my sad countenance and be of good cheer,' / I become afraid of all my suffering, / for I know you will not hold me innocent. / I shall be condemned; / why then do I labor in vain? / If I wash myself with soap / and cleanse my hands with lye, / yet you will plunge me into filth, / and my own clothes will abhor me. / For he is not a mortal, as I am, / that I might answer him, / that we should come to trial together. / There is no umpire between us, / who might lay his hand on us both."

In my years as a pastor, I did my share of grumbling about the way merchandising seems every year to seek an earlier beginning for the Christmas season. But preachers aren't alone in this complaint. A fair share of the general populace feels the same way. "Any year now," someone says, "I expect to see a Christmas promotion connected with the Fourth of July ads." Even some merchants are uneasy with what is happening. "I like the profits," a businesswoman confides, "but as soon as I get out of my store, I feel a little sad about the whole thing."

So what's my position in all of this discussion? To be honest, in my own way I'm much worse than the merchant, the advertising guru, and the people who develop the mail-order catalogs. I vote for an early Christmas. A *very* early Christmas. I submit that Christmas would mean a great deal more to us if we stretched our thinking to look for the Christmas story in places earlier than the Gospels of Matthew and Luke.

There Was Isaiah

Isaiah would understand what I mean. He was a prophet in Judah over twenty-seven centuries ago, which means that he went about his work some seven centuries before the birth of our Lord. But he got a preview of Christmas, a preview so good that it can help correct and enlarge our perception of Christmas still today.

Isaiah was the patrician among the ancient Jewish prophets. He dated his prophetic call from the year that King Uzziah died, because for him, Uzziah's death was more than just a change in the monarchy: Isaiah had been close enough to the throne that later he would write a biography of the king (see 2 Chronicles 26:22). When Hezekiah, perhaps the greatest of the late kings of Judah, was in power, Isaiah was his spiritual advisor. Being a spiritual advisor in a theocracy meant more than leading morning prayers and making occasional court appearances on religious holidays. By the nature of the nation's historic relationship to God, the spiritual advisor was also a primary advisor on international affairs, since it was especially through their relationships with other nations that the Jews were most likely to violate their commitment to God.

So Isaiah was accustomed to thinking politically, with a natural inclination for seeing the big picture. It isn't surprising that his prophecies so often dealt with a variety of nations, and sometimes with all the peoples of the earth. God generally uses people in ways for which the circumstances of their lives have prepared them, and Isaiah was prepared to spread out his message on a large canvas. He watched his nation go through good times and bad, and with it all, he envisioned an utterly better day. Listen:

> The people who walked in darkness
>   have seen a great light;

> those who lived in a land of deep darkness—
> on them light has shined. (Isaiah 9:2)

And what is this great light?

> For a child has been born for us,
> a son given to us;
> authority rests upon his shoulders;
> and he is named
> Wonderful Counselor, Mighty God,
> Everlasting Father, Prince of Peace. (Isaiah 9:6)

What did Isaiah have in mind? Clearly, he was envisioning more than just any ordinary ascendant to the throne. I think it's quite possible that he, himself, didn't fully grasp what he was saying. If, indeed, the Spirit of God was upon him as he spoke and wrote these words, he may have gotten far beyond his own boundaries of perception. As it happens, twenty centuries of Christians have believed that his words were fulfilled in Jesus, the Christ.

If so, Isaiah got an early start on Christmas. And ironically, we're still scrambling to catch up with his vision. So many things are good about the times in which we live, and I am grateful that I can enjoy them. But even so, our world seems so much of the time to be walking "in darkness," and most of us will acknowledge that we know great numbers of people who live "in a land of deep darkness." A century and a half ago, Henry David Thoreau said, "The mass of men lead lives of quiet desperation." At this moment, as I look out at a body of trees in all of their May loveliness, I find it easy to think that Thoreau was unduly pessimistic. But when I watch the late news this evening, or look at the faces in passing traffic tomorrow, I'll know that Thoreau was right. And I will know that although Christmas has come to our world, it still hasn't come, in any deeply effective way, to vast numbers of people. That is, it hasn't come in the measure that the prophet Isaiah had in mind twenty-seven hundred years ago.

Nearly eight hundred years later, when John set out to tell the story of the first Christmas, he used Isaiah's figure of speech. "What has come into being in him [Christ] was life, and the life was the light of all people. The light shines in the darkness, and the darkness did not overcome it" (John 1:3*b*-5).

Isaiah went on an early Christmas shopping expedition. *Very* early! He knew what the people of his day needed, and as history has demonstrated, the need is the same in every generation. We humans were made for light, and we don't do well shriveled into some place of subterranean darkness.

Isaiah also knew that we needed more than a new political system, even though he couched his story in political terms. As the King James Version put it, "And the government shall be upon his shoulder" (Isaiah 9:6). But it's a government with a high God-content, with results that will go far beyond our usual political platforms. Isaiah is talking about more than jobs and working conditions, food and world trade, significant as these issues are; indeed, he is reaching even into matters of heart and thought.

We humans have always dreamed of a world of such perfection. In truth, it's the kind of dream that keeps our political systems going. Those of us in democracies keep thinking we'll get it in the next election. In other political systems, there's always a ferment, even if deeply submerged, of hopes for some sort of revolution, some overturning of the old order that will make a new world possible. Plato envisioned it with his Republic, the English nobles with their Magna Charta, the Pilgrims with their dream of a city set upon a hill. Every political convention, however flawed it may be, is still informed by something of this wondrous dream of a better political establishment, and, from it, a better world. But of course all these dreams *are* flawed, because those of us who implement them are sinners. We need the One described in Isaiah's vision.

And Then There Was Micah

Micah was a prophet at roughly the same time as Isaiah. The two men were clearly different in so many ways, but they had this in common, that Micah, too, was voting for an early Christmas. We know little about Micah except the town from which he came, and the era in which he prophesied. I suspect this is partly because, unlike Isaiah, he wasn't a politically influential person. We remember him, not for any involvement with kings and empires, but for the words he spoke and wrote. Coming from Moresheth, a quite unpretentious village, Micah dared to begin his message:

> Hear, you peoples, all of you;
> listen, O earth, and all that is in it (Micah 1:2*a*)

And as it turns out, the whole world has, indeed, listened. Especially, it has listened to a particular verse, some three dozen words, that still thrill us more than twenty-five centuries later:

> But you, O Bethlehem of Ephrathah,
> who are one of the little clans of Judah,
> from you shall come forth for me
> one who is to rule in Israel,
> whose origin is from of old,
> from ancient days. (Micah 5:2)

We can only speculate what Micah himself had in mind. Obviously, the little town of Bethlehem was uniquely significant to the Jewish people, because their most revered king, David, had come from there. But now Micah was promising something beyond David, one "whose origin is from of old."

Sometime in the generations after Micah, Jewish scholars laid hold of this verse with hope born of longing. Thus, when the Gospel of Matthew tells how the wise men from the East came to Jerusalem in their search for the newborn king of the Jews, they learned from "the chief priests and scribes"—the major religious scholars—that when the Messiah came, he would be born in Bethlehem; and to make their point, the scholars quoted the words from the prophet Micah (see Matthew 2:1-8). Micah's prophecy came into play again during the course of Jesus' ministry, when some in the crowds said that perhaps Jesus was the Messiah. But others, familiar only with Jesus' boyhood home in Nazareth and not knowing of his birthplace, countered, " 'Has not the scripture said that the Messiah is descended from David and comes from Bethlehem, the village where David lived?' " (John 7:42).

So it is that Micah, the prophet from Moresheth, got a head start on Christmas. And much like Isaiah, Micah's was a head start of some six centuries.

But Also, There Was Job

I think my favorite early celebrant of Christmas was Job. My choice of words is questionable; Job didn't *celebrate* Christmas. But he *wanted* Christmas, and wanted it desperately. And again, I've used a questionable word, because Job didn't know that it was *Christmas* he wanted. Nevertheless, I won't apologize for what I'm saying. I may be putting words in Job's mouth, but I'm not putting ideas there; I'm just giving words to the idea.

Let me say a few words about Job before I go further. We don't really know when Job lived, nor where. The Bible tells us that he lived in the land of Uz, which was probably somewhere in the ancient land of Edom, and that he was "the greatest of all the people of the east" (Job 1:3), and that's as specific as the story gets. We do know, however, that Job's greatness was not simply a matter of his wealth and of his community standing. Above all, he was a truly fine human being, someone of whom God would say, " 'There is no one like him on the earth, a blameless and upright man who fears God and turns away from evil' " (Job 1:8).

In those days, it was widely believed that if you were good, God would bless you; and conversely, if things were going wrong for you, it was evident that you were not good. We still hear a good deal of that kind of thinking in our day. This is behind the question, "Why do bad things happen to good people?" and it's why, when someone enjoys particular good fortune, a friend will jokingly say, "Well, you must be doing something right!"

Being such a good man, Job seemed to live a charmed life. But suddenly it all changed. In a devastating series of tragedies, Job lost his considerable fortune, his seven sons and three daughters, and his health. He took refuge on an ash heap, apparently all that was left of his once-great resources. There he was visited by a small company of friends; we refer to them, sarcastically, as "Job's comforters," because once they began talking, they did nothing to comfort. Rather, they added indignity to Job's consummate pain.

Yet with his fortune, family, and health gone, and with his friends turned against him, the worst was this: Job felt he couldn't get a hearing with God. He sensed, rightly, that the distance between his state and God's was profound; there was no cozy familiarity in Job's religion, even though he was a man of prayer and holiness. And I suspect his present state of loss added to his sense of unworthiness; it's hard to think well of yourself when you're sitting on an ash heap, scraping your boils.

So Job told God of his dilemma:

> "For I know you will not hold me innocent.
> I shall be condemned;
> why then do I labor in vain?" (Job 9:28-29)

In fact, it seemed so hopeless to Job that he saw God as his enemy:

> "If I wash myself with soap
> and cleanse my hands with lye,
> yet you will plunge me into filth,
> and my own clothes will abhor me." (verses 30-31)

Then, having voiced his complaint to God, Job seems to turn to his friends, hoping they will understand his predicament, since they too are human.

> "He is not a man like me that I might answer him,
> that we might confront each other in court.
> If only there were someone to arbitrate between us,
> to lay his hand upon us both." (verses 32-33 NIV)

In truth, Job's request is a pretty hopeless one. He wants a very special kind of mediator, someone with enough standing to lay a hand on God, and understanding enough of our human condition to lay a hand on Job. Job was appealing for Christmas, the event that gives us the One described in the Apostles' Creed as "conceived by the Holy Spirit, / born of the Virgin Mary"—someone, that is, able to lay a hand on God, because he *is* God, and understanding of humanity because he *is* human.

So there you have it, Isaiah, Micah, and Job: three votes for an early Christmas. There are others, of course. Over the centuries, Bible students have found the voices of an early Christmas beginning in Genesis and continuing through much of the Old Testament. Some students of ancient literature see humanity's longing cry *outside* the Bible as well, in widely different documents—not with the clarity one finds in Job's cry, or in the words of Isaiah or Micah, but no less real. So Charles Wesley would describe Jesus in one of his hymns as "hope of all the earth thou art; / dear desire of every nation, / joy of every longing heart" ("Come, Thou Long-Expected Jesus").

I'm very sure that many a twenty-first-century person, driven by just such a "longing heart," is also looking for an early Christmas. Caught up in shopping, greeting cards, and party plans, and knowing how many days it will be until December Twenty-fifth, yet hoping for an early Christmas. And not clearly knowing what it is they're longing for.

Isaiah, Micah, and Job would understand. But they'd surely wonder why someone would still be waiting for Christmas on this side of Bethlehem's manger. After all, Jesus has already come.

CHAPTER 3

Christmas Comes to a Back Fence

LUKE 1:39-45: In those days Mary set out and went with haste to a Judean town in the hill country, where she entered the house of Zechariah and greeted Elizabeth. When Elizabeth heard Mary's greeting, the child leaped in her womb. And Elizabeth was filled with the Holy Spirit and exclaimed with a loud cry, "Blessed are you among women, and blessed is the fruit of your womb. And why has this happened to me, that the mother of my Lord comes to me? For as soon as I heard the sound of your greeting, the child in my womb leaped for joy. And blessed is she who believed that there would be fulfillment of what was spoken to her by the Lord."

Christmas comes at an intersection between that which is sublimely holy and that which is utterly common. It is the ultimate story of God's love for our human race, but it is acted out in a field where shepherds watched their flocks, and in a manger cave near a first-century inn. It is the eternal moment when "the Word became flesh and lived among us" (John 1:14), but it came to pass through a teenage girl from an insignificant village.

And part of it happened at a back fence. Not exactly, but figuratively speaking, a back fence.

I'm trying to say that Christmas shows us that no part of life is unimportant to God, and that none of it is beyond

God's interest. And if that be so, not one of us is beyond God's care and concern. The Christmas story dramatically reveals that God is not a far-distant, inapproachable object of worship, but one who chose to come into our world and live in our midst—and to do so in the most ordinary of circumstances.

So I'd like just now to take us to one of those common settings, a back fence. I reason that if Christmas can come to a back fence, it can come anywhere.

It's a scene from the first chapter of the Gospel of Luke. A girl in the village of Nazareth had received from God the extraordinary message that she would bring forth a Child born under unique circumstances. It was a beautiful message, but a quite overwhelming one—indeed, a frightening one. When this girl, Mary, received the word, she replied, " 'I belong to the Lord, body and soul. . . . Let it happen as you say' " (Luke 1:38 J. B. Phillips). Mary's answer was a classic statement of submission. But it isn't hard to read between the lines. It's obvious that Mary felt as much apprehension as she did joy and anticipation.

What do you do at such a time? When you're caught between unimaginable glory and inexpressible fear, what do you do? You find someone with whom you can talk—someone compassionate enough to listen, and wise enough to understand what you're saying, even to the very beat of your heart. That's what Mary did. The Bible says that she "went with haste to a Judean town in the hill country," to the house where Zechariah and Elizabeth lived (Luke 1:39-40). Mary knew she could tell her story to this much older cousin of hers, Elizabeth, and that Elizabeth would understand.

At certain times in our lives, nothing is as valuable as someone who understands. They may not verbalize their understanding; indeed, they may not know how. In some instances, we'd rather they didn't verbalize it. We're content to have a nod of the head, an embrace, a tear. And if they can also give us words that we can carry away, all the better.

So that day, Christmas came to a back fence. Now mind

you, the birth of Jesus was still nearly nine months away, but as we already know, Christmas was a long time in the making, and this particular portion of the story is at a point when the action is speeding toward its climax, even though we have nearly nine months to wait.

As I alluded to before, I confess that I'm not speaking literally of a back fence. The actual setting may have been a kitchen or a bedroom—or simply the open, large, all-purpose room of a first-century Middle Eastern home. Or it may have been a back courtyard. I'm just trying to say that it was a place where women might comfortably talk. If men had been the key figures, it might have been the village marketplace, or a place where men discussed the issues of their lives while trading for an ox or an ass. But for women in that ancient world—and in the world that many of us have known—it would be a cooking area or a back fence, a place where women might exchange confidences. In our time, in much of the Western world, it's increasingly likely that it would be a lounge area in a place where women work outside the home.

I suspect that at this point someone is wondering how I, a man, dare to venture opinions about woman-talk. It's because I was once a little boy, and little boys get in on a good deal of woman-talk during the early years of their lives; they did, at least, in my generation. I remember playing in a corner of the room while my mother and her friends talked over their coffee. Sometimes they forgot there was a child, or children, playing in the corner. When they realized my presence, my mother would say, "Little pitchers have big ears." I was never quite sure what this meant; I'm not sure yet that I understand that figure of speech. I only know that this signaled that the conversation should change, often to my disappointment. In any event, this is why I have some feeling about talk that goes on in kitchens and over back fences.

It was to such a setting that the glory of God came, in full Christmas splendor. Let me pause momentarily to ponder with you the marvel of this happening. Women are inescapably crucial to the Christmas story. There's Mary, of course, and because of her every woman can walk with a unique sense of dignity. But then there is also Elizabeth—a woman somewhat at the edge of the story, but important as the mother of John the Baptist, and important also as friend, relative, and confidante to Mary.

But you see, all of this happened in an age when women were generally downgraded. Among the documents of the first century, the century in which Christmas came to our planet, archaeologists have found a letter from an Egyptian workman to his wife. They were expecting a baby during his absence from home, so he wrote to his wife, "If it is a boy, keep it. If it is a girl, throw it out" (A. C. Bouquet, *Everyday Life in New Testament Times* [New York: Charles Scribner's Sons, 1954], page 3). Theirs was a brutal world (as is ours, in its own ways), but it was especially brutal to women. Yet the biblical Christmas story, the story of God coming uniquely to our human race, includes, early in its unfolding, *women*—two women who meet to talk in their kitchen or in their courtyard or at a back fence.

Several years ago, Paul Engle, for so many years the distinguished director of the Iowa Writers' Workshop at the University of Iowa, wrote a book about Christmas as he remembered it from his Iowa childhood. It seemed to him, he said, that "the Fourth of July was a man's holiday, loud, defiant, full of risk and explosion." But "Christmas was a woman's holiday, quiet, sharing, full of cheer and generosity." He comments further about the ways women made his early Christmases beautiful, then goes on to say, "Why should Christmas not have been the most womanly of all celebrations? It was a day of praise for woman's most desirable and unique aspect: birth. In the dead season came life" (Paul Engle, *An Old Fashioned Christmas* [New York: Dial Press, 1964], pages 43-44). Some of Dr. Engle's language might be offensive today to both men and women, but perhaps for that very reason we should give it a hearing, because in the long unfolding of our human development and our sensitivity, Christmas has played not only its obvious, direct role, but also some significant indirect roles as well.

Mary had done no more than call out a greeting to Elizabeth when something altogether remarkable happened. See how Luke describes it: "When Elizabeth heard Mary's greeting, the child [that is, the one who would be known as John the Baptist] leaped in her womb" (Luke 1:41). At that time, Elizabeth was in the sixth month of her pregnancy, and when she saw Mary, it was as if the baby in her womb responded with the excitement of holy recognition. The sequel to this scene comes some thirty years later, when John the Baptist, now the compelling wilderness prophet, says as Jesus approaches him, " 'Here is the Lamb of God who takes away the sin of the world!' " (John 1:29).

But now something more happens. Not only does the baby leap in Elizabeth's womb; Elizabeth herself is "filled with the Holy Spirit" (Luke 1:41). We read a good deal about the Holy Spirit in the New Testament, especially in the book of Acts. I'm fascinated to see that the first New Testament report of someone being filled with the Holy Spirit comes from this domestic scene, where two women are soon to compare notes on pregnancy and on the marvel of God's work in their lives. Mind you, I'm fascinated, not because the setting is so extraordinary, but because it reminds me that we ought more often to expect God's Spirit to be manifest in the kitchen, the bedroom, the boardroom, the classroom.

After Elizabeth had poured forth her praise to God, Mary spoke. " 'My soul magnifies the Lord,' " she cried, " 'and my spirit rejoices in God my Savior' " (Luke 1:46-47). Mary's speech, which follows, is often referred to by its Latin, churchly name, The Magnificat. It has inspired music, poems, and paintings. Some students of literature say it is as beautiful a poem as has ever been written. And where did it happen? As woman-talk over a back fence, so to speak.

Christmas, you see, makes any room of life consecrate,

brings a flame to a common bush, transforms a coffeepot into a sacrament.

So Christmas came to the world of the commonplace, the world of back fences and midmorning snacks. We're inclined to isolate it to a world of theology, something to be exposited in a seminary; or a matter of culture, to be sung by a choir. But God *did* it in an everyday place where people talk and cook, where they lay down their jacket when they return from the outdoors.

And God chose to do it with what society would call common people. The late Ernest Fremont Tittle once pointed out that people like Mary and Elizabeth were in that group known as "the quiet in the land." They were far from pretentious in their style of life or their religion. They were devout, but quietly so. They did not have the learning of the scribes or the power of the rulers. "But," Dr. Tittle continues, "these 'quiet' ones were, after all, the real strength of Israel. It was they who provided devout homes such as those of John the Baptist and Jesus, and who kept alive the moral and spiritual insight and the inspiring hopes of prophetic religion" (Ernest Fremont Tittle, *The Gospel According to Luke* [New York: Harper & Brothers, 1951], page 5).

Such persons are, indeed, the strength of a nation. They're also the strength of a church or a community. But don't mistake their quietness for detachment or indifference. I suspect that some of us might too easily classify ourselves among these "quiet ones." They were quiet because their cultural and political systems allowed them no voice. No voice, that is, in the customary human halls of power. It strikes me, however, that they had a substantial voice in the purposes of God.

As these women talked, the Holy Spirit came upon them. They were women in a world where women were expendable. They were powerless in a world that loved power (it always does). They were the kind of people who wouldn't ordinarily stand out in a crowd, except perhaps for the character in their faces. And they had come to an ordinary place—a kitchen, a back fence—to do an ordinary thing—talk. And there at a back fence, the glory of Christmas revealed itself.

But after all, where should we expect God to come into human life? If Christmas had come only to places of prominence, it would be the province of the powerful. And if it had happened only in a designated place of worship, Christmas might seem to be the property of priests or the clergy. I said earlier that Christmas comes at the intersection of the sublimely holy and the utterly common. Well, God supplies the sublimely holy, and we humans provide the utterly common. And lest we complicate the "common" by our attempts to improve on it, God has chosen, it seems, to make the scene so unmistakably common that the point cannot help being clear. God is not limited to the "out there," but has chosen to come among us. Christmas is an event for a crude manger, near a not very impressive first-century hotel, with preliminary scenes in a hillside town, over a back fence. God is not to be shut off in a corner of life—not even an ornately sacred corner; God chooses to be present in any and every scene, with no reluctance to enter our common life.

So if you're wondering where Christmas will happen this year, I'll answer with a question: Where do *you* expect to be? Because Christmas is meant to happen where we are. God enters our ordinary days, our routine patterns—sometimes a back fence, sometimes the world of shared confidences, sometimes the kitchen of a modest home, sometimes the carefully arranged dinner party.

Come to think of it, I may be giving you a warning of sorts. The first Christmas was full of surprises, and there seems no reason to think those surprises have come to an end. It just might be that the Holy Spirit will break in on your life this Christmastime, intersecting some common moment—in a kitchen or bedroom, while in the tedium of commuting, in a visit with a friend. Who can guess where your back fence may be?

CHAPTER 4

Celebrating Christmas in a Hotel

LUKE 2:1-7: In those days a decree went out from Emperor Augustus that all the world should be registered. This was the first registration and was taken while Quirinius was governor of Syria. All went to their own towns to be registered. Joseph also went from the town of Nazareth in Galilee to Judea, to the city of David called Bethlehem, because he was descended from the house and family of David. He went to be registered with Mary, to whom he was engaged and who was expecting a child. While they were there, the time came for her to deliver her child. And she gave birth to her firstborn son and wrapped him in bands of cloth, and laid him in a manger, because there was no place for them in the inn.

When Wilbur and Orville Wright finally achieved their historic airplane flight at Kitty Hawk, North Carolina, one mid-December day in 1903, they sent home a telegram reporting their success. The telegram concluded with the words, "Home Christmas."

Does such a commonplace message seem like an anticlimax for a telegram that announced one of the most revolutionary inventions in human history? Not if you've ever been in doubt about getting home for Christmas! Any of us who have ever sat in an airport, a railroad station, or a bus depot during the Christmas season, or anyone who has ever guided a car down an icy highway toward a Christmas destination, knows well enough that "home Christmas" is as lovely a brief declaration as human language can carry. *Of course* we want to be home for Christmas! Even those persons who seem neglectful of home throughout the year think about it at Christmastime. And those of us grown older, who no longer can return to a childhood home, still return there in memory at this season.

So it's ironical that the first Christmas came to a hotel, of all places. A hotel is where you stay when you can't be at home. A hotel serves its purpose very well through the rest of the year, but on Christmas Day or Christmas Eve, even the best hotel seems rather dismal. The few workers on duty are likely to act as if they've been drafted into service—and usually, they have. Most of the dining rooms are closed. There's a peculiar stillness about the building. Christmas decorations are everywhere, including perhaps a great tree in the lobby, but somehow these decorations seem inappropriately bright, like someone who's trying too hard to be cheerful. A hotel just isn't the place we choose to spend Christmas.

No matter; the first Christmas came to a hotel. It wouldn't have qualified for a modern chain, like a Hilton or a Marriott. As a matter of fact, it would have made even the most meager of our contemporary economy chains seem luxurious. But it was a hotel. It was probably a series of thatched rooms built around a central courtyard—looking more like covered porches than like rooms. Travelers brought their own food—and the pot in which to cook it—their own bedding, and often their firewood (Handel Brown, "When Jesus Came," in *The Light of Christmas,* Frances Brentano, editor [New York: E. P. Dutton, 1964], page 24). The hotel in Bethlehem was probably a shabby sort of place, perhaps several hundred years old. If so, it was like most hotels out in the provinces. They were usually dirty, uncomfortable, badly kept, and badly managed. Innkeepers in those days had a generally unsavory reputation, probably because their places were so often used for immoral and criminal purposes (A. C. Bouquet, *Everyday Life in New Testament Times* [New York: Charles Scribner's Sons, 1954], page 106).

This is the sort of place to which the young carpenter Joseph and his wife, Mary, came. They were tired and dusty from the road. Even though the voluminous garments of the Middle East were quite concealing, almost anyone could detect that the girl was soon to deliver a child. So the couple asked for a room. Have you ever traveled too long, wanting to make just a few more miles, and then come to a place without having a reservation? Even with an automobile and with money or credit card in your pocket, it's an unpleasant experience to have a desk clerk shake his head negatively. But how do you feel when you're traveling by foot, leading a donkey that carries your earthly belongings? And how do you feel when you simply can't go on to another town? And still worse, how do you feel when you're a woman, great with child, or the man who is responsible for her care? How is it, then, when the owner says, "Sorry, no room. We're all filled up," and perhaps adds, "Been filled since early this afternoon."

But I tell you, I'm glad Christmas came to a hotel. Hotels, and all that they represent as temporary lodging, are part of life. If Christmas isn't inclusive enough to come to a hotel, it would seem that some of the most inevitable elements of our human experience are somehow beyond God's concern and redemption.

But Christmas came to a hotel. That means, for one thing, that Christmas comes to the world of business. I'm glad. All of us have to spend a certain amount of our time on matters of business, whether in writing checks, signing contracts, settling accounts, or paying bills. And some of us spend a good share of our lives that way, through the working weeks of all our years. If Christmas bypassed the hotels of life—the world of cash registers, stock-market reports, computers, and business trips—it would leave us feeling that somehow the basics of daily life didn't matter to heaven.

Hotels not only represent the world of business, they

represent a particularly complex kind of business. Novelist Arthur Hailey says that hotel employees become used to seeing "an exposed slice of life." Most of what happens in a hotel is routine, of course, and not at all glamorous or shocking. It's mostly people on vacation, people attending a conference or convention, or people needing a room from which to carry on their business for a few days.

But there's a seamier side, too. Hotel managers know they must not inquire into the private conduct of their guests as long as their activities don't interfere with the rights of other guests. So for some people, a hotel is a place to go for a weekend of blind drinking, and for others, it's a setting for extramarital sex; and for many, a hotel provides the anonymity that allows conduct that would otherwise be forbidden. This is nothing new. Even in the first century, many hotels were "disorderly houses," frequented for immoral purposes.

Like it or not, that's part of the world in which we live. While the Christ Child was being brought to birth in the stable near the hotel, it's likely that several soldiers were gambling in some part of the hotel, and two government employees padding their accounts in another, while in still another area, a man was choosing a young woman for the night. When we think of the first Christmas, we usually think of angels singing for a group of shepherds, or "the cattle lowing" where "the baby awakes"; but in that Bethlehem hotel it was no doubt "business as usual." Through the years of Jesus' ministry, he never tried to isolate himself from the shoddy, shadowy side of life. Indeed, some condemned him for associating with what they would call the "less desirable elements of society." But Jesus was always trying to redeem human life, always seeking to restore it to its divine origins. His birth was appropriate to such a pattern, for he was born back of a first-century hotel. Christmas comes to the world of business, even to businesses that are disreputable.

Further, since Christmas comes to a hotel, it comes to the

lonely. A hotel may seem a lively, gregarious place when you're attending a convention, a wedding, or a family reunion, but for many people it's the loneliest place in the world. That's part of the story for the person behind the desk or for the sometimes nearly faceless people in the cleaning crew. The salesperson who spends half his life on the road will tell you that the four walls of a hotel room are the living definition of loneliness. Every city has some permanent hotel-dwellers. Often they're people with no family ties, living in the busy, crowded loneliness of a hotel.

Christmas comes to the lonely and says, "God loves you." The news media report at frequent intervals that the world is growing more crowded. Ironically, it's also growing more lonely. So many are learning that you can live in the midst of lights, action, and crowds, and yet be desperately alone. In a world where loneliness is almost epidemic, Christmas announces, of all things, that it's a friendly universe, because the Power at the center of the universe is a loving God who sends his Son into the world to embrace its lonely heart.

But let me say something still more important. When Christmas came to that first-century hotel, it reminded us that Christmas comes even to those who don't want it; specifically, for those who don't have room for it. You remember that this first Christmas story carried a poignant line: "There was no place for them in the inn" (Luke 2:7). Christmas comes not only to those who choose to seek it, like Simeon and Anna (Luke 2:22-38), but also to those who are indifferent and preoccupied. It invites them to share its benefits.

When I was younger, I thought of that ancient innkeeper in the Christmas story as a villain. As I've grown older, I've come to feel my own kind of kinship with him. I realize that probably he didn't refuse Joseph and Mary out of malice; it was simply a case of *no room.* In those days, government officials and soldiers on the march could claim free lodging in the hotels (Bouquet, *Everyday Life in New Testament Times,* page 106). It's quite possible that the innkeeper, if he was a sympathetic person, may have *preferred* to house Joseph and Mary—especially if the choice were against free guests. But his inn was full.

I understand the innkeeper. I've learned that so many of us shut God out of our lives, not necessarily because we're hostile to him, but simply because we are "filled up" with other things. Indeed, that's the tragedy of most of our lives, especially since so much of what fills our lives is trivia. So often persons who have passed through a crucial illness say that at the edge of death, they got a new understanding of what is worth living for. Everything seems to conspire to fill our days with life's transients—and then, when Eternity knocks at the door, seeking a place, we have to report that our rooms are all full. You and I are often like the innkeeper: We shut Christ out, not because we hate him, but because we're preoccupied. In fact, I ponder a quite uneasy thought. The innkeeper never knew, I'm quite sure, that he had shut out the very Christ; he was simply filled up. And this is just the way some of us go through life—not knowing that Christ has sought admission. We get so occupied with other matters that we don't even recognize the divine inquiry.

And so Christmas comes even to those who aren't seeking it, who don't even particularly want it. It comes to hotels that are filled, to lives that are crowded, to people who are preoccupied. And always, it comes saying, "I love you. May I come in?"

One word more. Because Christmas comes to a hotel, we know that Christmas comes to those who are away from home. I said earlier that Christmas is the holiday when we want most to be at home. But a hotel seems the opposite of home. It's a place of transience, a place that says we're away from home. And that's the peculiar glory of Christmas. It comes to those who are homeless.

Which is to say, *Christmas comes to all of us,* to all in our wandering, homeless human race. Remember how G. K. Chesterton said it?

For men are homesick in their homes,
And strangers under the sun,
And they lay their heads in a foreign land
Whenever the day is done.
("The House of Christmas")

And so it is. We human beings are never quite at home on this earth. We "lay our heads in a foreign land" each night. Something in us knows there is another home, an Eden we somehow lost long ago. I wonder if a great deal of our running may spring from the instinctive sense that we don't fully belong where we now live? Those who analyze the wide use of drugs, ranging from alcohol and marijuana to heroin and more, say that people are trying to escape. But from *what* and to *where?* Is it because we belong to a race that is condemned to wander all of its days? Is it because our hearts know that our address should be Eden, and we're constantly hoping to find our way home?

So Jesus was born away from home. Not in the village where Joseph and Mary had lived, and to which in time they would return, but in a town called Bethlehem, where they had gone to enroll for taxation. And he was born, not in a quiet peasant cottage, but back of a poor hotel. He was born away from home. Indeed! Because, as the New Testament writers tell us, his home was heaven, and he made himself homeless in order to restore us to our original Home.

So it is that Christmas comes to a hotel. It comes to the world of business, where sometimes we shut Christ out, and where the style is sometimes so very contrary to his. He comes to the lonely place. Yes, and even to the place where he may not be wanted, where there's simply no room for him. He comes (especially this!) to those who are away from home. To you and me.

And then, of course, the question comes, just as it did twenty centuries ago: *Will we make room for him?*

CHAPTER 5

How the Government Helped the First Christmas Happen

LUKE 2:1-7: In those days a decree went out from Emperor Augustus that all the world should be registered. This was the first registration and was taken while Quirinius was governor of Syria. All went to their own towns to be registered. Joseph also went from the town of Nazareth in Galilee to Judea, to the city of David called Bethlehem, because he was descended from the house and family of David. He went to be registered with Mary, to whom he was engaged and who was expecting a child. While they were there, the time came for her to deliver her child. And she gave birth to her firstborn son and wrapped him in bands of cloth, and laid him in a manger, because there was no place for them in the inn.

MATTHEW 2:1-8: In the time of King Herod, after Jesus was born in Bethlehem of Judea, wise men from the East came to Jerusalem, asking, "Where is the child who has been born king of the Jews? For we have observed his star at its rising, and have come to pay him homage." When King Herod heard this, he was frightened, and all Jerusalem with him; and calling together all the chief priests and scribes of the people, he inquired of them where the Messiah was to be born. They told him, "In Bethlehem of Judea; for so it has been written by the prophet: 'And you, Bethlehem, in the land of Judah, / are by no means least among the rulers of Judah; / for from you shall come a ruler / who is to shepherd my people Israel.' "

Then Herod secretly called for the wise men and learned

from them the exact time when the star had appeared. Then he sent them to Bethlehem, saying, "Go and search diligently for the child; and when you have found him, bring me the word so that I may also go and pay him homage."

There was a good deal of government involvement in the first Christmas. This will surprise some and anger others. I'm almost sure I can hear someone muttering, "What did you expect? Have you ever seen anything where politicians or the government couldn't work their way in?"

Most of us are ambivalent about government. Many of us complain that there's too much of it, but we're quick to call the police if our home is broken into, and we're glad for the fire department in the threat of emergencies. And if you think I'm staying close to those agencies of government that everyone favors (except, perhaps, when getting a traffic ticket), let me remind you of a phrase that so frequently slips into our conversations: "The government ought to do something about it!" We hear it from conservatives and liberals, from Republicans and Democrats. From what I can observe, the only difference is in the particular issues about which the mantra is recited.

In any event, the government got in on the first Christmas. And probably someone then said what someone says now: "What did you expect?"

The governmental involvement began with taxes. The Roman government was a big operation, and a very efficient one. But even efficient operations need a lot of money if they're to function; and ancient governments, like modern ones, were constantly under a strain to find new methods of taxation. Luke put it this way: "In those days a decree went out from Emperor Augustus that all the world should be registered" (Luke 2:1). The late British scholar William Barclay explained that censuses were taken periodically in the Roman Empire with two purposes—assessing taxation and locating persons who were eligible for compulsory military service (*The Gospel of Luke* [Philadelphia: The Westminster Press, 1956], page 15). Since Jews were exempt from the military operation, this census in Palestine would center on the tax factor.

It was this registering by the Roman government that forced Joseph and Mary to make the seventy-mile trip from Nazareth to Bethlehem at a most inconvenient time. Mary was great with child, and the trip, by foot and donkey, would take roughly five days over difficult terrain. There could hardly have been a less propitious time for travel. But there was no arguing with the Roman government. Joseph would have to return to his ancestral village, Bethlehem. And Bethlehem, as we noted in an earlier chapter, is where the Messiah was to be born; the prophet Micah had said so.

Which is to say, Emperor Augustus was being very helpful. He didn't know it, of course. I suspect he didn't even know that his far-ranging empire included a young carpenter and his wife; and if he had known, he could hardly have cared. But he did his thing, signing a routine document, following a pattern that existed in his government for three centuries or more, never knowing how big a matter this particular document would turn out to be.

In truth, Augustus was a very great ruler. He was an effective military leader, but he chose peaceful negotiation whenever possible. He famously said that he "found Rome brick and left it marble," and it was no idle boast. His roads, buildings, and bridges, and his encouragement to sculptors made Rome a worthy capital to one of the greatest empires of all time. But his name is known most widely today, in the roughly two thousand languages into which Luke's Gospel has been translated, for a routine governmental document that expedited the Christmas story. The emperor thought he was simply implementing a new tax program, but in the purposes of God, the point was to get Joseph and Mary to Bethlehem. If there had to be an imperial order to bring it to pass, so be it.

And then there was Herod. Where Augustus participated

in the Christmas story through taxation, Herod's issue was pure politics. On the whole, Herod was not a nice man. Let me use a strong word, and say that Herod was *insanely* fearful of losing his relatively small portion of the Roman Empire. So fearful, in fact, that over a course of time, he murdered his wife, his wife's mother, his eldest son, and two other sons, lest they take his throne. So it is that Emperor Augustus said that it was safer to be Herod's pig than Herod's son—a line that was a neat pun when Augustus said it, since the words *pig* and *son* are only a letter different in the Greek.

Mind you, Herod did some good and kind things. Remember that the Temple in Jerusalem in Jesus' day was known as Herod's temple, because it was one of his building achievements. In hard times, he was known to remit taxes, and on one occasion, even to melt down some of his own gold plate to feed those who were starving. But he took no chances when it came to his throne. At such times, he played politics in the meanest and most fearful way.

So when Herod heard from the wise men that a new king of the Jews had been born, he panicked. And, seasoned politician that he was, he turned his panic into ingratiating speech. "Go and search diligently for the child," he told the wise men, "and when you have found him, bring me word so that I may also go and pay him homage" (Matthew 2:8). Herod's idea of homage, of course, was the sort of thing he did for his wife, mother-in-law, and three sons.

Thus, where Augustus was an unwitting aid to making Christmas happen, Herod's aim was to prevent it; although, like Augustus, he had no idea what he was doing. But Herod's government wasn't the last to try to put a stop to Christmas. There's a fairly long list of countries in our own day where one had better not celebrate Christmas publicly. For that matter, the place of Christmas in American public life is becoming more and more complicated. Obviously, one can celebrate Christmas without restraint in church or home or private gathering, but in most secular gatherings we can celebrate Christmas only if the religious elements are removed. "Unreligious Christmas celebration" seems like the ultimate oxymoron, but our culture is working at it.

Herod played his own unique role in unfolding the Christmas story. He enters the plot through the wise men, who visit him because of their own interesting mix of mysticism and logic. They had followed a star, which was a pretty mystical thing to do; but when they got to Palestine, they went to the capital city, Jerusalem, which was a quite logical act, because they reasoned that of course any new king would be found in the capital. So it's Herod who calls together "all the chief priests and scribes of the people," to inquire "where the Messiah was to be born" (Matthew 2:4), and here it is made known that the Messiah is to be born "in Bethlehem of Judea" (2:5). Herod becomes the key link in the wise men's research project, somewhat like the helpful librarian who connects you with the volumes that make all the difference, or perhaps like the organization that underwrites the research. If it hadn't been for Herod, the wise men might have wandered around Jerusalem and never arrived in Bethlehem.

Herod then played another role in the story. As we noted earlier, he appealed to the wise men to bring him word when they had found the Baby. Instead, the wise men, "having been warned in a dream not to return to Herod," courageously ignored his orders, and went home "by another road" (Matthew 2:12). By his psychotic fears, Herod opened the door for a heroic decision by the wise men—a decision that, in its own way, evoked one of the first acts of allegiance to Jesus Christ.

So it is that two rulers, one the leader of a small province and the other the head of the greatest government of ancient times, each played his part in the first Christmas. I repeat, neither intended to do so; nevertheless, their roles were crucial in the unfolding of the plot. It's hard to imagine the Christmas story without them.

Nor was that the end of the intersection between politics and the continuing Christmas story. Thirty years after Bethlehem, when Jesus began to preach, his theme was "the time is fulfilled, and the kingdom of God has come near" (Mark 1:15). *Kingdom* is a word that sounds like politics and government, and it was Jesus' key word as he launched his ministry. Think how often Jesus said, "The kingdom of heaven is like . . ."—*How would* you *know,* they must have thought—and you realize that Jesus' religious enemies had good material to convince the Roman government that Jesus was a politically dangerous figure. So when he entered Jerusalem on the day we now call Palm Sunday, the crowds hailed him as "the Son of David." (See Matthew 21:9.) This was their way of saying, "Here's the king we've been waiting for." And when Jesus' enemies decided they must dispose of him, they did so by presenting him as an enemy of the Roman government, and it was to that government that he was brought for trial.

The presiding governor, Pilate, saw no legal reason for Jesus to be executed. But when he hesitated, the enemies of Jesus said, "If you release this man, you are no friend of the emperor" (John 19:12). So Jesus was killed not by an assassin, or by an unruly mob (though certainly the mob played its ugly part), but by a governmental decision that unfolded according to the general rules of the time. It was unjust, as even Pilate indicated, but nevertheless it was by the rules.

And the followers of Jesus have been dealing with governments ever since. The apostle Paul urged the early Christians to "be subject to the governing authorities" (Romans 13:1), yet during the first centuries of the Christian faith, governments again and again mounted persecutions of the church and its followers. Often in those early years the Christians were an easy scapegoat for emperors like Nero, or for rulers of smaller areas, because by persecuting the Christians a ruler could distract the population from more substantive matters.

As the church continued to grow in spite of persecution, rulers became increasingly apprehensive. True, Jesus had said, " 'My kingdom is not from this world' " (John 18:36), but when a body of people grows in the face of all opposition, and when they seem persuasive and winsome in spite of public disapproval, it's enough to make any ruler wonder where it might all end. Such a group can become a powerful voting bloc in a democracy, or a basis for revolt in a totalitarian state.

Then, in the fourth century, something special happened. Constantine, the most powerful ruler of his time, claimed to be a convert to Christianity, and he became a friend of the church. Suddenly the body that had dealt with intermittent persecution from the day of its birth now found itself welcome in the courts of power. And it has been that way in some parts of the world ever since. The history of Europe in the Middle Ages seems often to be little more than a continuing series of negotiations between papacy and kings. It is probably not unfair to say that one big reason that Martin Luther survived while John Hus, Savonarola, and William Tyndale were martyred is that Luther had some powerful political figures on his side. The Roman Catholic Church, the Eastern Orthodox, and several Protestant bodies have enjoyed being the state church in a variety of European countries.

A close relationship between church and government has not been an unmixed blessing. The church seems often to have lived closer to the teachings of its Lord when persecuted than when in power. Too much comfort has appeared at times to diminish the church's witness. Sometimes, unfortunately, when the church has had political power, it has used that power as inequitably as the secular state. I fear there have been instances when the church's voice of justice has been muted by the seductions of power and privilege.

On the other hand, when Christ is taken seriously, he is likely to make the rulers of this world quite uneasy. Power is a peril; even the best of leaders struggle with their moral imperatives when they have the upper hand, and especially when they feel that the future of their program or of their party is at stake. And by contrast, there's the issue of compromise. It is sometimes said that politics is the art of compromise. But how far can one go in the delicate business of compromise without sacrificing principles and persons? The Man of Galilee sometimes makes an uncomfortable presence in the halls of state.

Most of us expect that major political candidates in the United States—and probably in many other parts of the world—will invoke the name of God in the course of their campaigning. But it is quite another thing to fulfill Christian ideals, by whatever name you call them, in the tough arenas of government—and in all the other areas of life, too. I'm quite sure that someone reading this book remembers a time when he or she pressed earnestly for the high ground in some business discussion, community meeting, or dorm or neighborhood gathering, only to hear someone respond, "We're not running a Sunday school, you know."

So there's always a tension where Christmas and government meet, just as there was twenty centuries ago, when our Lord was born in Bethlehem. Caesar Augustus didn't know that he was a party to the Christmas story; Jesus was unknown to him, even though Augustus was cooperating in ways he didn't understand. Herod, on the other hand, was afraid of the Baby he never saw, and tried to destroy him.

Dorothy L. Sayers, the British novelist, playwright, and lay theologian, described Jesus as "the Man born to be King." Those of us who have accepted him as our Lord confess that he *is* our King. We cannot simply use him or manipulate him; we can only accept his Lordship. He seeks no alliance with ruler, legislature, power bloc, or political party, nor does he need such. He is King, by authority beyond any authorization this world can give. Tyrants do well to fear him, because when Christ comes into human lives, those he fills gain a dignity and a sense of self-worth that makes them inherently dangerous to those who would exploit human life. Those who truly acknowledge the lordship of Christ are the best of public servants, but they are no solace to those who misuse government or who are careless of justice.

The writer of Revelation promised that some day, "The

kingdoms of this world are become the kingdoms of our Lord, and of his Christ; and he shall reign for ever and ever" (Revelation 11:15 KJV). I'm very sure this will someday happen. And to think that it all began with an emperor who implemented a new tax law, and a provincial king who got the wise men in touch with scholars who would direct them to Bethlehem!

CHAPTER *6*

Christmas and the Impossible Dream

MATTHEW 2:1-12: In the time of King Herod, after Jesus was born in Bethlehem of Judea, wise men from the East came to Jerusalem, asking, "Where is the child who has been born king of the Jews? For we have observed his star at its rising, and have come to pay him homage." When King Herod heard this, he was frightened, and all Jerusalem with him; and calling together all the chief priests and scribes of the people, he inquired of them where the Messiah was to be born. They told him, "In Bethlehem of Judea; for so it has been written by the prophet: 'And you, Bethlehem, in the land of Judah, / are by no means least among the rulers of Judah; / for from you shall come a ruler / who is to shepherd my people Israel.'" Then Herod secretly called for the wise men and learned from them the exact time when the star had appeared. Then he sent them to Bethlehem, saying, "Go and search diligently for the child; and when you have found him, bring me the word so that I may also go and pay him homage." When they had heard the king, they set out; and there, ahead of them, went the star that they had seen at its rising, until it stopped over the place where the child was. When they saw that the star had stopped, they were overwhelmed with joy. On entering the house, they saw the child with Mary his mother; and they knelt down and paid him homage. Then, opening their treasure chests, they offered him gifts of gold, frankincense, and myrrh. And having been warned in a dream not to return to Herod, they left for their own country by another road.

People who get the Christmas story from an annual church pageant or from the music of the season think that the persons who brought gifts to the baby Jesus were kings. I'm sure that virtually every Christmas dramatization portrays these men in flowing robes, ornate headgear, and unabashed opulence; and they usually make their appearance as someone sings, "We three kings of Orient are. . . ."

Well, I know they weren't kings, because nothing in the biblical record even hints at such an idea. They were "wise men from the East," the Gospel of Matthew tells us (Matthew 2:1). But that's what bothers me. It would be easier to believe that they were kings. But *wise men?* I know, I know; the Bible says so. And I believe the Bible. But still I keep asking myself: How can we call them *wise* men?

It's not that I'm judging them by our twenty-first-century prejudices. When it comes to what passes for intelligence in our contemporary culture, I'm a bit of a curmudgeon. When people tell me how much smarter we are than previous generations, after they point to computers (which bewilder me) and modern plumbing (for which I'm grateful), I find the evidence of our brilliance a little hard to prove.

The first-century world into which Jesus came was actually quite remarkable. A large percentage of the people were in some measure able to read and write. Some say it was the period of the most widespread literacy the world was to know until some eighteen centuries later. In Palestine, for example, there were schools in every town, with compulsory education for all children over the age of six. Philosophy, law, and rhetoric were in some respects as developed in the first century as they are today. As for medicine, first-century rabbis practiced laws of health that were often far ahead of common standards in mid-nineteenth-century Europe and America. And as for dentistry, it was surely possible to buy false teeth in first-century Jerusalem!

The physical sciences were not so well developed, of

course, because the first-century world didn't have the mechanical apparatus for experimentation and calculation. Nevertheless, we should remember that the basic elements of mathematics and engineering existed in Mesopotamia thirty-five centuries before Christ. Three centuries before our Common Era, the librarian Eratosthenes had calculated the size of the earth and its distance from the sun with surprising accuracy, and efforts in chemistry and physics were already laying the groundwork for the research and discoveries of modern times. Books were not easily available, since they had to be hand-copied, yet already there were several great libraries. By the 200s B.C., the library in Alexandria, Egypt, had more than 700,000 scrolls, as its administrators sought to fulfill their goal of collecting a copy of every known existing scroll. (Much of the data in the two previous paragraphs is from A. C. Bouquet, *Everyday Life in New Testament Times* [New York: Charles Scribner's Sons, 1954], chapters 10 and 11.)

So it was not an illiterate world in which the first Christmas happened. In fact, it was an age with widespread learning, and one in which knowledge was prized and sought. It was in that world that a little group of scholars became part of the Christmas story.

We don't really know much about them. The Bible says simply, as we noted earlier, that they were "wise men from the East." We assume there were three, since they gave the Christ Child three gifts. They were students of astronomy, because they had taken their bearings from what was probably a dramatic star. We also could reason that they were political scientists, because they were coming in search of a new king. They were also interpreters of dreams; we might judge from this that they were simply first-century magicians, or on the other hand that they were forerunners of Freudian psychiatry.

We need to remember that lines defining fields of knowledge were not so sharply drawn, nor was knowledge as specialized, in that first-century world, as in ours. A literate person was likely to have a broad base of learning in a wide variety of fields. It is often concluded that these men were from Persia. The wise men of that country were the teachers and advisors of the Persian kings, and were usually skilled in philosophy, medicine, and natural science. They were generally known as good and holy men, admired for their search after truth.

I like to picture them as an ancient think tank. Basically supported by their own king, they probably took on projects from a variety of rulers and perhaps from entrepreneurs and other business people. And like any true scholars, they no doubt pursued independent lines of thought as new ideas captured their fancy or challenged their presuppositions.

But what in the world drove them on this strange mission in Matthew 2? Why would they invest so much time, money, and energy to find a new king of the Jews? The trip called for a substantial financial investment. As scholars, they probably had relatively modest means. Yet they entered on a research project that required traveling hundreds of miles over difficult terrain in a trip that no doubt took many weeks or months. The poet T. S. Eliot imagines their feelings:

> And the cities hostile and the towns unfriendly
> And the villages dirty and charging high prices:
> A hard time we had of it.
>
> ("The Journey of the Magi")

And since these men felt they were going to find a king, they couldn't build their venture on a shoestring. Perhaps our Sunday-school pageants are right when we dress them in our best bathrobes; after all, they would want to be fit for an audience with royalty. Their gifts, too, represented a substantial investment—gold, frankincense, and myrrh. Who underwrote such substantial costs?

Why would they do it? Were they perhaps driven by their

interest in astronomy? Our generation sometimes writes the wise men off as rather superstitious astrologers; and without a doubt, the astronomy of their day intersected astrology in ways we today would find unacceptable. Because even though astronomy was a well-developed study by the first century, it was also shot through with the idea that the stars sometimes marked major political and military events. It was not what we might call "pure science"—though when we use that kind of language, humility should remind us that some future generation may judge us to have been, in our own fashion, superstitious.

Or were they perhaps driven by some combination of faith and hope? The late British Bible scholar William Barclay reminds us that there was a strange sense of expectancy in the world in those centuries. Suetonius, Tacitus, and Josephus all say that the belief was abroad that a universal ruler was to arise in Judea. So, Barclay says, "When Jesus Christ came into this world the world was in an eagerness of expectation. Men were waiting for God. . . . They had discovered that they could not build the golden age without God" (*The Gospel of Matthew,* Vol. 1 [Philadelphia: The Westminster Press, 1958]; page 18).

But if there was such spiritual longing in that day, there was also aching despair. The literature that has come to us from that period reveals people living with little hope for the future. One man wrote that the world was perishing, reaching its last end. The Greeks, who were the intellectual arbiters of that age, were particularly depressed by the way things decayed, rotted, and vanished away. "So if they enjoyed life at all," A. C. Bouquet writes, "it was generally by not thinking too much about it, and by living for the day" (*Everyday Life in New Testament Times,* pages 2-3). But of course such a mix of hope and despair is not unusual. One thinks of the Bible story of Noah. His was a time when "the wickedness of humankind" was so great that "the thoughts of their hearts was only evil continually"; and yet it was in that dissolute climate that "Noah was a righteous man, blameless in his generation" (Genesis 6:5, 9). Perhaps the wise men were the Noahs of their day, persons longing for a golden age even in the midst of so much materialism and despair.

But we still come back to the same question: Why ever in the world would these wise men set out to find a king of the Jews? If they *were* wise men, surely they would pursue a more rational course. By the time the wise men began their journey, the Jews hadn't been a viable political entity for nearly six centuries. In truth, the Jews had been a significant military and political power for probably less than a century, during the reigns of King David and King Solomon. During the earlier periods, under the judges and under King Saul, they had struggled to hold their own against a variety of enemies, particularly the Philistines. After Solomon their nation was divided, and before too many years the Northern Kingdom simply disappeared after being conquered by the Assyrians. The Southern Kingdom, known as Judah, held its own until roughly 600 B.C., when it was conquered by the Babylonians, who exiled the surviving Jews to Babylon. Eventually those survivors made their way back to their homeland, but as a nation state they were not seen as a power to be reckoned with. At best, they were a frequent frustration to the several empires that included them in their domain, but not a force around which national greatness could be built.

So why would anyone from another place and culture want to see a new King of the *Jews?* What difference would he make? Why embark on a pilgrimage, with its months of preparation and its weeks of tedious travel, to see a king of a nation that was not considered very important, and which at that time was seen as only a troublesome province in a great empire? Travel to find a new Caesar, yes; but travel to find a new King of the Jews? An exercise in trivia!

But that's what they did. And we call them *wise men!* What made them do it?

I sometimes wonder if these wise men from the east were

driven partly by some knowledge of the Hebrew prophets. Not enough knowledge, mind you, that they knew they should go to Bethlehem; they needed help from the Jewish scholars to apply the writings of the prophet Micah to their journey. But they were learned men, and I venture that perhaps they may have read the prophet Amos, with his cry,

> But let justice roll down like waters,
> and righteousness like an everflowing stream.
> (Amos 5:24)

Or perhaps Isaiah:

> [The LORD] has sent me to bring good news to the oppressed,
> to bind up the brokenhearted,
> to proclaim liberty to the captives,
> and release to the prisoners. (Isaiah 61:1)

Perhaps as they read such passages, political scientists that they were, and advisors to kings, they pondered that nothing they had seen in all of statecraft resembled this kind of picture. And perhaps with that realization came a longing, and with the longing, a reaching out after a God they had never known; and then, the trip to Bethlehem. I wonder if that's the way it happened.

I can't say, of course, how it is that these wise men went on such a strange quest. I've often wondered, as have thousands of preachers and a fair number of poets and short-story writers, how the wise men must have felt when they came to the end of their journey and found themselves with a peasant family in a most modest dwelling. Did they think their whole trip was a fiasco? And how is it that they were persuaded, in spite of appearances, that this baby was, indeed, the point of their search? And how is it that they thought their gifts were appropriate, when it seemed so clear that there were several things this family needed more than frankincense and myrrh?

But in truth, none of these questions is much of an issue once you find some logic in the original venture. Anyone "foolish" enough to think a King of the Jews is important, in light of the history of the Jews as a national power and of their centuries out of the limelight, is ready to deal with what the wise men found when they got to their destination.

As for me, I've simply been forced to rework my definition of *wise*. I think of the words of the apostle Paul: "If you think that you are wise in this age, you should become fools so that you may become wise. For the wisdom of this world is foolishness with God" (1 Corinthians 3:18-19). And I think of Blaise Pascal, one of the epochal scholars of human history, and also a passionately convinced Christian, who said, "The heart has its reasons which reason knows nothing of" (*Pensees,* sect. 6, no. 347). I think of those thousands of persons who have chosen, over several centuries, to go to mission fields that contradicted all their natural sense of comfort and order, and who sometimes died there without apparently accomplishing anything. And I think of those persons who have labored for years in the pursuit of a worthy but hopeless cause. To say nothing of those who have continued loving a spouse, a child, a sibling, or a friend when everything demonstrated that the person didn't merit such love. I ponder all those persons who, in the words of Dale Wasserman, have "dreamed the impossible dream." I know then that *wise* is not easy to define.

I surely don't mean to make a case for irrational conduct. Nor do I recommend flying in the face of reason. As it happens, I'm generally a quite conservative person. But I'm convinced that we all should be very humble about our wisdom and our logic. The three wise men compel me to rethink my definition of *wise*. And they make me wish I were wiser. *Wise* the way the wise men were.

Amen.

CHAPTER 7

Christmas Comes to a Church

LUKE 2:22-32: When the time came for their purification according to the law of Moses, they brought him up to Jerusalem to present him to the Lord (as it is written in the law of the Lord, "Every firstborn male shall be designated as holy to the Lord"), and they offered a sacrifice according to what is stated in the law of the Lord, "a pair of turtledoves or two young pigeons." Now there was a man in Jerusalem whose name was Simeon; this man was righteous and devout, looking forward to the consolation of Israel, and the Holy Spirit rested on him. It had been revealed to him by the Holy Spirit that he would not see death before he had seen the Lord's Messiah. Guided by the Spirit, Simeon came into the temple; and when the parents brought in the child Jesus, to do for him what was customary under the law, Simeon took him in his arms and praised God, saying, "Master, now you are dismissing your servant in peace, / according to your word; / for my eyes have seen your salvation, / which you have prepared in the presence of all peoples, / a light for revelation to the Gentiles / and for glory to your people Israel."

And the child's father and mother were amazed at what was being said about him. Then Simeon blessed them and said to his mother Mary, "This child is destined for the falling and the rising of many in Israel, and to be a sign that will be opposed so that the inner thoughts of many will be revealed—and a sword will pierce your own soul too."

There was also a prophet, Anna the daughter of Phanuel of the tribe of Asher. She was of a great age, having lived with her husband seven years after her marriage, then as a widow to the age of eighty-four. She never left the temple but worshiped there with fasting and prayer night and day. At that moment she came, and began to praise God and to speak about the child to all who were looking for the redemption of Jerusalem.

Since this book is titled *Christmas from the Back Side,* you have a right to wonder about this chapter on which we now embark. "Christmas Comes to a Church"? *Where else?* you might ask. *And what's so out of the ordinary about that?*

I'm recalling a cartoon I came upon some years ago. I can't quote or describe it in full detail, but I remember it picturing two shopkeepers in a mall, looking at a Salvation Army worker and muttering unhappily, "What will those religious people try next? Now they're even horning in on *Christmas*!"

The impact of a cartoon, as with other forms of humor, often comes from its knack for giving an absurd twist to some element of truth. I suspect that most of us have no idea of the degree to which Christmas has been taken over by commercialism and secularism. We complain about what's happening, when Christmas promotions begin even before Thanksgiving, but that's only the tip of the iceberg. Consider, for instance, how greeting cards now feature the innocuous "Holiday Greetings" where once they announced "Merry Christmas." Indeed, see how I just used the generic term *greeting cards,* where formerly one spoke of *Christmas* cards. Survey the cards you receive this year, and see how few have an unapologetically Christian message.

I'm not appealing for something aggressively evangelistic, nor would you have thought in other days that I might be doing so. The truth is, we have watched one of the two major holy days of the Christian faith be so captured by the secular culture, and by our inordinate commitment to political correctness, that the cartoon message is correct. The main show at Christmas is commercial and diffused, while the church runs a sideshow. And worse, much of the Christmas activity in many churches is closer to the secular than to the sacred.

So—unfortunately—I'm true to my "back side" theme when I speak of Christmas coming to a church.

But let me tell you what happened on the first Christmas. It was a religious story all the way. The events unfolded in a magnificent variety of places, including a workplace conversation between cousins, scholars doing research in an ancient think tank, shepherds fulfilling their routine tasks on a chilly hillside, and an emperor developing a new tax plan. But the energy of the event, which tied together these disparate elements, was profoundly religious.

It began with human need, as our ancestors found themselves unable to deal with the problem of sin—an inability that is just as insistent today as it was when the human race was young. We may have made more sophisticated the way we describe the need for dealing with sin, and we may well have found some diversions that we like to think of as solutions, but the need is as clamant as ever. Then, ancient men of God found language to verbalize our human longing; we call them the prophets of Israel, and we marvel still at their uncanny grasp of our need and its solution.

And when Quirinius was governor of Syria, and Herod was running a small portion of the Roman Empire under the strong hand of Augustus Caesar, the plot of the ages began to unfold in its lovely, unlikely way in some small towns in a province no larger than the state of New Jersey. And it began with people who were admirably devout. Some of them were among what was known as the common people of the land, quite outside the ruling religious caste, but earnest in their pursuit of God. The womb that carried Jesus was that of a Jewish girl who said, "Here am I, the servant of the Lord; let it be with me according to your word" (Luke 1:38); and Joseph, the man who so faithfully watched over her, is described as "a righteous man" who denied his own plans in order to fulfill the purposes of God (see Matthew 1:19-25).

Luke's Gospel tells us how the Christmas event moved from its unlikely and miraculous beginnings into the traditional practices of the Jewish faith, climaxing at last in a house of worship. Eight days after Jesus was born in Bethlehem, and was heralded by the shepherds who had come in response to the angelic announcement, Joseph and Mary fulfilled the ancient laws of the Jewish people by having the Baby circumcised. It was at this point that he was officially given his name, Jesus.

Circumcision was probably the most sacred ceremony of the Jewish people. It was the symbol of their covenant with God, going back all the way to their key ancestor, Abraham. By this act, each new generation was declared part of the holy covenant. In Jesus' day, the rite was performed by the child's father (Abbott, Gilbert, Hunt, and Swaim, *The Bible Reader* [London: Geoffrey Chapman, 1969], page 732). Of the event, Luke says simply, "And he was called Jesus, the name given by the angel before he was conceived in the womb" (Luke 2:21). See the perfect blending of the elements of worship: a prescribed ritual is joined with a divine visitation. The structured ritual gives order to our lives; the divine visitation gives wonder and glory.

Several weeks later, probably when the baby was about six weeks old, Joseph and Mary went to the temple for two other ceremonies, the redemption of the firstborn and the purification after childbirth. For a devout Jew, these were routine religious ceremonies following the birth of a child, but steeped in heritage and awe. The purification ceremony applied primarily to the mother, but it's interesting to note that some modern medical researchers see values in this ceremony beyond its religious elements. The redemption of the firstborn reminded a Jewish family that God had delivered their nation from the bondage of Egypt centuries earlier, and that they owed each firstborn son to the Lord because of this deliverance. The devout practiced these ceremonies at the time of a child's birth in the same way a sincere present-day Christian family arranges for a baby to be baptized or dedicated to God.

So it is that Jesus was inducted into the faith life of his people from the very beginning of his life. He was the product of a conventionally religious home. When he was a boy of twelve, he made his first great pilgrimage to a religious festival, just as did all Jewish children who were following their faith. (See Luke 2:41-52.) No doubt it is significant that the only event the Scriptures report from the life of our Lord from the time of his birth until he began his ministry at age thirty was a celebration from their religious tradition.

And the practice of the traditional faith in Jesus' day was less than perfect, I suspect, as is true for us in our practice, in our time. Jesus' frequent controversies with the religious leaders of his people, for instance, make clear that many of them were missing the point. The most prestigious movement within Judaism at the time was that of the Pharisees; we remember them now for the way they sought to frustrate Jesus' ministry. The other major religious body, the Sadducees, not only was weak doctrinally, it dissipated whatever religious influence it might have had by the way its leaders compromised themselves to win favor with the pagan Roman government.

Now and then a contemporary writer will ask why Jesus stayed with the first-century Judaism into which he was born. I suspect that the average synagogue was not marked by admirable vitality. By the very nature of things, the synagogue services probably had a sameness, perhaps even a dullness. Nevertheless, the Gospel writer tells us that Jesus "went to the synagogue on the sabbath day, *as was his custom*" (Luke 4:16, emphasis added). Whatever the failures of organized religion, Jesus didn't decide that he could do it better alone. He brought himself under the weekly discipline of meeting with the people of God. They might be imperfect people in an imperfect world, but they were a people who were seeking, however unevenly, to follow God. And among them (just as it is today), there were some wonderfully *good* people.

It's not surprising that Jesus was impressed by the good people the traditional practice of the faith had produced. He was immersed in that spirit from his earliest infancy. When he was brought to the temple, as a baby of less than two months, there were good people waiting there to greet him. Luke's Gospel reports that on that ritual day, two special people were on hand, a man named Simeon and a woman named Anna.

Nobody had invited them, unless one acknowledges the invitation of the Holy Spirit. But Simeon and Anna were very remarkable people. Anna was some eighty-four years old and had been a widow since she was in her early twenties. Luke says that "she never left the temple but worshiped there with fasting and prayer night and day" (2:37). We sometimes say of certain persons, "They're at church every time the door is open." Anna was that kind of woman. The House of God was her heart's home, and she found her way there at every possible opportunity. It's no wonder, then, that she was there when the baby Jesus was brought for the high ceremony of dedication. She wasn't likely to miss the greatest hour that ever came to her place of worship, because she was there at all hours.

As for Simeon, the Bible says that he was "righteous and devout" (Luke 2:25), and that the Holy Spirit was upon him. We don't know how old he was, but he was so well advanced in age that he was living just to see a promise he had received from God, a promise that he would not die until he had seen the Messiah. On this particular day, he came to the temple under special inspiration from the Holy Spirit. When Joseph and Mary brought their baby for the act of dedication, Simeon took the child in his arms and blessed him. The words he spoke are still sung in thousands of churches every Sunday, and in the Roman Catholic Church they are said every night in the Compline, the final portion of the Divine Office. Listen: "Lord, now lettest thou thy servant depart in peace, according to thy word: For mine eyes have seen thy salvation" (Luke 2:29-30 KJV). Christmas came to Simeon while he was in the place of worship, because Christmas comes to a church.

Every Christmas season some writer or preacher or commentator raises the same question: Suppose Jesus Christ were born in *our* day; would we reject him again? Would everyone, including people of the church, turn their backs on him? Yes, probably the world as a whole would reject him again, just as we did nearly twenty centuries ago. And yes, no doubt many church people would reject him, even though we claim the name *Christian*; because, I suspect, many of us wouldn't recognize him for who he is.

But I can tell you who *would* receive him. It would be the Simeons and the Annas of our world. People like Simeon and Anna will always be waiting for God, and will always be seeking for the will of God. And those who seek, find.

Economists, sociologists, political scientists, and gamblers all agree that a wise person plays the odds. A wise person chooses the most likely prospects. Life produces some surprises, but don't build your life on the hope that surprises will happen for you. Plan instead on the predictables, the likely percentages. Believe me, in the Christmas story the predictable participants are Simeon and Anna. If you want to be sure to make the Christmas scene, follow their lead. The odds are all with them.

There are wonderful surprises in the Christmas story, as I've indicated in earlier chapters. You probably wouldn't expect Christmas to come to a hotel, or a barn, or a think tank. So it's exciting to see that God did, indeed, choose to unfold the Christmas story in such unlikely places. And it's a reminder that God can't be programmed, and that the grace of God can't be predicted. God is God, and God's ways are past our finding out.

Nevertheless, the church—that is, the committed people of God—is a predictable part of the Christmas story. Wherever else Christmas might or might not come, it will come to the people who have built an altar in their hearts. Simeon and Anna were that kind of people, the kind of people you would look for in a church.

I'm among the first to admit that the church has vast numbers of another kind. I know we have a discouraging percentage whose religion is perfunctory and indifferent. But for those who really give the church a chance, the Simeon and Anna type, the church produces the finest and most admirable human beings you can ever hope to find. I confess that I am sometimes distressed at the pettiness and half-heartedness I sometimes find among church members, but I'm far more often impressed by the kind, generous, godly people the church has produced. I've now lived long enough to know that goodness isn't easy to come by or easy to maintain. Becoming a truly good human being is the most complex of all human enterprises. I rank it with the under-four-minute mile or swimming the English Channel. As a result, I'm surprised at how often the church produces such beauty of character.

So I'm not surprised that Christmas came to Simeon and Anna. They're the very people who would be waiting for God to come into the world in a new, beautiful, unexpected, and redemptive way. In fact, they're the kind of people who help make Christmas possible, because they're working with God to bring the divine will to pass in our world. And that's a side of Christmas to which we all ought to give more attention. It's not enough to find Christmas for ourselves, not enough that we should be swept up in its love and beauty; more than that, we should bring its gladness to others. Simeon and Anna were that kind of people. They worked with God, by their conscious commitment, to make Christmas happen.

So the first Christmas came to a church. Jesus was born into the Jewish equivalent of a church family, and before he was two months old, he had passed through three major religious ceremonies. And he continued to be part of that religious tradition even though it was corrupt in so many ways, and even though its very leaders opposed him.

That's why you'll find me in church every Sunday. Because while God can be found any number of places, and while God is not about to be fenced in by our expectations, the Bible makes clear that God is found by those who seek him. And at its best, the church is just that: a body of people who are seeking to please God and to do God's will. They're not perfect, but they've caught the message and they're seeking to bring it to pass.

I know, because through the years I've met so many, many people like Simeon and Anna.

SUGGESTIONS FOR LEADING A STUDY OF

Christmas from the Back Side

JOHN D. SCHROEDER

This book by J. Ellsworth Kalas takes familiar Christmas stories and looks at them from a different angle. To assist you in facilitating a discussion group, this study guide was created to help make this experience beneficial both for you and for the members of your group. Here are some thoughts on how you can help your group:

1. Distribute the book to participants before your first meeting, and request that they come having read the first chapter. You may want to limit the size of your group to increase participation.
2. Begin your sessions on time. Your participants will appreciate your promptness. You may wish to begin your first session with introductions and a brief get-acquainted time. Start each session by reading aloud the snapshot summary of the chapter for the day.

3. Select discussion questions and activities in advance. Note that the first question is a general question designed to get discussion going. The last question is designed to summarize the discussion. Feel free to change the order of the listed questions and to create your own questions. Allow a set amount of time for the questions and activities.

4. Remind your participants that all questions are valid as part of the learning process. Encourage their participation in discussion by saying that there are no "wrong" answers and that all input will be appreciated. Invite participants to share their thoughts, personal stories, and ideas as their comfort level allows.

5. Some questions may be more difficult to answer than others. If you ask a question and no one responds, begin the discussion by venturing an answer yourself. Then ask for comments and other answers. Remember that some questions may have multiple answers.

6. Ask the question *Why?* or *Why do you believe that?* to help continue a discussion and give it greater depth.

7. Give everyone a chance to talk. Keep the conversation moving. Occasionally you may want to direct a question to a specific person who has been quiet. "Do you have anything to add?" is a good follow-up question to ask another person. If the topic of conversation gets off track, move ahead by asking the next question in your study guide.

8. Before moving from questions to activities, ask group members if they have any questions that have not been answered. Remember that as a leader, you do not have to know all the answers. Some answers may come from group members. Other answers may even need a bit of research. Your job is to keep the discussion moving and to encourage participation.

9. Review the activity in advance. Feel free to modify

it or to create your own activity. Encourage participants to try the "At home" activity.

10. Following the conclusion of the activity, close with a brief prayer, praying either the printed prayer from the study guide or a prayer of your own. If your group desires, pause for individual prayer petitions.

11. Be grateful and supportive. Thank group members for their ideas and participation.

12. You are not expected to be a "perfect" leader. Just do the best you can by focusing on the participants and the lesson. God will help you lead this group.

13. Enjoy your time together!

SUGGESTIONS FOR PARTICIPANTS

1. What you receive from this study will be in direct proportion to your involvement. Be an active participant!

2. Please make it a point to attend all sessions and to arrive on time so that you can receive the greatest benefit.

3. Read the chapter and review the study guide questions prior to the meeting. You may want to jot down questions you have from the reading, and also answers to some of the study guide questions.

4. Be supportive and appreciative of your group leader as well as the other members of your group. You are on a journey together.

5. Your participation is encouraged. Feel free to share your thoughts about the material being discussed.

6. Pray for your group and your leader.

Chapter 1
The Scandal of Christmas

SNAPSHOT SUMMARY

This chapter explores how the need for Christmas can be traced to the disobedient behavior of the first humans.

REFLECTION / DISCUSSION QUESTIONS

1. What insights did you receive from this chapter?
2. What is the connection between Adam and Eve and Christmas?
3. Reflect on / discuss and list any similarities between the biblical Christmas story and a secular Christmas story such as Charles Dickens's *Christmas Carol*.
4. Why is it necessary to fully comprehend the scandal in Genesis 3 in order to get the full impact of the significance of Christmas?
5. In what ways do most people not fully understand sin? Why, as the author suggests, do we have such a strong tendency to excuse or deny our sin?
6. Give some examples of scandals and behavior that qualify as a sin.
7. How do people sometimes hold God at a distance?
8. The author suggests that we tend to rush past or ignore Advent—the seasonal time of preparation for Christ's coming, when we are to be in a spirit of prayer and repentance—in our haste to get to Christmas. Why do you believe this is so?
9. How do people try to hide from God?
10. What key learning from this chapter will you most reflect on in your life today / this week?

ACTIVITIES

As a group: Locate other scandals in the Bible that end in conversion.

At home: Reflect on the connection between sin and Christmas.

Prayer: *Dear God, thank you for the gift of Christmas, which reminds us of your love for the entire human race. Help us be close to you and far from sin, and always mindful of your forgiveness. Amen.*

Chapter 2
Three Votes for an Early Christmas

SNAPSHOT SUMMARY

This chapter examines how, long ago, Isaiah, Micah, and Job offered a preview of Christmas to come.

REFLECTION / DISCUSSION QUESTIONS

1. What insights did you receive from this chapter?
2. According to the author, what do Isaiah, Micah, and Job have in common?
3. Explain how Isaiah got an early start on Christmas.
4. "God generally uses people in ways for which the circumstances of their lives have prepared them"; how may this be the case in your life or in the lives of others you know?
5. What are the benefits of and drawbacks to our dreaming of a world of perfection?

6. Why has Christmas not yet come to vast numbers of people; what is missing?

7. What was Micah's prophecy?

8. Why are previews of Christmas by Micah and Isaiah meaningful to us today?

9. In what way was Job making an appeal for Christmas?

10. What key learning from this chapter will you most reflect on in your life today / this week?

ACTIVITIES

As a group: Locate other "votes" for an early Christmas in the Bible. What longings are expressed in the Old Testament?

At home: Begin your own preparation for Christmas by examining your heart.

Prayer: *Dear God, thank you for people like Isaiah, Micah, and Job, who saw the need for and believed in the coming of Christ, even when they could not put a name to their longing. Help us not to lose the true meaning of Christmas, but to prepare for the coming of Jesus into the world and into our lives. Amen.*

Chapter 3
Christmas Comes to a Back Fence

SNAPSHOT SUMMARY

This chapter reminds us that Christmas came—and comes today—to the world of the commonplace.

REFLECTION / DISCUSSION QUESTIONS

1. What insights did you receive from this chapter?
2. What does the author mean by the term "back fence"?
3. Why do you think Mary sought out Elizabeth to talk to?
4. Who do you go to when you need someone to talk to, and why?
5. What commonplace elements were a part of the first Christmas?
6. How were women regarded in the time of Mary and Elizabeth? What were their roles? How do women's roles of today compare?
7. Who are persons you would describe as "the quiet in the land"—persons devout in their faith, yet unpretentious; persons who might be described as the strength of the church, community, or nation?
8. How does Christmas show that "no part of life is unimportant to God"?
9. Explain what the author means by the statement "Christmas is meant to happen where we are."
10. What key learning from this chapter will you most reflect on in your life today / this week?

ACTIVITIES

As a group: List "unexpected" surprises of Christmas.

At home: Meditate on where Christmas will happen for you this year.

Prayer: *Dear God, thank you for the common places of life and how Christmas comes even there—and* especially *there. Help us open our eyes that we may see Christmas throughout the year and prepare for it in our hearts. In Jesus' name. Amen.*

Study Guide

Chapter 4
Celebrating Christmas in a Hotel

SNAPSHOT SUMMARY

This chapter provides insights about the birth of Jesus and making room for Christ today.

REFLECTION / DISCUSSION QUESTIONS

1. What insights did you receive from this chapter?
2. Share your best or worst hotel experience. What made it memorable?
3. Why do people prefer spending Christmas at home rather than in a hotel?
4. Explain how hotels represent the world of business and also loneliness.
5. Share a time when you were away from home at Christmas. What did you miss (or if you have never been away from home at Christmas, what *would* you miss)?
6. What do Christians have in common with the Bethlehem innkeeper?
7. The author says that while the world is growing more crowded, it also is growing more lonely. What evidence do you see that would support this view?
8. How is it symbolic that Jesus was born away from home?
9. In what ways are all of us homeless and wanderers?
10. What key learning from this chapter will you most reflect on in your life today / this week?

ACTIVITIES

As a group: Discuss what needs to happen for us to make room for Jesus.

At home: Meditate on making room for Jesus in your life.

Prayer: *Dear God, thank you for being close to us when we are far from home. We always need you, and we thank you for surrounding us with your presence and love. Help us rid our lives of some of the clutter in order to make more room for you. Amen.*

Chapter 5
How the Government Helped the First Christmas Happen

SNAPSHOT SUMMARY

This chapter explores the relationship between government and Christianity across the centuries, beginning with the first Christmas.

REFLECTION / DISCUSSION QUESTIONS

1. What insights did you receive from this chapter?
2. What was the involvement of Emperor Augustus in the first Christmas? What was his motivation?
3. What was the involvement of King Herod in the first Christmas? What was his motivation?
4. The author describes how neither Herod nor Augustus was aware of how his actions were serving the greater purposes of God. To what degree do you believe God acts or refrains from acting in human governmental matters today?
5. Why was the adult Jesus considered a dangerous political figure?
6. Why were early Christians persecuted by the government and by others?

7. In your view, what is the government's current relationship to Christians and Christianity, in this country or elsewhere?
8. In what ways is Christmas becoming more secular, and for what reasons?
9. What does it mean when we confess Jesus as our King?
10. What key learning from this chapter will you most reflect on in your life today / this week?

ACTIVITIES

As a group: Compare and contrast human government with the kingdom of God.

At home: Meditate on how you can best serve your Lord and King, Jesus Christ.

Prayer: *Dear God, thank you for ruling our world with justice, mercy, and love. Help us open our hearts so that we may better serve you and others. Remind us of the true meaning of Christmas, that we may be moved to celebrate your presence each day of the year. Amen.*

Chapter 6
Christmas and the Impossible Dream

SNAPSHOT SUMMARY

This chapter explores the strange journey of three wise men in search of a king.

REFLECTION / DISCUSSION QUESTIONS

1. What insights did you receive from this chapter?
2. What is known about literacy and the standard of living in the first century?

3. What is known about the three wise men?

4. What were the wise men expecting to find in Bethlehem, and why?

5. Reflect on / discuss and list the costs and preparation that would have been involved in the wise men's trip to Bethlehem.

6. What does the author indicate is so peculiar or unusual about the wise men's search for the King of the Jews?

7. Explain the "aching despair" and "eagerness of expectation" the author attributes to the times in which the wise men lived.

8. What does the word *wise* mean to you? Why might it be thought of as not easy to define?

9. Explain the meaning of the title of this chapter.

10. What key learning from this chapter will you most reflect on in your life today / this week?

ACTIVITIES

As a group: Assume that the wise men are trying to decide whether to make the trip to Bethlehem; present to them both the drawbacks and the benefits to their making this trip.

At home: Meditate on the impossible dreams of life. What are you searching for?

Prayer: *Dear God, thank you for seeking us out as we seek to be closer to you. Be with us on our journeys and help us carry your love with us. Amen.*

Chapter 7
Christmas Comes to a Church

SNAPSHOT SUMMARY

This chapter looks at the significance of Jesus' involvement in the traditional faith of his people, as well as the faith of Anna and Simeon, who welcomed Jesus at the Temple.

DISCUSSION QUESTIONS

1. What insights did you receive from this chapter?
2. What is the author's explanation for why "Christmas Comes to a Church" may be seen as an out-of-the-ordinary idea?
3. Share what you know about Anna and Simeon. How had Anna and Simeon obtained such a strong faith and relationship with God?
4. If Jesus were born in our day, who would be likely to recognize him and receive him? Explain your answer.
5. In what way was Jesus the product of a conventionally religious home? What steps were taken to ensure that the young Jesus was inducted into the faith life of his people?
6. What religious ceremonies, rituals, or other practices have been important in your life?
7. Imperfections aside, what is good about the church today? How has the church been important to you and your faith?
8. Who are the godly people of faith you know, and what example do they set for others?
9. The author states: "It's not enough to find Christmas for ourselves . . . we should bring its gladness to others." What does this mean to you, and in what ways could we accomplish this?

10. What key learning from this chapter will you most reflect on in your life today / this week?

ACTIVITIES

As a group: Reflect on / discuss how Christmas challenges and encourages you. Share favorite highlights from this book, or meaningful Christmas stories or reflections that have enriched your faith in some way.

At home: Reread the Christmas story (found in Matthew chapters 1–2 and in Luke 1–2), and meditate on its meaning and significance in your life. Make a list of new insights you have gained into Christmas, and pray about how you might be shaped by the Christmas experience in new and lasting ways.

Prayer: *Dear God, thank you for the birth of your son, Jesus. Thank you for the gift of salvation, peace, and love he brings to the world through your grace. Thank you for opening our eyes to new truths, so that we may become more effective Christians and walk closer with you, not only in the Christmas season, but every day of the year. In Jesus' name. Amen.*

Allegra

Allegra

SHELLEY HRDLITSCHKA

ORCA BOOK PUBLISHERS

Library and Archives Canada Cataloguing in Publication

Hrdlitschka, Shelley, 1956-
Allegra / Shelley Hrdlitschka.

Issued also in electronic formats.
ISBN 978-1-4598-0197-4

I. Title.
PS8565.R44A64 2013 JC813'.54 C2012-907454-3

First published in the United States, 2013
Library of Congress Control Number: 2012952952

Summary: Allegra wants to dance, but when her music-theory teacher insists she undertake a composition project, their collaboration brings unforeseen changes in both their lives.

RECYCLED
Paper made from recycled material
FSC® C103567

Orca Book Publishers is dedicated to preserving the environment and has printed this book on Forest Stewardship Council® certified paper.

Orca Book Publishers gratefully acknowledges the support for its publishing programs provided by the following agencies: the Government of Canada through the Canada Book Fund and the Canada Council for the Arts, and the Province of British Columbia through the BC Arts Council and the Book Publishing Tax Credit.

Design by Teresa Bubela
Cover photography by Getty Images and dreamstime.com
Author photo by Leslie Thomas

ORCA BOOK PUBLISHERS
PO Box 5626, Stn. B
Victoria, BC Canada
V8R 6S4

ORCA BOOK PUBLISHERS
PO Box 468
Custer, WA USA
98240-0468

www.orcabook.com
Printed and bound in Canada.

16 15 14 13 • 4 3 2 1

In memory of a gentle soul and voracious reader,
Rachel Marie Sharman, 1990–2009

One

Ms. Jennings taps her fingers on the desk as I glance at my course-selection sheet.

English 12
History 12
Modern Dance Technique (Senior)
Visual Arts (Senior)
Choreography (Senior)
Ballet (Senior)
Hip-Hop/Jazz (Senior)
Music Theory 11-12

"There's a mistake here." I push the sheet back across the desk.

"There is?" Snatching the paper, she runs her eyes down the list. "Everything looks in order to me."

"I don't need to take any music classes, remember? I just want dance classes, and whatever academics I still need to graduate. I did math and biology in summer school to get them out of the way. My mom and I talked to you about this last spring, when I registered."

"Ah, yes," she says, leaning back in her chair and whipping off her glasses. "Allegra. Allegra Whitford. You're the girl who has completed all the levels in the National Music Academy. Your mother is the harpist in the Deer Lake Symphony Orchestra and your father is..."

"Bass player for the group Loose Ends."

"Right. Loose Ends. I think I've heard of them." She sits up straighter. "What you'll need to do, then, is go see Mr. Rocchelli, the music-theory teacher. Explain your situation to him. Then get his signature on a Drop form." She hands me the form and a map of the school, then stands up, dismissing me.

I stay seated. "Why don't you just take me out of it now and put me in another dance class?"

"Sorry. School rules." She moves to the door of her office. "Without his permission to drop the class, your records will show that you simply didn't complete it."

"That's stupid." I get to my feet.

Her eyebrows arch, and then she glances at the wall clock. "You'll find him in portable number four, at the back of the building. You've got time to get out there now and see him before the start of classes."

"And once he's signed off on it?"

"Come back here at lunchtime. We'll see what dance classes are offered in that block."

I brush past her in the doorway and am just about through the main office when I hear her say, "*If* there are any."

"What?" I turn back, but another student is already following her into the small room.

Disappointment nudges aside the anxiety I'm feeling about being here. I'd had such high hopes for Deer Lake School for the Fine and Performing Arts. Because it's a high school for the arts, I'd assumed the counselors would be more creative, more energetic and just generally nicer than the ones from Maple Creek High, my previous school. Ms. Jennings seems as burned-out as any other teacher. Not a good sign.

I find my way to portable four, which is behind the school. The door's ajar, so I peek into the room. There's a guy on the far side, opening and shutting cupboards, probably checking inventory. His back is to the door. I know it's the right room—the chairs and music stands are set out, ready for rehearsal—but this can't be Mr. Rocchelli. From the back, anyway, he looks like a student, in faded jeans and a T-shirt.

I clear my throat. "Excuse me..."

He jumps, startled, and whirls around. His sudden reaction surprises me, and I step back, but not before I notice that he looks a little older from the front, probably in his early to mid-twenties.

"Sorry," I say. "I didn't mean to scare you. I'm looking for Mr. Rocchelli."

He clutches at his chest. "I think my heart stopped for a moment there." He laughs. "Can you imagine what a dramatic start to the term that would be? I can see the headlines: *New teacher dies of heart attack before first class.*" He chuckles again, and that's when I notice the dimples in his cheeks. "I'm Mr. Rocchelli. And you are?"

So it is him. I step farther into the classroom. "I'm Allegra Whitford. I'm here to—"

"Allegra!" He looks pleased. "What a great name. In music, the term *allegro* means 'lively, with a happy air.' Does that describe you?" His smile lights up his face.

"I think that's what my parents were hoping when they named me."

"And?"

"I let them down."

He studies me, his smile fading. "Oh. Well, then, what can I do for you, Allegra?"

I approach him, holding out the Drop form. "I just need you to sign this form giving me permission to drop your music-theory class."

His eyebrows spring up. "Why would you want to drop my class? Have I already offended you?" The smile is back, along with the dimples.

"No, it's just that I don't need it. I've been studying music for years. I want to take extra dance classes."

"Ah, you're a dancer." He takes the form, scans it and then passes it back to me.

"But you haven't signed it."

"I don't intend to."

"But if you don't, it will appear on my records that I didn't complete your class."

"Then I guess you'll have to complete it."

I can't decide if he's joking around again. "I want to take a dance class in this block."

"I see that you already have four dance classes on your schedule," he says. "This is a fine *and* performing arts school, Allegra, not a dance school. You need to take my music-theory class to bring balance to your schedule. You know that balance is important in dance, right? It's important in life too. And at school."

I sigh. "I've already completed all the levels in the National Music Academy. I talked to Ms. Jennings and she's okay with it too. Please just sign the form." I'm aware that I haven't concealed my irritation very well, but he's being so annoying.

"That's great that you've mastered the National Music Academy curriculum," he says way too enthusiastically.

"And if that's the case, I'll design your assignments to challenge you. There's always something new to learn. I can explain that to Ms. Jennings."

"But I'm not interested in any more music theory," I tell him. "I want to dance!"

He turns away, but not before I notice the clench of his jaw. He continues opening and closing cupboard doors. "I expect to see you here in block seven, Allegra," he says over his shoulder. "And I promise you this." He turns to look at me again. "My class will challenge you and quite possibly help you with your dance too."

A bell rings, announcing the start of classes. I hear students entering the room, but my eyes remain locked with Mr. Rocchelli's, challenging him. The classroom fills with that back-to-school buzz. I break eye contact and turn away, fighting the urge to slam the door as I return to the main building. This school isn't going to be any better than the last one.

Two

"New here?"

I turn and look at the girl sitting at the next desk. Her brown skin is flawless, like her eye makeup. Her hair has been braided into perfect cornrows, and I wonder if she has extensions. "Uh-huh." I open my notebook to the first page and lay my pen along the spine.

"What's your focus?"

"Dance." In my peripheral vision I see that her dark eyes are sizing me up, all of me, and I don't like it.

"How d'you like Ms. Dekker?"

Ms. Dekker is the dance teacher. I met her in first block, but we only talked about her expectations. We start dancing tomorrow. I shrug and allow my own gaze to check my classmate out, noting the slight bulge at the waistband of her jeans. Clearly she's not a dancer. "She seems okay."

"You just wait." She pulls a pen out of her backpack and places it beside a decorated binder.

"Wait for what?"

A small smile tugs at her mouth. "You'll see." She turns to face the front of the room, just as the teacher arrives. I stare at her another moment before turning to face forward myself. I make a mental note to sit somewhere else when English class comes around again.

I have to shoulder my way through the crowded hallway to get back to the office. Lockers bang open and kids reach inside them to grab their lunches. The energy is tangible, and it ricochets off the walls as classmates who haven't seen each other all summer greet one another. Inside the office it's much quieter, but a long line of students snakes around the room. It looks as if everyone is waiting to speak to Ms. Jennings, who is standing behind the main counter. I take my place at the end of the line and think about what I'll say to her. I have to be convincing when I explain that Mr. Rocchelli is dead wrong, that staying in his class is a total waste of my time and that she needs to make an exception for me. It's imperative that she take me out of his class, even without his stupid signature. I'll tell her that without another dance class I won't be properly prepared for my chosen career. I'll ask her to think creatively, and I'll point out that even if there isn't a dance class offered in that block, my whole schedule can be altered once I'm out of music theory.

We don't seem to be moving. I crane my neck to see what's going on at the front of the line. Ms. Jennings is speaking to a tall skinny guy with a tidy ponytail and small frameless glasses. Her arms are folded across her chest, and she's shaking her head.

"Sorry, Spencer, there's nothing I can do for you," she says.

Spencer jabs his finger at the paper on the counter, but she's not willing to budge on whatever the problem is. Finally he smacks his hand on the counter. She simply stands taller, folds her arms even tighter and then peers around him to the next student. He kicks the counter and stomps out of the office.

Oh great, I think. Ms. Jennings is not in a cooperative mood, and I don't think she warmed to me after our chat this morning. Things are not looking good.

From my backpack I pull out the form Mr. Rocchelli has refused to sign. I stare at the line where his signature is supposed to be. The signature Ms. Jennings says I need to get out of his class.

I think back on my visit to his classroom. Had I heard him correctly? Is he new to this school too? Will Ms. Jennings even know what his signature looks like? Most people just scrawl something illegible when they have to sign something.

I pull out a pen and a textbook to write on. When the attention of the students on either side of me is elsewhere, I quickly scrawl a signature. I make a big fat *R* at the start, and the rest is just a long squiggle. There. Now I won't have to convince her of anything. She'll just have to put me in another dance class.

The line inches forward. My stomach growls. I watch Ms. Jennings's face as one student after another slides a form across the counter to her. She glances at each one, sometimes making changes in the computer and sometimes just pushing the forms back at the students.

When there are only two students to go before I reach her, a tall figure passes behind me, heading toward the end of the counter where he can go through to the staff-only side. It's Mr. Rocchelli. My stomach clenches.

I drop my head and let my hair fall around my face, but in my peripheral vision I see him walk to the rear of the office to check a bulletin board. He stands there studying the messages, his back to us. The student at the counter moves away, and there's only one more person before it's my turn. I keep my eyes glued to Mr. Rocchelli's back, willing him to stay put until I'm safely out of there.

I listen to the conversation going on in front of me. The girl's babbling away about her summer holiday. Ms. Jennings is smiling. Her face has softened. Bad timing—she likes this girl, and their conversation doesn't seem like it's going to end anytime soon.

I clear my throat. *Get on with it*, I want to say. *There are people waiting*. The girl glances back at me and then leans forward to speak more softly to the school counselor. In that moment I see Mr. Rocchelli swing around and move toward a bank of narrow drawers. He pulls one open and reaches inside for a stack of papers. Then he pushes the drawer shut and leans back, rifling through the pages in his hand.

Ms. Jennings is now consulting the computer screen beside her. "Well," she tells the girl, "if we move you into the chamber choir, that would free up block seven and then you could take music theory."

The girl's face lights up. "Perfect!"

Ms. Jennings types something into the computer. "*Voilà!*" She smiles at the girl. "It's done."

The girl turns to leave, and my heart leaps. I'm going to get away with it. I step up to the counter, but then the girl is back, nudging me aside.

"Sorry," she says to me, then turns to Ms. Jennings. "Could you please print me out a new course-selection sheet?"

"Of course," Ms. Jennings says.

I clench my jaw again as Ms. Jennings reopens the girl's file and hits the Print button. The printer farther down the counter whirs to life. Ms. Jennings walks toward it, and that's when she notices Mr. Rocchelli standing at the back of the office. Suddenly her shoulders straighten, her face settles into a pleasant expression, and she pushes her glasses up into her hair, using them as a hair band. "Mr. Rocchelli," she says, raising her voice so he can hear her across the room. "I've just enrolled another student in your music-theory class."

He looks up from his papers. "You have? Great!" He walks across the room toward her. "I'm so relieved to hear that," he continues. "The enrollment for that class is so low, I was afraid it might get cancelled. Students seem to be put off by the word *theory* for some reason. My other classes are all full."

"Maybe that's because it sounds like work," she says with a roll of her eyes. She starts walking back to the counter, motioning for him to follow her.

The girl waiting for her course-selection sheet has stepped aside, and now I'm standing there, totally exposed. I'd already placed the sheet with the phony signature onto the counter, in a futile attempt to get the process over with as quickly as possible. Now I feel the blood draining from my face, and I reach for the Drop form, knowing I have to get out of there fast.

But Ms. Jennings is faster. In a single motion, she places the other girl's printout on the counter and snatches up my form.

"Allegra!" Mr. Rocchelli says, seeing me.

I nod but don't look at him.

"Mr. Rocchelli, this is Julia," Ms. Jennings is saying. She motions to the girl standing beside me. "She's the student who just enrolled in your class."

Mr. Rocchelli's attention turns from me to the other girl. "Hello, Julia," he says. "I look forward to seeing you in block seven. It's going to be a great class."

Part of me is aware that Julia is blushing, but most of me is trying to figure out how I can slink out of here without being noticed.

"Allegra here is in that class too," he says, turning back to me.

Now I feel *my* cheeks burning.

Ms. Jennings glances at my form. "Actually," she says to Mr. Rocchelli, frowning, "it appears you've just given her permission to drop your class."

"I have?" he says. I finally look up, and he holds my gaze a moment longer than I expect. Then he takes the form from Ms. Jennings and glances at it. I look back down at my feet and feel my heart sink. I wonder if I'll be the first student in history to get expelled on the very first day of starting a new school.

Mr. Rocchelli doesn't speak for a few moments. Those five or ten seconds feel like an eternity. Finally, I can't take it any longer. I look back up. He's staring at me, his head tilted. My heart is now pounding. He nods. "You're right, Ms. Jennings," he says. "It seems I did give Allegra permission to drop my class."

I'm vaguely aware of Ms. Jennings looking back and forth between me and Mr. Rocchelli. I'm waiting for him to bust me, but he just continues to stare. Finally he holds the paper up and very slowly rips it in half.

"But I have since changed my mind. I think Allegra needs my class. Actually, I *know* Allegra needs my class. I take back my permission for her to drop it."

Ms. Jennings keeps glancing back and forth between us; then she shrugs. "Whatever you say." She cranes her neck to look to the person in line behind me. "Can I help you?" she asks.

I step to the side but keep my eyes fixed on Mr. Rocchelli. He seems to be waiting for something. Probably an apology. He's not going to get one.

"I guess I'll see you in block seven then," I say finally, turning and walking toward the door. I can't help myself: I have to look back. He's dropped the ripped-up paper into a recycling box, but he's still watching me.

I leave the office and start walking down the hall. That's when I notice how bad my hands are shaking.

The sharp smell of cleaning solution assaults me when I walk through the door. Something's wrong. My mom is a lot of things, but a clean freak isn't one of them. I find her in the kitchen, on her knees, scrubbing the floor. She looks up when she sees me standing in the doorway. "Well?" she asks, rocking back into a squatting position. "How was it?"

"It sucked."

Mom sighs and rolls back onto her butt, her back leaning against a cupboard. "Why did it suck?"

"They're making me take music theory. I don't need it. I've done the work already. You know that."

She nods thoughtfully. "Okay, so how were the rest of your classes?"

I just shrug. They were fine, actually, but that awful situation in the school office—getting caught forging that signature—well, the whole stupid thing unsettled me. "So what's with you?" I ask, motioning to the floor.

"Your dad called. He'll be home tonight."

I should have guessed. Dad's visits always throw her into a cleaning frenzy. It's not that he likes a clean house—not at all. It's just that his imminent arrival stirs something up in her, a weird kind of nervousness that she works off by cleaning.

Mom gets to her feet as I open the fridge. "Are you working tonight?" I ask. Mom landed her job with the orchestra about a year ago. It was a huge deal for her. Before that, she worked from home, teaching harp and piano. She still teaches but not as much.

"Just a rehearsal," she says. "But there are five performances a week for the rest of the month." She watches as I pour myself a glass of nonfat milk. "At least you'll have your father for company."

"How long will he be home?"

"Who knows?" She sighs.

I nod, heave my backpack over my shoulder and take my milk and an apple down the hall to my room. I drop the food on my desk and flop onto the bed. Rolling over,

I stare at the ceiling. Like Mom, hearing that my dad's coming home unsettles me too. The truth is, I really don't know him that well. He's been touring with his band since I was a small kid, and he's on the road more than he's here. I've come to think of his visits home as crash landings. He'll sleep for most of the first few days, and then, as he emerges from his stupor, he'll start glancing at me, shyly, more like a stranger than a father. I think he'd like to know me better too, but I haven't figured out how to help him with that. He's full of confidence when he's onstage performing, dancing around, being goofy, but he's like a self-conscious kid with me. He tries, I'll give him that. When he's home, he comes to a lot of my dance classes and sits in a chair watching hours of tedious barre work and exercises. My teachers at the studio let him hang out there because Sonia, the owner, is a big fan of his band, Loose Ends, and she gets seriously weird when he's around. He's rarely home for my performances, but he's definitely seen the rigors of training.

Mom appears at my bedroom door. "I'm leaving," she says. "I've got a ride. The car's all yours, if you need it."

I nod.

She turns to leave, then swings back around. "No dance tonight?" she asks.

"No, it's registration night. Dance classes start up tomorrow."

"Oh, okay." She hesitates. "Well, then, I guess I'll see you in the morning."

"Yep."

She studies me for another moment, blows me a kiss and is gone.

I spend the evening waiting. I do homework, eat, chat online with Angela, my friend from dance, all the while expecting to hear Dad come through the door. I pace and peer out the window. I wish he'd carry a cell phone like every other parent does so I could phone him and see where he is. I try to plan what we can talk about when he does get here. Maybe I can tell him about my problems with Mr. Rocchelli. Not the forgery part, but what a stubborn jerk he is. Dad would get it. He wouldn't have the time of day for a guy like Mr. Rocchelli. Dad is a self-taught musician and doesn't believe in spending years studying music theory and all that. It's a running joke between him and Mom. She's classically trained, but it's only recently that she's found work performing. He's been a performing musician for years.

One of the great things about Dad is he doesn't question my desire to study dance, which Mom only let me take seriously once I'd completed the highest level of piano performance at the National Music Academy. It was the deal we had. Once I'd mastered the music, she'd support my dream of being a dancer. That's how I ended up at a performing-arts school. It's finally my turn.

The hours tick by. I take a long bath. I read. Eventually I give up waiting and go to bed. I don't hear either of them come home.

Music theory is my second class on Wednesday morning. It's the one class I can find easily, having been here just yesterday. I pause at the door, feeling nauseous, but force my legs to propel me into the room. I almost wish Mr. Rocchelli had busted me for the forged signature, because now I feel indebted to him, and that makes the whole thing even more awkward.

A quick glance around, and I realize he's not here yet. The music stands have been shoved into a corner, and the chairs are arranged in a small circle. A few kids are already seated. I groan inwardly. It looks like he's trying to create one of those intimate, "safe" places to learn. I just want to hide behind the rest of the kids, do the work and get out of here.

I sit in a chair away from anyone else. A moment later a backpack plunks onto the chair next to mine. Glancing up, I see that it belongs to Julia, the girl who was in line in front of me in the office yesterday. She's chattering away to someone a couple of chairs over. She plants herself on the chair next to her backpack. Inhaling deeply, I slouch lower in my seat, staring at a point on the floor in the center of the circle, not wanting the others to see how uncomfortable I am about being here, not knowing anyone, and mad because I shouldn't be in this class in the first place.

I let my thoughts drift back over my morning, and they settle on my mother's strange behavior. When I got up she was already in the kitchen, putting coffee on. I noticed dirty wineglasses standing beside the sink. Two glasses. She must have come home and waited up for my father, or perhaps it was the other way around. As I popped bread into the toaster, I watched as she wiped the already clean counters. She was still on edge, for some reason. I'd have thought she'd be happy to have him home.

My thoughts are interrupted by Mr. Rocchelli's arrival. The nausea I felt earlier intensifies, and I wonder if I might throw up. I glance about, wondering where the nearest washroom is.

Mr. Rocchelli takes the remaining chair and smiles at the circle of students. I won't meet his eyes, keeping my gaze on the window behind him.

"Welcome to music theory," he says. "I'm Mr. Rocchelli, your teacher. My friends call me Rocky. If you feel comfortable with it, you can call me that too."

Despite myself, I look at him to see if he's serious. Whoever heard of a teacher giving students permission to use a nickname? Mr. Rocchelli must be even newer to the teaching profession than I'd guessed.

"We're a small group," he says, "which is awesome. It'll allow ample opportunity for one-on-one instruction."

I swallow a groan and sink even lower in my chair, noticing that Julia sits up a little straighter in hers.

"So, let's get going," he says. "I want us to build community in this room, and in order to do that I have some games for us to play, to jump-start us."

The morning careens from bad to worse. I hate this touchy-feely stuff.

The first game is one I'm sure I played in third grade. We each have to tell two truths and one lie about ourselves, and the others have to decide which statement is the lie.

"I'll go first," Mr. Rocchelli says.

He thinks for a moment. "I have a collection of over a thousand vinyl LPs. I am a wannabe jazz musician. My father is a beekeeper." He points to the guy on his left. "Well, which is the lie?"

We each take turns guessing. I go last and guess that he's lying about the LPs.

He smiles. "Those of you who guessed the LPs are right, though I do have over seven hundred." A murmur runs through the circle. "Why don't you go next?" he says to me.

I take a deep breath and spew out the first three things that come to me. "I was only three pounds when I was born, my dad is the bass player for the Loose Ends, and I have four brothers."

Without exception, everyone guesses that the lie is my dad being the bass player for the Loose Ends. For some reason, when it's his turn to guess Mr. Rocchelli passes and doesn't say why. When I tell the class I'm an only child, I see looks of surprise and even disbelief cross a few faces.

"Are you serious?" a guy asks. He looks familiar, but I can't place him.

I just nod.

"That is so cool," he says.

"It looks like Allegra got you all on that one," Mr. Rocchelli says. "Well done. Julia, why don't you go next?"

The game continues, and I have to admit, some of the truths are pretty interesting. One guy has actually swallowed a live goldfish, and the boy who asked if I was serious about my dad has the autographs of two hundred well-known musicians. I'm impressed.

When everyone has had a turn, Mr. Rocchelli explains the next game. He asks one of the boys to stand and then takes away his chair. "In this game, the person without a chair has to name one thing that they have never done. Everyone else who has never done the same thing has to get up and take an empty chair from someone else who has also never done it. The person who ends up without a chair goes next." He looks around the group, then adds, "And please keep the activities clean and legal."

"I have never eaten snails," the first boy says. Most of us jump up and scramble to find a chair. My butt hits a chair at the same moment that Julia's butt hits the same chair. She gives me a shoulder-check and I slide off, barely managing to stay on my feet. "Looks like you're up next," Mr. Rocchelli says to me.

"I have never owned a dog," I say. A few chairs are exchanged.

"I have never worn braces."

"I have never colored my hair." Mr. Rocchelli jumps into the fray on that one and, not wanting to shove any of his students, ends up losing.

"I have never been fishing," he says. About half of the group scrambles to get to an available chair.

"I have never been on a diet."

"I have never broken my curfew."

"I have never made my curfew."

The game gets slapstick and silly, and even I find myself laughing. One guy keeps losing on purpose so that he can say ridiculous things. "I've never kissed a girl." All the girls switch chairs while none of the boys move, despite the goading a few of them get.

"I've never cheated on an exam." A surprising number of kids stay in their seats.

"I've never cheated on my girlfriend."

"Okay, that's enough," Mr. Rocchelli says, clapping his hands to get our attention.

Reluctantly, we settle back into our chairs, but the chatter continues. The game has prompted a lot of silly conversation. As I watch him hand out the course outline, I realize that the tension I'd felt at the start of the class has subsided. Maybe Mr. Rocchelli knows what he's doing after all.

He goes over the units we'll be studying, outlining some of the assignments, and then asks for questions.

"Rocky, what percentage of our grade will the final exam be worth?" Julia asks. "I'm, like, *so* bad at exams," she adds.

I scan the faces of the other students, wondering if anyone else feels like rolling their eyes. The guy who looks familiar makes eye contact with me. That's when I realize he's the guy from the office yesterday, the one who was arguing with Ms. Jennings. Spencer. He smirks and nods in Julia's direction. I nod in return, feeling a sense of silent camaraderie. Neither of us likes Ms. Jennings or Julia. After a few more questions, Mr. Rocchelli dismisses the class, but he adds, "Allegra, will you stay behind a moment, please?"

Oh man, I think. Here it comes, the lecture about how lucky I am that he hasn't turned me in. I'll probably have to apologize before he'll let me leave the room. The relaxed mood brought on by the games evaporates in a single moment.

I remain in my chair, trying not to act as nervous as I feel. Spencer smiles when he passes by me, and I try to smile back, but I think it comes off as more of a grimace. When everyone is gone, Mr. Rocchelli goes to his desk and comes back with a file folder. He hands it to me and then takes a seat a couple of chairs away.

"What's this?" I ask.

"Open it up."

I flip it open and read the words on the top of the page: *Music Theory 11-12. Final Exam.* I look at him, confused.

"I forgot to mention," he says, "that you can challenge the course. Take the exam early and be done with it."

As the words sink in, I become angry. Why didn't he mention this at the start? It would have saved me from embarrassing myself the way I did in the school office yesterday.

I guess he can see the flush working its way up my cheeks, because he leans forward and says, "I owe you an apology, Allegra."

I still don't say anything. I'm too dumbfounded at the direction this conversation is going.

"I should have told you yesterday that you wouldn't have to redo all the work you've already done."

I find my voice. "Yeah, you should have."

He just nods.

"So all I have to do is write this exam and pass it, and I'm done with your class?"

"Not quite."

I look at him, waiting.

He takes back the file with the exam. "You'll be done with Music Theory 11-12. But you won't be done with my class."

"What are you talking about?"

"Like I told you yesterday, Allegra, this is not a dance school. If you pass the exam, I have another project in mind, one I think will challenge you to actually apply all the music theory you know. You may even want to call on your knowledge of dance."

"Why won't you just let me sign up for another class?" I know I'm whining, but I don't care.

"I've read your file, Allegra. I know that both your parents are musicians. That's why I said *Pass* in your round of the two-truths-and-a-lie game. I believe you do have a sound background in music. That said, I am committed to the philosophy of this school. We are about all the arts. I want you to push yourself in more areas than just dance. Believe me, it will help you bring even more to the dance studio." He pauses and leans forward. "You have to trust me on this one, Allegra."

For the first time all morning, I meet his gaze and stare back at him. I feel a sense of defeat.

"Your other option would be to take drama, I guess. Or painting."

There's not a chance I'm doing that.

"Well?" he asks when I don't respond.

I sigh. "How soon can I write the exam?" I nod at the file.

"Attagirl!" he says, beaming.

Despite myself, I notice how nice he looks when he smiles. "Whatever," I say.

Three

Ms. Dekker teaches all of my dance and movement classes. She's the one the girl from my English class told me about. During my first ballet class, I can feel her eyes assessing me during barre. I try to ignore her and focus on the exercises, but she keeps hollering out instructions. "Shoulders down, Allegra! Stretch your feet! Pull up, chest bones to the ceiling! Ribs closed, soft neck!" I try to do everything she says, but there are too many things to think about at once. When I'm thinking about my arms, I forget to point my toes, and when I'm worrying about my legs, my posture sags.

With a click of Ms. Dekker's remote, the music stops and our exercise comes to an abrupt halt.

"Allegra," she scolds, "I see that you've picked up some bad habits along the way. Where have you been studying up until now?"

"Turning Pointe," I tell her.

"Well, the teachers at Turning Pointe should be ashamed of themselves," she says. "Your feet are terrible and your turnout needs a lot of work."

I stretch out my leg to do a *grande rond de jambe* and she bounds right over to where I'm working. Bending down, she grabs my inner thigh and rotates it upward. "There," she says, standing up and assessing my new position. "That is proper technique."

It feels all wrong. My *développé* is overcrossed, and the way she's twisted my leg makes my hip feel out of place. "Are you sure?" I ask. "It doesn't feel right this way."

"I'm sure," she says. "And I expect to see you use your turnout from your hips from now on, not forced from the knees."

In the mirror, I make eye contact with the girl from English class. She tilts her head, eyebrows raised in a question. I nod and decide that I might not avoid her in English after all.

Mom and Dad swing around to look at me when I enter the living room. I've just arrived home from school, and they obviously haven't heard me come into the house. They smile, and Dad gets to his feet, but I feel the tension in the room and note their stiff postures. "Hey, Legs!" Dad says, using the nickname he gave me when I was a little girl. He pulls me into a hug. I relax into his arms. The smells of the road cling to his sweatshirt—another musician's stale cigarette smoke, the greasy fumes of coffee-shop food and the body odor from nights on the tour bus, sleeping in his clothes. He must not have done his laundry yet or showered. He probably slept all day.

"How's your new school?' he asks, pulling away but letting his hands rest on my shoulders. I notice his sleep-mussed hair and the stubble on his skin.

"Well, it's not what I expected. They have stupid rules, just like at Maple Creek, and the dance teacher,"—I pause, wondering how to describe her—"she's kinda high-strung."

"Aren't all dance teachers high-strung?" He laughs. "You know what they say: those who can, do; those who can't, teach." His hands drop to his sides.

"Jerry!" Mom says sternly. She loves teaching.

He shrugs, still grinning. "I'm just repeating what I've heard."

Mom crosses her arms. "Those who can think for themselves do, and those who can't repeat ignorant things that other ignorant people say," she says, flushing. I look from one to the other, wondering what's really going on here.

"It's just a joke, Cindy," Dad says, crossing the room and settling back into the couch, facing Mom. "Relax."

"Not a funny one," Mom answers.

There's a long, awkward silence, and then Mom stands up. "I'll get dinner started. I have to leave early for the theater."

She leaves the room and Dad and I sit across from one another. I'm acutely aware of the silence.

"How was the road trip?" I ask.

Dad stretches, a full-body one. "It was good."

"How good?" I ask, repeating something he often asks me.

"Pretty good," he answers, now parroting my usual response. He grins.

"Better than the last one?"

"I can't honestly say." He looks thoughtful. "I don't remember anything about the last one." He hesitates, then adds, "They're all starting to run together in my head."

We sit quietly for another minute, but this time it's a comfortable silence. Dad's probably thinking about past road trips, trying to remember the details, and I'm wondering how I might get to know him better, how I might get him to talk about his experiences. He stretches again. "I guess I'd better shower," he says. "Before your mom sends me back on the road. We'll talk later."

I nod, and as I watch him leave the room I notice the slight stoop to his shoulders. He's finally starting to show his age.

I set the table while my mom tosses the salad and then spoons sauce over the pasta. I find a couple of candles in a drawer, place them in the center of the table and rummage around in another drawer, looking for matches.

"Special occasion?" Mom asks, putting the food on the table.

"Yeah. Dad's home." I strike the match.

After cleaning up the dinner dishes, I get changed and grab the car keys from the hook beside the door. A couple of months ago, when I first got my driver's license, Mom began riding to work with another musician so that I could use the car to get myself to dance classes. It was a huge relief, as the bus late at night is sketchy. Besides, I hate getting on the bus when I'm all sweaty from class.

I've just climbed into our Mazda when a little red sports car pulls into the driveway behind me. Looking in the rearview mirror, I'm surprised to see that the driver is a man. For some reason, I've assumed Mom's been getting rides from one of the other women. I've never thought to ask, and I haven't noticed the driver until now.

Mom must have been watching for him, because she steps right out of the house, wearing her black floor-length performance dress, and the driver steps out of the car to open the passenger door for her. He's wearing a black tux. They look more like a couple going to a fancy charity event than two musicians heading to work. She waves at me and flashes a smile. The driver waves too, and then they're off. That's when I notice Dad standing at the living-room window, mug in hand, watching. He's changed into clean clothes for dinner, but they're his comfy clothes, baggy sweatpants and an old T-shirt. His hair is tousled from the shower and not yet combed. His face is thoughtful as he watches them drive away. "See ya tonight, Dad," I say to myself, waving. I just like the sound of it.

I can see lights on in the house when I pull into the driveway. This cheers me up considerably after a painfully tough jazz-tech class at Turning Pointe. Then, as I step into the hallway, I hear music floating up from the studio in the basement. Live music. Dad's band is already rehearsing. I'm surprised they haven't taken at least a night off. It can only mean one thing: they aren't staying in town for long.

My damp dance leotard sticks to my skin, but it's so nice to hear Dad's music that instead of heading straight to the shower, I pour myself a bowl of cereal and plunk myself down at the kitchen table. The Loose Ends have a Celtic sound with a rock beat. It appeals to a wide variety of people, young and old. I'm still amazed at the reaction I get from people when I tell them that my dad plays with the Loose Ends. I'm proud of him, but I'd still rather he had a job where I'd get to see him more often.

The band is practicing something new. It's catchy. I can hear Dad on the sax, really jazzing it up. He calls himself the bass player, but he actually plays a whole range of instruments. As I cross the room to the sink, I find myself responding to the music. My hips swing back and forth as I bend down to put my dishes in the dishwasher, and by the time I've straightened up, my whole body is moving. Warmed up from three hours in the dance studio, I get right into it, my hips leading the way. A solo turns into a duet as I catch a glimpse of myself in the reflection of the dark window. We whirl around the kitchen, arms stretched overhead, leaping, spinning. I throw everything I know into the mix: drag step, chaîné, axel turn, kick layout to the ground, roll and stand-up. The pulsating beat, the complicated rhythms, the wail of the singer—it all energizes me, and I feel free and safe enough to simply let go. I dance faster, harder, in total abandon.

When the music slows, my movement follows: chassé, attitude turn, fondu into arabesque, brushing through into a pirouette. I'm left gazing at my own reflection. I curtsey, and my reflection curtsies back, the perfect dance partner.

A sudden clapping of hands startles me, and I spin around. The band's manager, Steve, steps out from the shadows near the top of the basement stairs.

"You were watching me?"

"I didn't mean to," he says apologetically. "I just came up to grab some beer, and there you were. You were so… so into it." His face takes on a different expression, one I can't quite read but that makes me a little uncomfortable. "Anyway, I didn't want to disturb you," he says.

How stupid had I looked? Steve stays put, staring at me, and I stare back, not knowing what to do next. I struggle to catch my breath.

And then we hear footsteps coming up the stairs. "Where's that beer, Steve?" Dad's voice breaks the spell of our strange standoff seconds before he appears in the doorway. He glances at Steve, puzzled, and then steps around him and into the kitchen. That's when he sees me standing there, zombie-like. "Legs, you're home!" he says. He looks me over, a crease deepening between his brows. "Looks like you should be hitting the shower." He glances behind him at Steve, who's still glued to his spot in the shadows. "What are you staring at?" Dad asks, his eyes narrowing. "Never seen a girl in ballet tights before?" He looks back at me; I'm standing equally still. "Go on, Allegra," he says, using my full name. He must be serious.

Steve steps back so I can slide past him into the hall. I shut my bedroom door and pull off my leotard. This is the first time in ages that my dad has actually behaved like a father, acting all protective. I slip into my housecoat. It's too late, really; I'm practically a grown-up myself.

But my heart expands in my chest. I like Dad telling me what to do.

I poke my head into the hallway and check to see that the coast is clear before I scurry across to the bathroom. I shut and lock the door behind me.

As I turn on the shower, I remember the expression on Steve's face when I caught him watching me dance. At first he looked guilty, like he'd been caught doing something wrong. But then his expression changed. He looked almost smug, as if he'd liked what he'd seen and didn't mind that I knew it.

My housecoat drops to the floor and I step into the warm stream of water. As I let it pummel my sore muscles, I think again of Steve's expression. With a slow wave of understanding, I realize that I liked that he liked it.

Four

The warm summer weather has stretched into fall, so I spend my lunch hour walking around the school's neighborhood, listening to music on my phone. It's better than eating my lunch alone in the cafeteria. I'm a little concerned about what I'll do when winter sets in, but for now this is the perfect way to pass the time.

English class follows lunch today, and I go to the classroom early and flip through my music-theory textbook. It's just as I expected: I've already studied all the material they're going to cover this year. But I want to review it before I take the exam, just to brush up. I turn to the unit on harmony. It's been a long time since I've studied that.

Thump. A textbook lands on the desk beside mine, and the girl with the cornrows slides into the seat.

She places a can of diet cola on the corner of the desk and flips open the English textbook. "You're early," she says.

"You too."

"Yeah. Thought I'd get ahead on some reading. I'm Talia, by the way."

I look at her and nod. "Allegra."

Today all her braids are pulled into a ponytail. It accentuates her flawless skin, her perfectly chiseled features. We both turn to our respective textbooks, but I'm distracted, too aware of her presence. The classroom is empty except for the two of us, and we're sitting side by side, as if we're old friends or something.

"Is Ms. Dekker always so anal?" I ask suddenly.

She turns to look at me. "Ballet's kinda anal, don't you think? Do it right, or don't do it at all."

I think about that, then nod. I don't mind ballet, but the truth is, I only take it because it's a prerequisite for all the other dance classes. I was confident with my form, though, until my first class with Ms. Dekker. Now I'm wondering if she'll find fault with all my technique.

"How long have you been at this school?" I ask.

"I transferred in last winter. A spot came open and I didn't want to lose my place on the waiting list so I took it, but it was hard, coming in the middle of a term."

I haven't noticed that it's particularly easy at the start of a term either, but I don't say so. "I was on the waiting list for almost two years," I tell her.

"Yeah, that's about average."

"Do you dance outside of this school?"

"No," she says. "I'm here for visual arts: painting, sculpting, stuff like that. But you know how they like you to balance out your schedule here. I like the precision of ballet. I took dance classes when I was younger, so luckily I got put in the senior class here."

"What music classes are you taking?" I ask.

"Chamber choir."

"Who teaches it?"

"Mr. Rocchelli," she says, and then she smiles. "Rocky."

"What do you think of him?"

Her perfectly arched eyebrows pop up. "You ask a lot of questions, Allegra. What do I think of Mr. Rocchelli?" She considers. "I think he's kinda cute."

"You do?" I glance at her, wondering if she's kidding. "I think he's a goof."

She studies me for a moment. "I'm willing to overlook a little goofiness." She grins.

Other students are trickling into the classroom, taking their seats. Talia returns to reading. I close my book, knowing I won't absorb anything with all the chatter around me. Talia glances over at me and does the same. "We should hang out sometime," she says, picking up her pen, her thumb repeatedly popping the button at the end.

"Sure," I say. Stay calm, I tell myself. I study my nails. Was it just two days ago I wrote her off as being too smug?

I turn my attention to the teacher who has just entered the room and vow not to blow it this time.

Mr. Rocchelli excuses me from music-theory class to study in the library. By the end of the hour, I feel I'm ready for the exam. I've been studying music since I was five years old, and most of the material is second nature to me. Intervals, chord recognition, timing, scales... I'm as familiar with the language of music as I am the English language.

I find myself trying to slide back through the classroom door just as the rest of the class is coming out. When I pass Spencer in the doorway, he says, "Hey, we missed you."

I look at him, not sure if he's serious. I keep moving into the classroom.

"Where'd you go?" He has stepped back inside in order to talk to me.

I turn to him and hold up my theory textbook. "I was in the library, studying. I'm challenging the course because I already know all the material."

He looks disappointed. "So you're not going to be in this class?"

"No, apparently I'll still be here, but doing something different."

"Good." He smiles. "See you next time."

"Yeah."

Wow, two potential friends in one afternoon. Don't screw up, Allegra.

Mr. Rocchelli glances up from his desk, where he's typing on a laptop. "So, are you ready?"

"Yep."

"Do you want to take it right now?"

I glance at the students filing into the classroom, carrying instruments. The school day is officially over, but some group must be meeting for a rehearsal.

"We're practicing," he says, gesturing to the students, "but you can take the exam in the sound room. It's quiet in there."

I think about that. It means I'll miss my bus, but it would be nice to get the exam over with. There will be later buses. "Okay."

He hands me the folder and leads me to the soundproof room. "If you finish before I'm done rehearsing, you can leave it on my desk."

I nod.

He looks right at me and smiles. "Good luck."

"Thanks."

The small room has a desk and a couple of chairs. I sit down and look around. There are computers and various recording machines and headphones. It's all very high-tech. One of the walls is made entirely of glass, and I can see Mr. Rocchelli moving about the classroom, assisting students. I open the folder and scan the exam.

It's long—fifty questions—but it doesn't look too hard. I take out a pencil and start with the first one, transposing a mini-composition.

After about half an hour I sit back and stretch. Through the glass I watch the woodwinds rehearsing. Mr. Rocchelli stands in front of them, leaning forward, arms in motion. He glances from the music to the students and back to the music. His whole body is moving. It's like he's trying to draw music out of the students with his hands and arms. He's working hard. Eventually he drops his arms, and the students lower their instruments. He talks to them, though I can't hear what he's saying. The students laugh, and then the instruments are back in their mouths and Mr. Rocchelli's arms are in the air again. I notice a tattoo trailing down the inside of his right arm. With a bend of his knees, he's back at it—the music extractor. I smile and return to my exam. At least he's one teacher who really gets into his job.

The next time I look up, I've finished the exam and the students are packing up their instruments. I'm determined to ace this exam—I have something to prove—so I return to the top of the first page and begin checking my answers. There's a knock on the door, and Mr. Rocchelli pokes his head into the room. I see through the window that the portable has emptied.

"How's it going?" he asks.

"I'm done. Just checking it over."

"Good girl. Bring it out when you're finished."

I nod.

A few minutes later I collect my things and leave the sound room. Mr. Rocchelli is back at his desk. I'm aware of how quiet the portable has become while I was in the sound room. Creepy quiet.

Mr. Rocchelli leans back when he sees me approaching. I hand him the exam. He flips through the pages.

"So what will I be doing in this class?" I ask.

He looks thoughtful for a moment. "I have something really special in mind," he says. "But maybe I should mark this before I tell you about it."

"I passed."

He chuckles. "You're one confident young woman."

I try to mask my surprise. I don't think of myself as confident, not most of the time, but I do know my music theory.

"We don't have theory class tomorrow," he says, "so could you come back after school tomorrow to talk about your assignment?"

I think about that. It means staying late at school two days in a row, but I'm intrigued now. *Something really special...*

"Okay."

"Good. See you tomorrow."

I turn and walk toward the door.

"How are you liking the school?" he asks.

I pause and turn back, thinking about it. "It's too soon to say, really," I tell him. "But I think it'll be okay."

"I hope your experience will be better than okay."

I don't know what to say to that, so I turn to leave again.

"Allegra…"

I swing around.

"I'm sorry we got off to a rough start."

"Whatever."

"No, seriously. I feel bad about being such a tyrant, but I really believe you'll be challenged in this class. Creatively challenged."

I think he just wanted to be sure there'd be enough students for the class to run, but I don't tell him that. "See you tomorrow." I escape quickly, not wanting to prolong the conversation. There's something about him that makes me anxious.

I hear raised voices before I even enter the house. Letting myself in quietly, I stand in the hallway and listen.

"You can't just drop in here any old time you please and tell me how to run my life!" My mother's voice.

"I'm not doing that." Dad. He sounds a little more reasonable. "I'm just concerned about her."

Her? They must be talking about me!

"Oh yeah? You want *me* to stay home more, but what about you? Maybe it's my turn to have a life finally."

"I just think she shouldn't be alone so much. It's not right."

"It's a little late to worry about that, don't you think? Ten more months, and she could be living on her own. I have to have something in place for myself, and I'm not going to get an opportunity like this again."

I step into the kitchen. Mom is standing at the stove, wooden spoon poised in the air like a conductor's baton. Dad is across the room from her, holding a mug. Their backs are to the door.

"What's going on?" I ask.

They swing around to look at me, embarrassed. They glance at each other. "It's nothing," Mom says, turning back to the pot on the stove.

"Sounds like something to me."

"How was school?" Dad asks.

"Were you talking about me?" I ask.

Dad sighs. "Yes, we were."

I see my mom glance sharply at him.

"What were you saying?"

"I was saying I'm a little concerned that you're alone so much now that your mom's working nights." He looks back at her, but I can't read his expression.

"I'm seventeen, Dad, not seven. And I'm fine. Better than fine."

"I don't see you hanging out with any friends."

"I made two new friends today, as a matter of fact."

He smiles, but it's forced. "That's good."

"Do you want me to hang out at the mall or, even better, at the park, drinking and doing drugs?"

"No, of course not, but you need to have some fun."

"I'm having fun. Dance is fun. I don't have time for hanging out."

He nods. "Okay, Legs." But I know he doesn't buy it. He thinks I'm a geek who can't make friends. The truth is, I haven't had time for them. Between music and dance and school, it's all I can do to keep up. Athough I do hang out with Angela between dance classes.

"I'm going to my room to study."

"How 'bout we go to a movie tonight?" he asks.

"Can't. Dance class."

"Tomorrow night?"

"Dad, I dance every night except Saturday, Sunday and Monday."

"And now you're dancing at school too?"

I nod.

"Then maybe you could skip the odd evening class when I'm at home."

I realize he's telling me that he wants to spend more time with me. Or maybe he's just feeling sorry for me. For some reason, tears spring to my eyes. "I'll think about it."

I leave the kitchen, but I don't go to my room. Instead I go down the stairs to the music studio. Hearing them argue like that—about me—is too weird. It's the second time this week I've walked in on something. There's so much tension between them.

Mom's harp stands majestically in one corner of the studio. I sit down at the piano and stare at the keys.

My right hand rests on them, and I pick out a simple tune. I haven't practiced in six months, maybe more. I completed the academy exams and then quit, cold turkey. The last argument around here was back when Mom wanted me to continue studying. I told her I'd completed my part of the bargain. I was done with studying music.

My left hand automatically joins my right on the keys, and I find myself playing Grieg's "Morning Mood." It comes back to me as if I'd played it just yesterday. I lean into the piano and pound the keys, enjoying the full range of emotion the music triggers. It comes so effortlessly, and for a few minutes I enjoy the sensation, completely losing myself just as I do when I dance.

But then the piece is over. My hands drop to my lap after the last trill.

"That was beautiful, Legs."

Dad has come down the stairs and is sitting on the bottom step. "Can I join you?"

"What do you want to do?"

"We'll jam. You play whatever you like, and I'll join in."

I have a flashback to a time when I was much younger and had to practice the piano every evening. I didn't like coming down to the studio alone, so Mom always sat close by, reading on the old couch. Once I'd mastered a piece, she'd accompany me on the harp. If Dad was home, he'd pick up an instrument too, and we'd all play together.

I nod at my dad and let my hands decide what to play next. They choose a dreamy Satie piece, "Gymnopédie No. 1." I don't think I've played it in years. A moment later, the soulful sound of a wooden flute has joined in, filling in the blanks, and the music floats around the room, so much richer with the addition of another instrument. I finish the song, and a flute note lingers after the final piano chord. I love the mood we've created together. He puts his hand on my shoulder and smiles down at me. "We make beautiful music together."

I laugh, and the melancholy spell is broken. Mom calls down the stairs that dinner is ready.

Both of them try to keep the conversation light while we eat, and then Mom rushes away to get ready for her evening performance. I clear the table and leave Dad with the dishes so that I can get ready for dance. The tension from earlier is almost gone.

"Will you be home later?" I ask him as I head out the door.

"I will," he says. "Maybe we can jam some more."

"Maybe," I reply, and I smile to myself. We're finally finding a way to connect.

I break the speed limit on my way home, looking forward to hanging out with my dad and playing music. The drone of the TV is loud when I step into the house.

I slip out of my jacket and wonder if I should shower before we get started. I decide against it; I'm too excited about getting back down to the studio.

I find Dad lying on the couch, fast asleep. He's snoring softly, more like purring. His face looks older when he's asleep, the creases deeper. I consider waking him but don't. I have homework to do anyway. I gently lay a light blanket over him and head down the hall.

Five

When the last bell of the day rings, I shove my dance shoes into my pack and pull shorts and a T-shirt over my dance leotard. I head back out to the music portable. The afternoon is hot, and I worked up a serious sweat in my modern-dance class. Ms. Dekker is just as particular about modern as she is about ballet. I swear we repeated the same routine across the floor twenty-five times, and I still couldn't please her. "Hit it harder, Allegra! Sharper lines! Tuck your bum under." I hope Mr. Rocchelli doesn't get too close to me. I feel like a furnace, and I'm not sure how well my deodorant is holding up in this heat. I take another long swallow of water before I enter the portable.

He smiles when he sees me. "Been dancing, Allegra?"

"How can you tell?" I wipe away a drop of sweat that is prickling at my hairline.

"How many hours of dance do you do a week?"

I think about it, calculating the hours in my head. Before I can come up with the answer, he says, "Never mind. If you can't figure it out, it must be a lot. I look forward to seeing you perform in the spring gala."

The Deer Lake Spring Gala. In the past few days I've discovered that it's the annual event every class works toward for the entire year. It's a charity fundraiser; all the dance, music and theater classes perform, and students' art is sold at a silent auction. I gather the hype is huge in the weeks leading up to it.

"So, come and have a seat," he says, pulling a chair up beside his desk.

I take it and watch while he pulls a folder out of the file cabinet. I can see now that the tattoo on his arm is a name with two dates separated by a dash written beneath it: the span of someone's life. I wonder whose. It's written in beautiful script. From the look of his arms, Mr. Rocchelli spends some time at the gym. Or maybe they just get like that from all the conducting he does.

He places the folder on his desk and lays his hand on top of it. "Your exam is in here."

"And?" I ask, fighting back a smile.

He sits in his chair and studies me for a second. "You really do know your music theory," he says. He opens the folder and hands the paper to me. Written across the top is *110%*.

Now I do smile. "What's the extra ten percent for?"

"For giving me such detailed answers, far beyond what I would expect from a student completing my class."

I lean back, relaxed. "So? Will you sign my release now?"

He chuckles and leans back too. He runs his hands through his hair and then clasps them behind his head. "Do you really want out that badly?"

I shrug. "I really want to dance—as much as possible."

"But you just told me that you already take so many classes you've lost count of the hours."

"That's the only way to get good."

He nods. "But you don't want to do anything to excess. We talked about how it's important to find balance in our lives."

"*You* talked about that."

He nods and smiles. "I guess you're right." He pauses. "The thing is, Allegra, you've shown me, without a doubt, that you know your theory. What I want to know now is whether you can actually apply that theory to a composition."

"I have to compose something?"

"No, not exactly. You see, I've written a simple melody. What I want you to do is expand it and write the conductor's score, including every instrument in the orchestra."

I just stare at him.

"My melody is like a black-and-white sketch. I want you to turn it into a full-color painting. You'll need to learn the range of each instrument and write notes that the instrument is capable of. You'll need to know the key of each instrument and its clefs. The final music score should also be written without a thousand ledger lines, with each instrument written vertically on the page."

"But I don't play all the instruments."

He points to the sound room. "All the equipment you'll need is in there. I'll teach you how to use it. You won't actually need to know how to play the instruments. The computer program will do that for you."

I try to process what all this entails.

"For bonus marks, you can prepare the sheet music for each instrument and its various parts—for example, first clarinet, second clarinet, etcetera. And then, for extra bonus marks, we'll give it to the senior orchestra and you'll rehearse it with them and then perform it at the spring gala."

"Anything else?" I ask. I hope he realizes I'm being sarcastic.

"Yeah, if you really want to impress me, you can choreograph a dance to go with it too. I'm sure Ms. Dekker would help you gather a group to perform it."

I just stare at him.

"You could even add an eight-part choral arrangement. I'll provide the chamber choir." He smiles. "What do you think?"

"I think you're out of your mind."

He throws back his head and laughs. "Miss Allegra doesn't sound so confident anymore."

"What's in it for me?"

"An A-plus."

"Hey! I should already get an A-plus! I aced the exam."

"Oh c'mon, Allegra. You're not at this school for the grades. You're here to learn, to grow. I want you to dig deep. I don't want this to be a superficial exercise. I'm looking for a masterpiece here."

A masterpiece? I study his face, trying to determine how serious he is.

"Okay, maybe not a masterpiece." His smile is apologetic. I decide Talia is right: he *is* kind of cute. "But I do want you to really stretch yourself, show me what you are capable of."

I suddenly feel overwhelmed.

Mr. Rocchelli must read my reaction. "Come and listen to the tune," he says, getting up. "That will help you decide whether you're up to the task."

He motions for me to follow him. I do, but when I see him heading to the sound room, I hold back. I've just finished two hours of dance. I'm still sweating. I can only imagine how I smell. I can't go in there with him.

"Allegra?" He looks over his shoulder. "Are you coming?"

"I just remembered that I have to catch my bus," I say, looking up at the wall clock.

He looks disappointed. "That's a shame, because I'm not sure when we'll get time to meet again." He thinks about it. "Perhaps I could just drop you off at the bus exchange. Do you switch buses there?"

I do, but I don't want him to know that. I pause, trying to come up with a response, but I'm too slow.

"Good, that's settled then. C'mon."

I feel the tingle of a fresh onslaught of sweat breaking out in my armpits. It's stifling in the portable. I can only imagine what it will be like in that tiny sound room. I consider telling him I have to use the washroom, but that would mean going back to the main building. I follow him inside, but I stand as close to the door as I can. I keep my arms pressed firmly against my sides. My underarm sweat rings are probably creeping down to my waist by now.

Mr. Rocchelli plugs a flash drive into the computer and then sits in the chair that I sat in yesterday to write my exam. There's another one beside it, and he pushes it with his foot, rolling it toward me, and indicates that I should sit in it. I do, but I roll myself as far from him as is possible in this small space. I do it slowly, hoping he won't notice. Then I keep as still as I can. Maybe if I don't move, my BO won't waft toward him.

Piano notes begin to fill the room. The melodic line is simple, lyrical. I find myself relaxing. Then the melody is repeated, but the phrase lengths have changed and it's higher in pitch. I see Mr. Rocchelli glance at my foot. I look down and discover that it's tapping. I stop. Mr. Rocchelli smiles. His eyebrows arch. I ignore him and go back to staring at the computer. The tune is really catchy. It moves into a bridge and then drifts back to the same quiet melody but with a slight variation, an echo of its former self.

The room goes still again. I realize my mood has changed. I feel lighter.

"Well?" Mr. Rocchelli asks. "What do you think?"

I glance at him. What do I think? "I like it." I know my words are trite, not giving any clue as to what I really think. "Can you play it again?"

His eyes widen momentarily, but then he clicks the mouse and the small room is once again filled with the sound of piano notes delicately picking out the gentle tune. I close my eyes and hear what it could be with the addition of other instruments. I would extend the middle section, repeating the melody but building on it, evoking more passion. I would draw out the crescendo as well as the resolution. The song makes me think of longing, but not painful longing. More like the ache you feel when you experience a beautiful sunset, or when you watch a litter of kittens romping and you so badly want to scoop one up and snuggle it to your face.

The piece ends. I open my eyes and find myself smiling at Mr. Rocchelli. He smiles back and tilts his head. "So?" he asks, breaking into my thoughts. "Do you think you can convert my little melody into real music?"

I don't know exactly what happens in that moment. Maybe the endorphins created from dancing are still active, or maybe the music actually moves me, but whatever it is, I find myself feeling somewhat excited at the challenge.

"I think"—I hesitate, but only briefly—"I think I'd like to try."

His face breaks into a wider smile, and he clicks the mouse again. He pulls out the flash drive and hands it to me. "She's all yours."

When Dad's on the road with his band, Mom and I are totally casual about our meals. Mom cooks things and puts them in the fridge, and we eat whenever we're hungry, sometimes together but usually alone, depending on our schedules. It works for us, but when Dad comes home, Mom makes an early dinner so we can eat together before she goes to the theater and I go to the dance studio. We used to treasure these times, but tonight Mom and Dad sit poker straight in their chairs, assembling wraps from food that is laid out in the center of the table. They don't say a word to each other. I glance at them, concerned, but I don't dare ask what's going on. Eventually, they turn their attention to me, neutral ground.

"How's school?" Mom asks.

"It's pretty good." I think about it. "But the dance teacher, Ms. Dekker, thinks I've developed bad habits at Turning Pointe."

"Do you agree?" Mom asks.

"I don't know. Maybe. But now I have to dance one way at school and another way at the studio."

"Different teachers focus on different things," Dad says. "It's good to have variety."

Mom changes the subject, not acknowledging Dad's comment. "What happened with the music-theory class?"

"That's actually turned out okay."

They both stop their wrap-making to look at me.

"The teacher, Mr. Rocchelli, has given me a different assignment than the rest of the class. He wants to challenge me." I shrug. "It *will* be a challenge."

"What's the assignment?" Dad asks, returning to the task of rolling his wrap into a tidy package, without much success.

I smile at him as he takes a bite and all the stuff inside the wrap falls back to the plate. "I've told you, Dad, you put in too much food. I'll make your next one."

"Thanks," he says. "I never did like these things. Too sloppy. I like to eat with a knife and fork." He picks up the bits of food with his fingers and pops them into his mouth.

Mom rolls her eyes but, to her credit, doesn't comment.

"So, this music-theory assignment," Dad prompts. "How did this come about?"

"Oh, yeah. Well, I challenged the course already and aced the exam."

Mom and Dad finally exchange a glance, and I notice a softening in their faces. Good. Maybe this dinner can be saved after all.

"So he's asked me to develop a piece of music using all the theory I know."

They're both looking at me again, waiting for more. This is a subject that interests them.

"He gave me a melody, and I have to expand it, write the score for the full orchestra."

"Wow!" Mom's eyes are wide. I just have to mention the word *orchestra* and she's sold on the project. "This sounds like a very wise teacher," she adds.

"I don't know about that. He's pretty young, and a bit too intense, but he's okay." I think back on the afternoon and how he gave me a ride to the bus exchange after our meeting. He drives an old Toyota, but it was immaculate inside and out. He talked the whole way—about the project—so the ride wasn't as awkward as I'd imagined it would be.

"Maybe I could help you with this one," Dad offers.

I'm swallowing a mouthful of food, about to tell him how much I'd like that, when Mom butts in. "What do you know about orchestration?" she asks.

He studies her. "You're right, Cindy. Not much." He gets up and takes his plate to the dishwasher. I frown at Mom, ticked that she's shut him down that way.

"You don't want another wrap, Dad? I'll make it for you."

Dad pats his stomach. "Watchin' my weight," he says. "Too many French fries on the last trip."

I help Dad load the dishwasher and put the remaining food in the fridge. When Mom leaves the room to get dressed, I turn to Dad again. "I'd really like your help with my music-theory project," I tell him.

He smiles sadly. "Your mom's right, honey. I know nothing about orchestration."

"But you know a lot about music, Dad, and song-writing. You'd be a big help."

"We'll see," he says. "Your mom will probably be a bigger help to you."

"I didn't hear her offering," I point out.

"It goes without saying," he says. "She's your mom."

I don't answer. I like the idea of working with Dad more. Mom would try to make it her own project instead of just helping.

"Can I come and watch your dance classes tonight?" he asks.

"Sure."

He smiles and nods, and in that moment I forgive him for falling asleep on me last night. I also decide to find a way to include him in my project. It will be a collaboration. I just know Mr. Rocchelli would approve.

Six

It's been one of those mornings. I woke up late and had to skip breakfast in order to get to school on time. My stomach competed with the driving rain all morning to see which could make the most noise, and now, for the first time, I have to face the school cafeteria, because I also didn't have time to make myself a lunch. The lineup for food snakes along the side wall. I join the end of it and glance around the overflowing room. Not a single familiar face. I try not to think about where I'll sit when I get my food. Maybe a table will come free by then. I look at the long line ahead of me. Maybe not.

I sense someone stepping up behind me in line and then a finger pokes me in the back. I spin around and come face-to-face with Spencer from music-theory class. I melt with relief. A familiar face.

"How's it going?" he asks.

"Not bad. How 'bout you?"

"Pretty good. But I sure missed you in music theory. Julia is *so* annoying."

I laugh. He makes it sound like we've been in theory class together for months, not just a few days. "I figured she was going to be a pain."

He scans my face. "So what's the project you get to work on?"

"I'm writing some music." I decide to leave it at that. I don't want to sound like I'm bragging.

"Why don't you just take a different class?"

"Mr. Rocchelli, *Rocky*"—I roll my eyes—"wouldn't sign my release form."

"Really? What a jerk!"

"That's what I thought."

The line creeps forward, and I move with it. Spencer moves up to stand beside me. I wonder if he has friends to sit with, but I don't ask.

He clears his throat. "Is it true that your dad is Jerry from the Loose Ends?"

I nod and shuffle forward again. He's been doing some research. I consider telling him that my mom is the harpist with the Deer Lake Symphony Orchestra, but I don't.

"I'm a huge fan of the Loose Ends."

I glance at him. His face is open, eyes shining. He looks sincere. "Then you should come over and meet him sometime," I say.

"Really?"

I nod. Something about this conversation depresses me. I'd thought maybe Spencer and I had made a legit connection. Now I wonder if it's just my dad he's interested in. It wouldn't be the first time.

"So what's good to eat here?" I ask, looking up at the menu that hangs above the food counter. There's a picture of each selection. At least the menu's a little more creative than at my last school, which specialized in burgers and pizza. My eyes rest on the picture of a spinach salad.

"I always get the mac and cheese," he tells me. "But I hear the soups are good."

I check the soup-of-the-day sign. Broccoli and cheese. Perfect.

We've reached the counter, and I place my order. I push my tray along to the cashier and pay. Spencer is still right behind me. I take my tray and look around the room.

"Follow me," he says, pushing past me.

Relieved, I follow him across the cafeteria and toward a bank of doors leading outside to the courtyard. I'm surprised when he shoves one open with his shoulder and waits for me to catch up.

"It's raining," I tell him, as if he hasn't noticed. Actually, it's not just raining, it's like a monsoon has hit. The heavy raindrops are bouncing off the courtyard tables like thousands of Ping-Pong balls.

"Follow me," he repeats.

He stays pressed along the outside wall, under an awning. It's not cold out here, just incredibly wet. I feel my shoes soaking up water.

When we reach the far end of the courtyard, Spencer balances his tray on one hand and pulls open another door, this one leading back into the school. He glances over his shoulder to check that I'm following. We enter a part of the school I haven't been in before. It's a large room, with wide steps leading down to a kind of pit. "This is the multipurpose area," he tells me. "It's not as noisy as the cafeteria."

There are students sitting in clusters on the steps or at round tables on the top level. Right away I spot Talia. "Allegra!" she calls, motioning me over.

I smile and walk over to where she's sitting, and Spencer follows me.

"Hey, Talia," he says, plunking himself down on the step she's sprawled on.

"You two know each other?" I ask.

"Yeah," Spencer says. He places his tray on the floor. "We're both in photography."

I lower myself to the floor too, between them but one step higher. Talia introduces me to two girls sitting on a lower step. "Molly and Sophie." Molly is small and round, with a freckled, friendly face. A mass of curls is pushed off her face with a hair band. Sophie is the opposite: long, lean and slightly more aloof. I notice her French manicure and the diamond stud in her nose.

"Hey," I say.

They both nod and smile.

"Did you get your photo story turned in?" Talia has turned to Spencer. He's picked up his bowl of mac and cheese and is shoveling it into his mouth. I begin to eat my soup but find the melted cheese keeps stretching into long strings. I have to really concentrate on each mouthful in order to keep from wearing the gooey stuff, but I'm aware of the interactions between the others. I can tell by their glances that Molly and Sophie are sizing me up. They don't think I notice, but I do. *Be cool*, I tell myself.

After a few minutes, Molly climbs up a step and settles herself next to me. "Are you in photography too?" she asks.

"No, I met Spencer in music theory, and Talia in ballet and English."

She nods. "What do you think of Ms. Dekker?"

It's the same question Talia first asked me. "She's tough. I can't do anything right."

Molly smiles. "She'll grow on you. She gets results from her dancers. The ones who take the exams always ace them."

"Do you dance too?" I ask.

"I did last year, but it wasn't a good fit. Look at me."

She lifts an arm and pinches the soft flesh of her upper arm, jiggling it. "This is not a dancer's body. But I have her for musical theater."

"That sounds like fun."

She laughs, a sweet, high-pitched giggle. "You'd think, wouldn't you? But she even manages to make musical theater feel like work."

I scrape up a last spoonful of soup and look around the room. The walls are painted with colorful murals, most likely done by students, and there are display cases filled with various pieces of art. The floor of the pit area would work as a small stage.

"So, tell me more about your music-theory project," Spencer says.

I feel everyone turn to look at me. *Deep breaths*, I remind myself. *Remain calm*. I shrug. "Mr. Rocchelli's given me a simple tune and wants me to expand it, write a full orchestrated version."

I look at Spencer. He tilts his head, encouraging me to continue, so I babble on.

"It'll be interesting. I've never done anything like it before. The trouble is, I don't know how to get started." That came out of the blue. I haven't even thought about starting it yet.

"Maybe your dad could help you," Spencer suggests. He turns to the others. "He's the bass player for the Loose Ends."

Everyone turns to stare at me again. "He could, I guess, but it's my mom who is the classically trained musician. She's the harpist in the Deer Lake Symphony Orchestra."

No one responds. Have I said too much? Does it sound like I'm bragging about my family? I didn't mean to.

"So when can I meet your dad?" Spencer asks, changing the subject.

"The sooner the better," I tell him. "I haven't heard when he's going back on the road, but it's probably soon. I've heard them rehearsing some new material."

Spencer pulls a phone out of his pocket. "Call him," he says.

I laugh. "Persistent, aren't you?" I take my own phone out of my purse and press the first number on my contact list. "I'd like to meet him too," Talia says.

"Me too," Sophie and Molly say in unison and then laugh.

"Hi, Dad," I say when he picks up. "No, no, everything's okay. It's lunch hour. I'm sitting here with"—I hesitate; do I dare call them friends?—"with some kids from school who are Loose Ends fans. They'd like to meet you."

Dad, gracious as ever, suggests they come over on Monday evening, my night off from dance, and sit in on a Loose Ends rehearsal. He puts the phone down to consult with Mom. "Monday night?" I ask the group. "To watch the band rehearse?"

Spencer's face lights up. He high-fives me. The girls smile and nod. Then Dad comes back on the phone. "Your mom will put on a pot of chili so we can all visit beforehand, your friends and the band."

"They're in," I tell him. "Thanks."

Before the lunch break is over, we've all exchanged phone numbers. I've remained calm. I've also pushed away the niggling worry that this is really all about my dad, and not about me making friends, but then, maybe that's why I was able to invite them over. The focus is not on me.

First thing Saturday morning, I take Mr. Rocchelli's flash drive downstairs to the music studio. I plug it into the computer and play it over and over, picking out the tune on the piano and jotting the notes on music staff paper. Once I have the melody down, I begin tinkering with it. I try to imagine where other instruments will blend in, but nothing seems right. I sit and stare at the music. It's true. I really don't have any idea where to start with this. I remember having some thoughts when I first heard it, but they've vanished.

The door to the upstairs creaks open and my dad's slippered feet appear on the stairs, followed by the rest of him. He's carrying a mug of steaming coffee. I take in the sleep-tousled hair and dark shadow of whiskers.

"What's up, Legs?" he asks.

"Just working on my music-theory project," I tell him. "Do you need the studio?"

He shakes his head. "No, I heard the piano and was wondering what you were working on."

"Listen to this, Dad." I turn my back to him and play the simple tune on the piano. When I'm done, I turn to look at him again. He has settled himself into the couch that squats in a corner beside Mom's harp. He nods. "Did you write that?"

"No, that's what the teacher gave me. My job is to rewrite it for an orchestra."

He takes a sip of coffee. "It's a great project."

"But I have no idea where to start!" I throw the sheet of music into the air, and we both watch as it floats to the floor.

"Starting is hard," he says. "But at least you're not starting from scratch. You've got a skeleton here. Adding the flesh is the fun part."

"Easy for you to say. You've written tons of songs."

"There was a first one for me too."

"So how *do* you get started?"

He swirls the coffee in his cup, looking into it as if he'll find the answer to my question there. He looks up and studies me for a moment. "First of all, Legs, I think you need to forget that this is a school assignment. You'll be far more creative and have more fun if you tackle it with a spirit of playfulness, rather than just seeing it as a project you need to complete."

I stare at him. *A spirit of playfulness?*

"And you have to work from your heart and not your head." He places his hand on his chest. "Finding the emotional core of the music is what will make it appealing to an audience."

I can only sigh.

"You dance from your emotional core, Legs. I've watched you. Go to that same place when you're working on this piece."

Now he's beginning to make some sense. "I'm still hoping you'll help me with this, Dad."

"I will, honey, as much as I can, but I've just confirmed the dates for our next tour. We're leaving again at the end of the month."

"You are?"

He nods. "We're touring in Europe."

I hear myself sigh. That won't be a short one.

He nods and places his mug on a table. "But it may be my last tour for a while."

That's news. "How come?"

He hesitates before he answers. "Because..." He stumbles, looking for the right words. "Because I'm finally beginning to understand the impact touring's had on my family." He looks back into his mug.

"What are you talking about? We're fine."

Now he heaves a sigh."I need a break from the traveling. I'll concentrate on writing for a while too. And I'll take local gigs."

"Have you told the rest of the band?"

"Not yet. I haven't told your mom yet either. I'm waiting for the right time."

Dad's looking so sad that I go sit next to him on the couch. "I don't want you to quit touring because of us,"

I tell him gently. "But it will be nice to have you around more."

He looks at me, a little smile tugging at his lips. "Really?"

"Yeah, really."

"It's good to hear you say that. I know I've been a lousy father."

"No, you haven't! And at least your work is something you enjoy. If you were doing something you didn't like just to stay home, well, then you'd be a grouch, and none of us would be happy." I smile at him.

He studies my face and then picks up my hand and squeezes my fingers. "How did you get to be so wise? You grew up so fast. I don't know when it happened. I guess I thought you'd be my little girl forever."

"I'll always be your daughter, Dad."

"I know that, honey." He lets go of my hand and we sit quietly for a few moments. Then he turns to face me. "Has your mom seemed okay these past few months?"

I think about it and realize that yes, she was happy—until Dad came home. That's when she got all prickly. I don't tell him that. "Yeah, she really loves her work."

He nods. "One more road trip," he says quietly. "And that's it."

Seven

Dad and I spend all of Saturday morning working on my project. Together, we decide to divide the piece into four distinct sections, each with a different mood. Each part will be about two minutes long, so it feels almost like writing four different pieces of music.

"I think I'll call it *Etude in B minor*," I tell him after a while.

He rolls his eyes. "What a cop-out," he says.

I just laugh and play the intro again. Dad picks up his flute and plays along. When I stop, he continues, and I like what I hear.

"Hey, can you do that again?" I ask, reaching for a pencil and the music score.

He plays something, but it's not the same.

"No, exactly like you did it the first time."

He tries again, but still it's not right.

"Dad!"

"I'm trying, I'm trying."

Eventually he gets it, or something close to it, and I'm satisfied. I play it on the piano after I've recorded it on the page. Dad gives me a few pointers on how to use his computer program, Logic Pro, for music composition. I try to imagine which instrument in the orchestra would have the best "voice" for this part. Possibly the oboe. "Let's work on the second section next," I suggest. "This leads nicely into it."

We spend another hour trying different variations, and I begin to understand what he means by approaching it with a spirit of playfulness. One musical thread seems to lead effortlessly to another, and it feels like a kind of musical brainstorming. As I watch Dad picking out the melody on his guitar, I realize I don't want the morning to end.

The door to the upstairs opens again and this time Mom's feet appear on the stairs.

"How's it going?" she asks. She's carrying a tray with three mugs on it.

"Good," I tell her.

Dad nods. "This girl knows something about music."

"I should hope so." Mom hands out the mugs and sits down on the end of the couch, beside her harp. Her hands run along the strings. Dad and I sip our tea and listen to Mom play. For a change, there's no tension in the air. I take a deep breath and sigh, letting the gentle sounds of the harp wash over me.

"I have an idea, Cindy," Dad says after a few minutes.

She looks up but keeps playing.

"Why don't Legs and I drop you off at the theater tonight, and then we'll carry on and catch a movie?"

Mom's hands drop to her lap and my contented feeling vanishes. It's not that I don't want to spend time with him, but going to a movie with my dad on a Saturday night...well, it just seems a bit pathetic. Playing music in the studio is one thing; going to a movie is quite another.

Mom doesn't like the idea either. "I don't need a ride, Jerry," she says. "Marcus drives right past here. He's happy to pick me up."

Marcus. So that's his name.

"I know he does, but I thought it would be nice for Legs and me to do something together. Marcus can drive you home after your concert."

They both turn to look at me. I shrug. "I was going to use the evening to study," I say, but I can't meet his eyes. "I usually have Monday night for that, but it's out this week because of the rehearsal."

There's a long silence. I don't dare look at Dad.

"Then I'll drive you anyway," he says to Mom. "Maybe we can get some dinner on the way."

"That won't work," she tells him. "I'll be dressed for my performance, and there's really no point in your driving all the way to the theater."

"Maybe I'd just like a date with my wife," he says quietly. "And you could change into your dress at the theater."

Mom collects the empty mugs and goes back up the stairs without saying a word.

Dad stares at the door she's just gone through, then suddenly climbs the stairs after her. I hear the front door slam.

I'm left with a sick feeling in the pit of my stomach.

There is no family dinner on Saturday night. Dad hasn't come home, and Mom helps herself to a bowl of corn chowder that she made earlier. Later on, she tells me to have a nice evening and then climbs into Marcus's sports car. I watch as they back out of the driveway and speed away.

We don't have a Sunday-night dinner together either. I spent the morning back in the music studio, working on my project, but Dad didn't join me. I don't blame him. I'm not even sure he came home last night.

I help Mom prepare a couple of pots of chili for Monday night's Loose Ends rehearsal. It was my idea to make two, one veggie and one meat. I stand at the counter, chopping onions and green peppers while Mom fries meat at the stove behind me. I want to talk to her, ask her what's going on, but I don't. It just feels like too big a topic to broach. She's unusually quiet too. When we're done, we sit at the table, sampling our creations.

"How are you feeling about tomorrow night?" Mom asks gently.

I shrug. "Okay, I guess." I know exactly why she's asking. Having friends over is not something I usually do. It's strange. I can dance in front of a theater filled to the rafters with strangers, or play at a piano recital, but… well, I just don't "do" friends. Except for Angela, and our friendship never leaves the dance studio. "They're here for the rehearsal, not to hang out with me."

She nods. "It'll be fine."

Thankfully, the subject is dropped. I've been trying not to think about it too much.

Mom leaves for work while I finish cleaning up. I notice that she drives herself. I still haven't seen Dad. I hope he shows up for Monday night's dinner. I'm not sure what I'll tell Spencer and the girls if they arrive and Dad's not here.

But he does show. When I get home from school on Monday afternoon, I can hear him in the studio, practicing. I don't recognize the song; it must be new. Mom has tidied up the kitchen and put a stack of bowls and spoons on the counter.

Steve arrives first. I let him in, but I can't look him in the eyes. The last time I saw him was the night he caught me dancing alone in the kitchen. "So?" he says, hanging his jacket in the closet. "How's the dancing?"

"Good," I tell him and leave it at that. He follows me into the kitchen and greets my mom, joining her at the counter where she's chopping up vegetables. They begin catching up on news. Dad's soulful saxophone music wafts up the stairs. Steve looks at Mom, eyebrows raised. She just shrugs, but I sense she's retreating into herself again.

I keep a watch on the street, waiting for Spencer and the girls. Eventually an old Volvo pulls up to the curb, and they all pile out. They wave at the driver when the car pulls away. I can see that they're laughing about something. Sophie applies lip gloss as they walk up the steps. I take a few deep breaths, open the door and invite them in. I introduce them first to my mom, then to Steve. Dad comes into the kitchen and I see Spencer's eyes light up. I make the introductions.

"I'm a huge Loose Ends fan," he tells my dad. "I saw you perform when you opened for the Tragically Hip."

"Cool," Dad says modestly. He always acts like he doesn't get what the fuss is all about. He cracks open a can of soda and takes a long swig. He glances around the room, spots Mom, then quickly turns back to Spencer.

"I think my favorite album is *Room to Move*," Spencer continues. "You really explored some new stuff on that one."

"Interesting that you say that," Dad answers, wiping his mouth with the back of his hand. "I think it's my favorite too. It was the first time the guys let me experiment a little."

"Yeah?"

"Yeah." He nods and elbows Steve, who has moved over to join the conversation. "Before that, they thought I was just a bass player. I finally got up the nerve to show them I could play a few other instruments—and write too," he adds.

"Cool," Spencer says.

"And that's how it got its title, that album; they finally gave me room to move."

I can see that Spencer is trying to act nonchalant, as if talking to one of his favorite musicians and getting the scoop behind the album is something he does every day, but his posture is a dead giveaway. His arms are crossed tightly across his chest, and he's rocking back and forth.

I exchange a look with Talia, and we smile. I feel myself relax. Sophie and Molly begin chatting about something else, their voices high-pitched. Eventually the other band members begin to arrive. I introduce everyone. The men act as shy as my friends do. Without their music and instruments to hide behind, they're just regular guys. I think people forget that.

Mom starts handing out bowls, and everyone eventually helps themselves to the food. The girls and three of the band members sit around the table and talk while they eat. I lean against the counter and eat chili with my dad,

Spencer, Steve and Randal, the drummer. Mom stands slightly apart from us and simply listens.

"Spencer has an autograph collection, all musicians," I tell Dad.

"Really," Dad says, tilting his head.

Spencer nods. "I'm up to two hundred now."

"That's great," Steve says. "Would you like to make it two-oh-five? I can give you signed head shots of each of these guys."

"Maybe we're not famous enough for his collection," Dad teases.

"Are you kidding? That would be awesome! Thanks," Spencer says.

I glance at Mom and wonder if this is the moment to remind them that she, too, is a musician, but I decide against it.

After everyone has had a second bowl of chili and the platter of veggies is emptied, Dad asks, "Well, Legs? Is it time?"

"Legs?" Spencer looks at me, puzzled.

I shake my head and roll my eyes. "That's what *he* calls me." I frown at my dad, who just laughs.

Spencer laughs too. "Because you're a dancer, and your legs are so long?"

"No! It's short for Allegra. A-*lleg*—gra." I sound the word out slowly, embarrassed by his interpretation. "He started calling me that long before I started dancing."

"Or grew the long legs," my dad adds. "C'mon, everyone, time to get started." He leads the way to the studio.

Spencer follows me down the stairs. He pokes me in the back. "Legs. I like it," he says.

I just shake my head again.

Talia and the girls squish together on the couch, and I prop myself on its wide arm. Spencer sits on the floor, leaning against a wall.

The band members consult with Dad and decide to warm up with some of their oldies. "Any requests?" Dad asks Spencer.

"'It's a Day For Dancing,'" he says, without hesitation.

Dad smiles, switches guitars and counts off the beat. In a united motion, each musician plays the opening chord, the drummer hits the drums, and the rehearsal begins.

Spencer's face breaks into a huge grin. His foot taps along, and when the band gets to the chorus, I hear the girls joining in. It's a lively song, and the musicians are relaxing as they warm up. When the song ends, they move immediately into the next one. John, on fiddle, really gets going. The girls begin bouncing on the old couch. Christopher puts his guitar down and reaches for Molly's hand, pulling her off the couch. She doesn't resist and begins dancing to the steady beat. Talia and Sophie leap up and join in; then Spencer grabs my hand, and suddenly we're all bouncing together in the tiny space.

Christopher picks up his guitar again, and I feel like I'm at a party. My first.

When that song is done, they slow it down a little. The girls return to the couch, and I sit beside Spencer on the floor. He leans his shoulder into mine, and I feel all the tension that has built up over the previous days simply melt away. The song is fairly new, and the musicians stop and start, trying to get it right. There's a discussion among them about which rhythm pattern should be used. They can't agree, so Dad turns to Spencer and asks his opinion.

"I like the first version," he says.

"Why?"

"The tempo's a bit faster…it fits better."

Dad nods. "Let's try that one again."

They continue working on new pieces for the next forty-five minutes, and then Dad turns to Spencer again. "Do you play the keyboard?"

Spencer nods.

"Wanna sit in?"

Spencer jumps to his feet while Brian, the keyboard player, slides off the bench to let Spencer take over. Brian picks up another guitar and strums a chord.

"What song?" Dad asks.

"'Found My Way,'" Spencer says. He bangs out the first couple of bars, then the band joins in, and a moment later the girls are off the couch again, dancing. I watch Spencer, impressed by how well he plays the song. He truly is a fan. And good on the keyboard.

When the song ends, the musicians applaud Spencer. "Keep it up, kid," Steve says, "and we may find a spot in the band for you."

Dad and I exchange a glance, but I quickly look away. I wonder how hard it will be to replace him when he stops touring.

The rest of the rehearsal becomes more of a jam session, with each of the girls choosing rhythm instruments and playing along. That's something I've noticed about the students at the performing-arts school: they're not shy about joining in. I sit beside Spencer on the piano bench and we take turns, improvising when we don't know the notes. The band chooses Loose Ends' biggest hits, and we put our hearts into it, my shyness from dinner completely gone.

Finally Dad calls for a break. We clomp up the stairs and into the kitchen, where Mom has left a platter of brownies on the counter. They disappear quickly, and I drop slices of lemon into a pitcher of ice water before pouring it into glasses.

"That was so awesome," Spencer says, nodding. His eyes are shining and his cheeks are flushed.

Dad smiles at him. "Glad you enjoyed it. You're a fine musician yourself."

Spencer's cheeks flush even redder. "Thanks. I can't actually believe I was just playing with the Loose Ends." He shakes his head. "I was so shocked when we were playing two truths and a lie at school and Allegra said that her dad was in this band. I thought for sure it had to be a lie." He looks at me and we both laugh.

"Okay, guys, party's over," Steve tells the group. "We need to meet and go over some details for the tour. Back to the dungeon."

The girls and Spencer all thank the band again.

"I'd love to see your autograph collection sometime," Dad says to Spencer as he follows Steve out of the room.

"Sounds good," Spencer calls to his back, obviously pleased.

Talia slides into her jacket. "That was so much fun." Effortlessly she reaches out and pulls me into a big hug. Molly does the same, followed by Sophie. When it's Spencer's turn, he follows the hug with a kiss on my cheek. They tumble out the door, chatting all the way to the curb, where the Volvo is idling.

Stepping back into the house, I smile to myself. The evening was perfect. Maybe I'm finally ready to "do" friends.

At school on Tuesday, Mr. Rocchelli suggests I work in the sound room while he teaches the rest of the class. "Do you have everything you need?" he asks.

I pull the flash drive from my pack. "It's all on here," I tell him, "but I don't really know much about how to operate this equipment yet."

"Hmm," he says. "I forgot about that." He studies me for a moment. "How about you help me out with the class today; then we'll meet at lunchtime and I'll start tutoring you on the composition program we use."

I don't mind at all. I'm still on a natural high from the rehearsal last night, and I can see Spencer watching us from the side of the classroom. "Sounds good."

Spencer smiles when he sees me approaching the circle of chairs. "You're with us today, *Legs*?" he asks.

I punch him lightly. "It's Allegra to you, buddy. And yes, I am."

"Why can't I call you Legs? I like it."

I shrug. I don't know, really. It's just that it's always been my dad's nickname for me, no one else's, not even Mom's. It's his way of being affectionate. Yet I have to admit, it sounds completely different coming from Spencer, and not in a bad way.

"Whatever. You can call me anything you want."

"Thanks, Legs," he says.

My cheeks feel warm as I sit down beside him.

"And thanks again for last night," he says. "That was totally amazing."

"You're welcome. Let's do it again before they leave on tour."

"I still can't believe they asked me to play with them!" He shakes his head. "I thought I'd just be watching."

I look up and see Julia entering the room. Her eyes zero in on Spencer, and she does a double take when she notices me beside him. She takes the chair on his other side. "I didn't think you were taking the class with us," she says, leaning across him to talk to me.

"I won't be, usually, but I am today."

"Oh." She doesn't look happy. "Are we still going to be partners?" she asks Spencer.

He glances at me and shrugs. "I guess," he says. "Whatever."

The rest of the class trickles in, and Mr. Rocchelli joins us in the circle. "We're going to warm up this morning by continuing our work with ear training and music intervals. I've asked Allegra to help me, as she has already mastered it. We're going to circulate and help out where we can. Any questions?"

"Should we stay in the same pairs as last time?" Julia asks.

"That's up to you," he says. He glances at Spencer, who is picking at a hangnail. "Though it's always good to switch it up too. Move about and use any of the instruments. Remember, well-trained ears are essential for all musicians."

Spencer doesn't stand a chance. The moment Mr. Rocchelli is finished speaking, Julia says, "Spencer, let's use a xylophone today instead of the piano. C'mon."

I smile sympathetically as he gets up to follow her across the room. He looks back at me but just shrugs and shakes his head. I know he doesn't like her, but he must be too kind to do anything about it. I'm not sure I'd be so nice.

I join the two students nearest me, who are using a keyboard. They glance at me but continue working. I just listen in and don't offer any suggestions. It suddenly feels really odd to be in this position. I wish I hadn't agreed to help.

After about ten minutes, in which I do nothing but watch, Mr. Rocchelli asks the students to return to the circle. He's moved the chairs so that they are all facing a portable whiteboard.

"Great," he says, when everyone is seated. "I heard some really awesome stuff going on. How about you, Allegra?"

I just nod.

"So let's continue our work on transposition—changing a piece of music from one key to another. What is the most important thing to remember when we are transposing?"

My mind wanders as the lesson continues. I watch as Mr. Rocchelli draws responses from his students. He does it in such a way that if they make a mistake, they still feel okay about it. "That's not quite right, Zoe, but you'd be absolutely correct if we were working in a minor key." "You're so close, Conner. Want to give it another try?"

Spencer answers a question correctly, and Mr. Rocchelli praises him. My mind wanders back to last night. I remember how his shoulder pressed against mine while we listened to the music. I hadn't felt panicky at all, just completely comfortable. Spencer sees me studying him and smiles. I smile back, then look away. Where has the easiness from last night gone?

Mr. Rocchelli hands out sheets of music. The students are to transpose them into the key indicated at the top of the page. Each student receives a different sheet. They spread out around the room, most of them using music stands to write on.

I walk around, feeling totally self-conscious about my role as teacher-helper. Why did I agree to do this? It won't happen again. I try to avoid Spencer—I feel especially awkward about helping him—but eventually I find myself near the table he is working at. I pull up a chair and look at his work. He's finished, and his transposition is flawless.

"Looks like you know what you're doing," I whisper.

"I do," he admits.

"Maybe you could challenge the course too," I suggest. "You could help me with my project. A team effort."

"I'd like that," he whispers. "But I'm afraid there's still a lot of stuff I don't know."

"I'll tutor you," I say.

He just smiles and looks away. Then a funny expression crosses his face. I follow his gaze to see what he's looking at. It's Julia, and she is clearly unhappy to see us talking together. I won't be a bit surprised if she accuses me of doing Spencer's work for him. I get up and wander around the room some more, being especially careful to avoid Julia.

Eventually Mr. Rocchelli collects the assignments, and then he sits at the piano. "Call out the name of the scale I'm playing," he says.

For the last fifteen minutes of class, I watch as he challenges the students to name harder and harder scales and chords. He makes it fun. I find my gaze constantly returning to Spencer, but I quickly look away if he glances at me.

As agreed, I meet Mr. Rocchelli back in the portable at lunchtime. I follow him into the sound room, and once again I'm aware of how tiny it is and how close we have to be to work together.

"I'll leave the door open," I tell him. "It gets so warm in here." Nodding absently, he sits down and plugs my flash drive into the computer. I sit in the other chair to listen to what I've done.

"It's just a bunch of ideas right now," I tell him when the piece ends.

"I realize that," he says, looking up at me. "But I'm impressed anyway. I can barely recognize my own simple tune. What program did you record this on?"

"Logic Pro. That's what my dad uses. He helped me record this."

"Great! That's what we have here too, so you'll be able to work at home as well as at school. How much do you already know about Logic Pro?"

"Hardly anything."

"Okay, well, I'll start at the beginning and you stop me if you already know what I'm teaching you."

He turns back to the computer screen and shows me how my music scrolls across it. It almost looks like a hospital heart monitor. Each additional instrument and rhythm that I add will show up on the screen as a new track, either beneath or above the ones already recorded. I can even assign each one a different color to distinguish it from the others. I can record multiple tracks and adjust each one individually without affecting the others. I can raise the volume of the flute or soften the beat of a drum.

"What do you think?" he asks.

"It's pretty cool. I didn't know you could do all that."

"Now you know."

"It looks complicated."

"Just play with it for a while. You'll get the hang of it."

I shrug, not convinced.

"You've got a whole year to finish the project, you know."

"How often can I use the sound room?" I ask.

"It's all yours during music-theory classes. And there"—he points at the wall—"is a sign-up sheet for other hours. I've blocked off the times that the composition class meets, and we have some eager recording-studio-engineer types in this school, but you'll have plenty of time to get the project done."

"I don't know about that."

He tilts his head to regard me.

"You said you wanted a masterpiece. How long did it take Beethoven to write the Fifth Symphony?"

He smiles but doesn't laugh. He's studying me a little too closely, and I feel the urge to move back, get some space, but there's no room.

"That was a joke," I tell him.

"I know." He gets up, and his hand squeezes my arm as he directs me into the chair he's just vacated. "Have a seat," he says. "Let's try adding a trumpet track to your composition."

I sit down, still aware of where his hand was on my arm. It felt nice. Gentle but firm. Just enough pressure to guide me, the way a perfect dance partner can guide you around the dance floor without being aggressive.

"Okay, now find the trumpet under the Options menu," he instructs.

I scroll through the list of instruments, distracted by his presence as he stands close behind me, bent over and peering at the computer screen.

We spend the next half hour playing with the composition program. Occasionally his arm brushes against mine as he reaches to point at something on the screen. I can feel his body heat through his shirt, and his breath is warm where it hits the back of my neck. The scent of his spicy aftershave wafts past me. I have trouble concentrating on his instructions.

Eventually he stretches and steps toward the door. "I need to eat something before the next block," he says. "But you go ahead; keep playing with the program.

We can schedule another lesson once you've had a chance to experiment a little."

I should be relieved that he's no longer right behind me, but I'm not, and I'm bothered by the fact that I actually enjoyed having him so close.

My stomach growls. I slap my hand to it, embarrassed.

He smiles. "There's only one rule," he says. "No eating or drinking in here. You can't damage anything by clicking on the wrong icon, but a spilled drink..." He leaves the sound room, and through the glass I see him walking toward his desk. I save the work we've done and put my flash drive in my pack. I give him a little wave as I walk across the classroom toward the door. "Thanks!"

"Allegra," he calls.

I spin around. "Yes?"

"You're not a perfectionist, are you?"

I'm not sure what he's getting at. "Of course I am." I smile.

"I'm serious," he says. "When I said I wanted a masterpiece, I should have added, 'Within reason.' I don't want you getting bent out of shape over this."

Now I get it. It was my Beethoven remark. I laugh. "No worries. I'll just write an average masterpiece."

He smiles at my joke. "It's just that, well, I know how seriously you take your dancing. I don't want you getting an ulcer or anything."

I roll my eyes. "No ulcers, I promise."

I sense him watching me as I leave the room, and I like it, but I know that's stupid. What is going on with me?

I find Spencer and the girls lounging on the steps in the multipurpose room.

"Are you hot? Your cheeks are flushed," Talia comments.

I put my hand to my face. My skin *is* warm.

"Where have you been?" Spencer asks, moving over to make room for me beside him. He's sitting a level higher than the girls.

"In the sound room, with Mr. Rocchelli," I tell him. "It does get warm in there."

"Reeeally," Talia says, dragging out the word. She studies my face. "Do you still think he's a goof?"

I feel my cheeks burn even more, recalling my comment a week or so ago. "No, not really," I admit. "He's pretty cool."

"And *hot*," Talia adds. "Don't you think?"

"Very funny," I say, but I'm remembering how I felt when his hand squeezed my arm. I pull my sandwich out of my pack and change the subject. "Have you studied for the history quiz?" I ask her.

She doesn't answer and keeps smiling, a sly smile as if she knows something, which she doesn't. She gives Spencer's leg a little punch. "I think you've got competition, buddy," she says.

Sophie laughs and Molly says, "Woo hoo!"

"Shut up, Talia," I say, a little more harshly than I intended. I take a swig of water. I can't look at Spencer, but I can feel him watching me.

"Hey, I'm just kidding, Allegra," Talia says more softly.

I nod and keep eating.

"Seriously," she says, putting her hand on my leg. "I'm always goofing around. Nobody takes me seriously."

"Nobody," Molly agrees, and Sophie nods.

I shrug, and the bell rings. We all collect our things.

"Are we okay?" Talia asks quietly.

"Yeah, of course." But I can't meet her eyes.

She hesitates before joining Sophie and Molly, who have walked on ahead.

I know I'm overreacting, but I can't seem to help it. I also know that her comment wouldn't have bugged me so much if Spencer hadn't been sitting there, and...well, if there wasn't some truth to it. I feel my cheeks start to burn again.

I catch up to Spencer, who is pushing through the door that leads into the courtyard. He holds it open for me. We walk across the courtyard together and through the doors on the other side. I can't think of a thing to say.

"Can I call you tonight?" he asks, stopping at the door to the art room.

"Sure," I say, feeling my heart speed up a little. "I'll be home from dance class by nine thirty."

He smiles and squeezes my arm before slipping into the art room. That's two arm squeezes in one lunch hour, and I can't help but notice that I don't have the same response to this one as I did to Mr. Rocchelli's.

Eight

I find Dad in the music studio when I get home from dance class. He's wearing headphones and strumming his guitar, keeping time to whatever it is he's listening to. He doesn't hear me come down the stairs. His brow is creased, and he's either concentrating deeply on the music or angry about something.

He looks up and smiles when I plunk myself on the couch. He pulls off the headphones. "Hey," he says. "How's it going?"

"It's going good," I tell him. "What are you working on?"

"Not much," he says. "Just chilling, really."

He looks back down at his guitar and plays a couple of chords. The frown has returned to his forehead.

"Have you told anyone about your plans?" I ask. "To give up touring?"

He sighs deeply. "Yeah." He plucks a guitar string, and we watch it vibrate. "I told your mom."

"And?"

"And"—he plays an intricate little riff—"I thought she might be happy about it."

I stare at him, trying to make sense of what he's saying. "She wasn't?"

He shakes his head and keeps picking out notes.

"What did she say?"

"She didn't say much. But she clearly wasn't happy to hear it."

He plays for another minute while I sit in shocked silence.

"That kind of changes everything," he says finally.

"What do you mean?" I think I know, but I need to hear him say it.

He sighs again and stares at his guitar. "I might as well be honest with you, honey." There's a long pause while he decides what to say. "Your mom and I are going to have to figure out where we go from here." He puts his guitar down and looks directly at me. "We'll make a decision when I get back from the tour."

"What do you mean…a decision?" I hear the tremble in my voice, but I don't care.

He looks away. "About our marriage, Legs."

I feel like I've been knocked in the head, hard, and have just woken up to a new reality, one that doesn't make sense. I stare at him as the meaning of his words sinks in.

Dad comes over to the couch and sits beside me. He puts his arm around my shoulder, but I pull away. His arm drops back to his side. "Legs," he says, "it's not what I want either. Your mom and I are going to get some counseling right away and...consider our options."

"What about me?" I feel icy cold all over.

"Nothing much will change for you, Legs. You're already used to me being away a lot."

Suddenly I get what this is all about. "It's that Marcus guy, isn't it?" I stand and walk over to the harp. I pull hard on a string, and then another one. Their combined sounds made a jarring, unpleasant sound. "I should have known!"

Dad leans back and sighs again. He folds his hands in his lap. "That's something you'll have to ask your mom," he says.

I'm still too shocked to move. I'm breathing hard and my feet feel glued to the floor. I can hear my cell phone ringing upstairs, but I ignore it.

Dad moves back to his chair and his guitar, but before he can play anything, the home phone rings. When I don't move to get it, he leans over to pick up the studio extension.

"I'm not home," I whisper.

He looks at me, frowning, then picks up the receiver and says hello.

"Hey, Spencer," he says a moment later. "I'm afraid she can't come to the phone right now. Yes. I'll give her your message."

He hangs up and turns back to me. "He says he'll see you at school tomorrow."

I just nod.

"It's going to be okay, honey," he says quietly.

I don't answer, but I can move my feet again so I climb the stairs, shut myself in my room and curl into a small ball under my blankets.

A long time passes before I hear a soft knock on my door. It opens and someone crosses the dark room and carefully sits on my bed. A hand touches my shoulder.

"Allegra?" Mom says.

I don't answer. I have nothing to say.

"I heard you had a...a conversation with Dad tonight."

A conversation. That's an interesting way to put it.

"I'm sorry, honey. I wanted to be there when we talked to you about...about things. I didn't think it would come up so soon. We haven't made any firm plans yet."

I shrug; I still have nothing to say.

"Everything's going to be okay, honey."

"Whatever." Once again, it's the best I can do.

She rubs my back, then suddenly pulls back my blanket. "Allegra. You're still in your dance leotard."

I don't respond.

I hear her sigh and feel the blanket return to my shoulder. The mattress springs up as she gets to her feet. "We'll talk more tomorrow," she says, and I hear my door close.

I flip over and pull my knees up into my chest. The icy-cold sensation continues, radiating from my core out, and my breathing becomes ragged. Tears spill down my cheeks, followed by sobs, and I just let go, not holding anything back. I cry until I feel empty, mercifully pain-free. Warmth returns to my body, and finally, finally, I fall into a deep sleep.

I don't bother to get up in the morning except to use the bathroom. Mom comes into my room with a mug of tea. "Not going to school today?" she asks.

I sit up and accept the mug, but I don't look at her. "Maybe later."

"Do you want to talk?" she asks, sitting on the end of my bed again.

"Not really." I do, but I'm afraid of what I might say. I'd like to tell her there wouldn't be a problem if it weren't for her.

And Marcus, the guy with the sports car. I bet he's a bassoon player. I never did like the bassoon.

"Dad's going to move in with Steve, for the time being," she adds.

Now I do look at her. "How come?"

"It's just easier that way," she says.

Easier for who? I think, but I don't dare say it. Certainly not easier for me. And not for him either. His studio is here.

"He'll still be around," she says. "To rehearse and to see you, of course."

"Of course," I say, more sharply than I intend. I feel Mom's gaze.

"Are you sure there's nothing you want to talk about?" she says again.

I shrug. How do you go about asking your mother if she's having an affair?

I don't bother going to school after all. Late in the morning I hear my parents leave. They return a few hours later. I'm still in bed. Another knock on my door. This time it's Dad's face that appears.

"Can I come in?" he asks.

I nod.

He sits on the end of my bed, not looking at me. He pulls a pillow into his lap, and his fingers twirl the decorative fringe. We sit in silence for a moment.

"I've never been very good with words," he says quietly. "I tend to express myself in music."

"You write great lyrics," I remind him.

"That's different. I can fiddle around with those words until I get them just right." He hesitates. "But talking with my daughter...well, I'm still struggling with that, though I feel we've been connecting better since I've been home this time."

I nod. I think so too. Silence fills the room. He goes back to twirling the pillow fringe.

"Will you write out your dance schedule for the next couple of weeks so I can watch your classes?" he asks.

I nod. "I was hoping you'd keep on helping me with my music composition."

"I will when I can," he says. "But that's a year-long project. There's not much I can do when I'm on the road."

"You'll be back, and besides, there's still a couple of weeks."

"We'll set up dates," he suggests.

"I still don't see why you can't stay here. There's a sofa bed in the studio. You could sleep there if you don't want..." The sentence is too awkward to finish.

It's his turn to shrug. "I'm trying to do everything the way your mom wants things done. This is her idea."

"You're going to be gone soon enough."

"It's complicated, Legs. Relationships are always complicated. That's why there is so much music written about love and heartbreak." He smiles sadly.

I have a sudden idea. "Why doesn't she move out until your road trip? That's only fair. You're gone enough already."

"She still has her harp students coming here."

"You still have your band rehearsals."

Dad finds my foot under the blanket and squeezes it. "We're going to do it your mom's way," he says, and I know he's closing the subject.

My cell phone jangles. I check the caller ID. Spencer.

"Take it," Dad says. "I've got to go pack up my things. Steve is coming to get me."

I take a deep breath. "Hello?"

"Hey, Legs!" Spencer's voice sounds chirpy, light, uncomplicated.

"Hey, Spencer."

"We missed you at school today."

"Oh. Thanks. I...I wasn't feeling well."

"Are you contagious?"

"No, why?"

"I wondered if...if I could come by for a visit."

I can hear my dad in the next room, opening and shutting drawers as he packs up his clothes. Sadness begins to well up in me again.

"No," I tell him, hoping he can't hear the quiver in my voice.

"Allegra?"

Uh-oh. He heard it. "Yeah?" I'm on the verge of losing it again.

"Are you okay?"

"Yeah." I try clearing my throat, but the lump in it is too big. "But I gotta go."

"Will you be at school tomorrow?"

"Maybe. Bye, Spencer."

I hang up before he can ask me anything else. How can I tell him that my dad is leaving?

Dad must have finished packing. The floor outside my room creaks as he carries his things to the front door. My heart sinks deeper than ever. I have to get out of the house. I can't be here when he leaves. I quickly pull on some clothes and running shoes, and when I hear Dad pass by my room and the screen door slams, I slip down the stairs to the studio and head out the basement door to the backyard. Pulling open the gate, I turn left into the alley. I begin to run, slowly at first, but picking up speed once I'm warmed up. I pound along the sidewalk, trying not to think about what's happening at home.

After a long time, I slow to a walk, and my breathing begins to return to normal. I wipe the sweat off my brow and turn, reluctantly, to begin the walk home. I wish I had somewhere else to go. Anywhere else. I grew up in this neighborhood; I should have friends I could drop in on. I wrack my brain. I don't.

The street I've run to looks familiar. I study the houses as I walk past them. A memory of a summer afternoon spent near here begins to surface in my mind. And then I see it, the large front yard with the rancher-style home set neatly back from it. I attended a birthday party here once. I must have been about ten years old, in grade five. All the girls in my class had been invited to the celebration. We started the party at an art studio, where we each chose a ceramic figurine to paint. I could handle that, simply withdrawing into myself while I painted. I listened to all the chatter around me but didn't join in.

When that was done, we returned to the birthday girl's house. It was a hot day, so the girls changed into bathing suits and ran back and forth through the spray of a sprinkler on the front lawn, screaming in delight when the water hit their skin.

I stood off to the side with the parents, mostly moms who'd helped with the driving. My dad was with me that day. He was the one who'd encouraged me to attend the party in the first place. Mom would have let me skip it.

As I stood there, not knowing how to join in, Dad gave me a little push. "Go on, Legs. Go have fun."

I took a timid step back. The girls looked so silly to me, squealing like piglets when the water hit them. Then they'd crowd together in a tight pack until one of them dared to run through it again, and the rest would follow.

I wanted desperately to escape from that yard. I realized I should never have listened to Dad. I'd only gone to the party because I wanted to please him, to spend time with him on one of his rare weekends home. But I knew he would be disappointed when he saw that I didn't fit in with those girls.

Suddenly Dad bolted from my side. I watched as he ran, fully clothed, through the spray of water. The girls shrieked and the mothers clapped in delight.

He turned and began to run back again, but this time he did a cartwheel over the spray. The blast of water hit him directly in the face. The girls screamed even louder and jumped up and down. The moms clapped harder.

I felt more isolated than ever. When Dad got back to my side, dripping wet, he said, "See, Legs? It's easy."

I knew he thought he was helping, but he'd only made matters worse, drawing more attention my way. I simply pulled my towel tighter around me.

Dad knew better than to push the issue. He put his arm around my shoulder, and we watched as the other girls did cartwheels through the spray.

We stayed at the party long enough to watch the birthday girl open her presents and blow out her candles and then I caught Dad's eye and motioned to the door.

His eyebrows arched in surprise, but he excused himself from the circle of women who were fawning over him, the local celebrity.

"Let's go," I whispered.

"You're not staying for a piece of that cake?" he asked, eyeing it hungrily.

I shook my head.

"Okay," he said. "Grab your things and we'll say our thank-yous."

Back home, I heard my parents talking in the kitchen when they thought I was in my room.

"I told you," Mom said. "She's just not social. There's nothing wrong with that."

"Maybe she needs to be encouraged a little more," Dad said.

"She is who she is," Mom said, coming to my defense as always. "Not all of us are party animals like you."

Dad didn't answer, and I felt sick. There was nothing I wanted more than to please him.

He wasn't really a party animal, but he *was* comfortable hanging out with groups of people, and I'm still not, despite the counseling Mom eventually agreed to take me to. Now, I realize, my parents had practically this same conversation about me just a few evenings ago. Some things never change.

I think that may have been the last birthday party I was ever invited to. I was never shunned by the other girls; I was simply left alone. That was fine with me.

I push the memory from my mind and continue toward home. I think of Angela, the girl I met when I was allowed to start dance classes. She also started taking classes later than most of the other girls, and she also takes nearly as many as I do. We are friends, but not outside the studio. I don't know why. Maybe she's like me; she knows that while we're at the dance school we can relate, but outside, who knows? I pick up the pace. Dance. I will go to class tonight. Dance will take me away from my worries, help me escape the painful situation at home. I begin to run again.

Nine

I'm so lost in thought the next morning that I just about hit the ceiling when Mr. Rocchelli taps on the sound-room window. He opens the door and steps into the room. "There, we're even," he says, grinning. "I just got you back for that first day of school, when you nearly gave me a heart attack."

I smile, remembering how high he'd jumped. It seems so much longer ago than just two weeks.

"What were you concentrating on so hard?" he asks.

I look down at the computer screen and realize I haven't done a thing over the hour-long class. "Just thinking about the music," I lie.

Through the window, I see the students filing out of the room. Julia is walking beside Spencer, chatting up at him. He pauses at the door, turns back to look at me and waves. I wave back. Julia's eyes flash.

Mr. Rocchelli glances at Spencer too. "So how's it going in here?" he asks. "Do you need some help?"

"I'm okay for now," I say.

"Your friend Spencer"—he nods toward the door—"is in my sound-engineering class and seems to know his way around Logic. He might be able to give you a hand with the technical stuff."

"Thanks. I'll remember that."

Mr. Rocchelli studies my face. I look down at the equipment.

"Is everything all right?" he asks.

"Yeah." I pull the flash drive out of the computer and put it into a pocket in my backpack. I take a step toward the door, assuming Mr. Rocchelli will move, but he doesn't. He stays firmly planted in the doorway. I glance up at him.

"You were away yesterday," he says. "Were you sick?"

"Yeah, but I'm fine now," I lie.

"You still look a little tired," he says. "Are you sure you're okay?"

I squeeze myself around him, being careful not to make contact. "Yes, I'm sure, but I won't be okay if I'm late for ballet. See you tomorrow." I turn and immediately collide with a guy who has seemingly appeared out of nowhere. Books go flying. Flustered, I apologize, help him pick up his things, check that he's okay and, with a last look at Mr. Rocchelli, who's still watching me from the sound-room doorway, race to class.

"Welcome back," Talia says when I sit down beside Spencer at lunchtime. It's become our habit for Talia, Molly and Sophie to sit on one step, and Spencer and me on the step above them. I'm not sure why they always save the space beside Spencer for me, but they do.

"Thanks." I smile as normally as I can and pull a sandwich and a bottle of water out of my bag.

"Were you sick?" she asks.

"Yeah, but I'm okay now." I leave it at that and hope she won't ask what I was sick with. I feign intense interest in my sandwich, lifting off the bread and rearranging a leaf of lettuce.

I can feel Spencer watching me, but I ignore him and turn my gaze across the room.

With a last glance at me, Talia goes back to a conversation she was having with Molly and Sophie when I arrived, and Spencer and I sit in uneasy silence for a few moments.

"You sounded kind of...funny on the phone yesterday," he says.

"Oh, that. I'm sorry. You caught me at a bad moment."

He stabs the last noodle in his Styrofoam bowl. "Has Steve dropped off those autographed headshots yet?"

"No, I don't think so. I'll ask my dad to remind him." My dad. Just thinking about him brings me down again.

"Thanks."

I nod.

"When's the next rehearsal?"

"I don't know." But I do know that I'm not inviting Spencer over for it. How would I explain why my dad is leaving with the others when the rehearsal is over? I don't know why this new living arrangement embarrasses me, but it does.

I glance at Spencer and wonder again if he has befriended me just to get closer to the Loose Ends. Did I imagine those moments when our friendship felt like something more? Right now, I feel too depressed to even care. "Mr. Rocchelli says you know how to use Logic," I say, changing the subject.

"I'm learning."

"He thought you might be willing to help me with it."

His face lights up. "No problem."

That makes me feel a little better. "Thanks. I'd appreciate it."

He glances up at the wall clock. "We've got time right now. Want to get started?"

That takes me by surprise. "Sure." I swallow the last piece of my sandwich and collect my things. We hurry out to Mr. Rocchelli's portable but find the door locked. "Shit," Spencer says, banging it with his fist.

That's the second time I've seen Spencer hit something when he's mad. It doesn't fit with his usually easygoing temperament.

"I guess he can't leave all that equipment unsupervised when no one's there," I say.

The school door bangs shut behind us, and we both swing around. Mr. Rocchelli is heading toward the portable, keys in hand.

"Spencer's already agreed to tutor you?" he asks, sliding the key into the lock.

"Yeah, and he doesn't like to waste any time."

"I see that." Mr. Rocchelli pushes the door open and steps aside to let us pass. "In the future, if you sign up to use the room I won't lock you out. As it was, I didn't think anyone was going to be here today."

"We didn't know either until five minutes ago," Spencer says, leading the way into the sound room.

Mr. Rocchelli smiles at me. "Go to it," he says.

I feel my heartbeat quicken. What is the matter with me?

Spencer is a patient teacher, and by the end of the lunch hour I feel way more confident with the program. He listens to snippets of what I've written and appears genuinely impressed. He watches as I tuck away the flash drive. "You look better than you did earlier," he says.

"Better?" I tease. "I wasn't looking well before?"

"No," he says seriously. "You were looking…sad."

That's because I *was* sad. But I'm not going to tell him that. Working with the program was a good distraction, just as dance class was last night. I'll have to remember this. Keep busy. Keep distracted.

"Well, I'm glad I'm looking better."

"Do you want to come back here after school?"

I think about it and glance at the schedule on the wall. No one has the room booked. "What I really need to do now is simply work on the music," I tell him. "I think I know enough about the equipment to get started."

He thinks about that. "I could do homework in the portable," he says, gesturing to the main room, "and you could work in here. If you have any problems with the program, I could help you."

I glance through the window at Mr. Rocchelli, who is working at his desk. I'd feel more relaxed about being here after school if Spencer was here too.

"Okay, thanks."

"Good. It's a date."

I glance up at his choice of words.

"You know what I mean," he says, looking away. I follow him out of the sound room. "We'll be back after school," he tells Mr. Rocchelli as he heads across the room.

"You've got a whole year to complete this project," Mr. Rocchelli reminds me. "It doesn't have to be done in one semester."

"Have you forgotten?" I ask him. "I'm working on a masterpiece. That takes time, lots of time."

He laughs. "See you after school."

My after-school session in the sound room is completely different from the hour I spent there during music-theory class. This time I'm focused, and only twice do I have to ask Spencer for help. I work on the second part of the piece and begin creating an entirely new segment of music, including a new melody that wasn't part of Mr. Rocchelli's original song. This section has some darker themes, and the notes come easily to me. I play it on the small keyboard that sits in the corner.

When I look up, I find Mr. Rocchelli standing in the doorway. "I don't recognize my song anymore," he says.

"Oh, you will," I quickly assure him. "I'm just adding to it."

He smiles. "It's wonderful. I like what I just heard."

"Oh, that. It's really rough."

"I know, but I still liked it."

"Thanks." I feel my face growing hot. I've never been good at taking compliments, especially about things I'm new at.

"I just came in to tell you that I'm off to a meeting, but I've given the room key to Spencer. He'll lock up and return the key tomorrow. I've got a spare key for the morning."

"Okay, thanks."

He studies me. "Why don't you guys go have some fun? You've worked hard enough today."

"I'm on a roll. Can't quit now."

He pats my shoulder. "Then I'll leave you to it."

I watch through the window as he speaks to Spencer and then heads out the door. Suddenly the portable feels very still and quiet. Creepy again. Spencer looks over at me. I give him a little wave and go back to work.

It takes a few minutes, but eventually I get back into the zone, that place where my mind thinks of nothing but the music. Using only the computer, I add a variety of instruments. I click *Playback* so often, I'm afraid I'll wear out the mouse. Eventually I sit back in the chair. I feel satisfied with what I've accomplished, but now I need some feedback.

"Want to take a listen?" I ask Spencer from the doorway.

He hurries in and I sit him in the chair and start the music. I stand to the side. He closes his eyes and listens. When it's over, I reach past him to shut it off. He opens his eyes.

"Wow," he says. "That was sad."

"Was it?"

"Yeah. But beautiful too. Haunting."

Hmm. I wonder if it's too different from the rest of the piece, the part Mr. Rocchelli wrote. "Will you listen to the intro and see if it flows into this?"

"Sure."

I play the piece from the start, and shut it off after the new section. Spencer's eyes flutter open. They look a little glazed, and he blinks again.

"That's amazing," he says.

At first I don't know whether to believe him, but his expression is completely sincere.

"I hear a whole section of string instruments playing that part."

I nod. That might just work.

He stands up, and I go to step back to make room, but his hands land on my shoulders, keeping me close. I fight the urge to shrug free. He looks directly at me. "This is really, really good," he says. His voice is as intense as his gaze.

"Thanks," I say and look down at my feet. The sound room is suddenly sweltering hot. Sweat breaks out all over me.

I feel his fingers under my chin, and he lifts my head so I have to look up at him. His eyes are questioning, his head tilted. I stand frozen to the spot. Part of me wants to flee, put as much distance between us as I can, but another part yearns to stay in this moment.

Spencer leans in and kisses me softly. His lips linger, looking for a response, but I feel only numbness and confusion. He pulls his mouth away, his arms circle me in a hug, and he pulls me close. "I'm sorry," he says. "It's too soon."

"It's okay," I say. And it is. The hug feels very nice, and I relax into his body.

By the time I get home, Mom has already left for the theater. There's a note on the fridge: *Sorry I missed you. Dinner is in the fridge. You can take the car to class.*

I slump into a kitchen chair. The house feels incredibly empty. It's amazing how fast I've grown accustomed to having Dad home in the evenings. I really want to see him tonight.

I look up Steve's phone number. I'll tell Dad I'm calling to see if he can bring over the autographed headshots. Then, when he's here, I'll ask him to listen to the music I wrote this afternoon. For some reason, I need to know that he approves, that he thinks it's good.

The phone rings and rings. No one answers. The voice mail clicks on. I hang up without leaving a message.

I think about eating dinner and getting ready for dance class, but I can't motivate myself to get out of the kitchen chair. For the first time ever, I don't feel like going.

I pick up my bag and jog down the stairs to the studio. Plugging my flash drive into the computer, I listen to what I've written so far. I cringe. How did I miss those mistakes? I grab my notebook and write down what needs to be corrected. Then I begin jotting down new ideas. I move to the piano and try a few variations.

When I hear what I like, I jot the notes down. I flip through my notebook and read through the sketches I've made for the third and fourth parts of the piece. As the outside light fades, I turn on the overhead lights and continue working.

The door to the upstairs swings open, startling me.

"Allegra? Is that you?"

"Mom! What are you doing home?" I struggle to drag myself back to the real world, feeling much the way I do when I'm suddenly awoken from a deep sleep.

Mom descends the stairs. "Honey, it's almost midnight. What are you still doing up?"

Almost midnight? Where did the evening go? I look at the music staff paper scattered across the floor, and I'm hesitant to quit. I really do feel like I'm on a roll.

"Did you eat anything tonight?" she asks.

My stomach answers with a loud growl.

She sighs. "Come upstairs. We'll have a snack and then you need to get to bed."

I consider arguing with her but then close my book, shut down the computer and put my things away. I walk past her down the hallway and into the kitchen.

It's still very early. I emerge from sleep tangled in a sweaty heap of blankets and sheets. It's like there's been a dog fight, or several of them, on my bed. My room is still pitch-black. The glowing red numbers on my alarm clock read 5:00. I should unravel myself, roll over and sleep for at least another hour, but my mind is alive with the vivid images of my dreams. Crazy, mixed-up dreams.

I tug my leg free from a sheet that's twisted around it and flop over on my side, pulling up on the blankets. The furnace rumbles to life downstairs. The house creaks, familiar noises I've known all my life. I settle back into a foggy, sleepy state, but the images from my dreams return.

I'm on a stage, in complete darkness. The stage lights burst on, the music begins, and I'm supposed to start dancing, but my mind is blank. I don't remember a single step. My heart pounds and my mouth dries up. I'm dizzy. I want to run offstage, but I can't make my feet move...and then I'm in the music studio downstairs. Spencer's kissing me and pulling me toward the couch. When I look up, Mr. Rocchelli is standing on the stairs, watching. He winks. I push Spencer away, embarrassed, but that only makes him cling tighter. Mr. Rocchelli goes to the piano and starts pounding away, old jazz standards. Spencer keeps kissing me, against my will. I look to Mr. Rocchelli for help, but he has morphed into my dad, who is now singing a sappy love song. I feel like I'm suffocating...I want to scream for help, but Spencer keeps pressing his mouth to mine so I can't make a sound...

I sit up with a start, breathing hard. My heart really is banging. If I go back to sleep, I'm sure the dreams will resume where they left off. Climbing out of bed, I cross my room and head down the hallway, running my hand along the wall in the dark. When I reach the door to the basement, I open it, flick on the lights and peer down the stairs, half expecting to find Spencer and Mr. Rocchelli there, but the room is empty.

In the studio, Dad's headphones hang from the wall. Plugging the cord into the keyboard, I place the headset over my ears and press my fingers into the keys. I start by playing phrases from my composition, but that feels like work, so I let go and play anything that comes to mind. My hands run up and down the keyboard, and with the headphones on, I know I won't wake my mom. Unlike when I had to practice for exams and be completely precise, I can now let the music pour out of me, unchecked. And it does. Chopin. Handel. Beethoven. The unsettled feelings from the dreams start to evaporate as I give myself up to the music. Finally, when daylight begins to appear though the slats of the blinds, I turn the keyboard off and remove the headphones. I slump lower on the bench, feeling like I've been through a mini-exorcism, banishing the demons that haunted me in the night.

I arrive at school early, hoping to find the music portable unlocked. It is.

"Allegra!" Mr. Rocchelli looks up from the papers he's marking at his desk. "What are you doing here so early?"

"I'd hoped to work on my piece."

"But what if I hadn't been here? The door would have been locked."

"Then I guess I would have done homework in the study hall."

He considers that. "Well, this is your lucky day. I'm trying to get caught up myself." With a flourish he gestures toward the sound room. "She's all yours."

"Thanks."

I feel him watch me cross the room.

"Allegra, are you sure you're not going overboard with this assignment?"

When I turn back to him, the image from my dream returns. I expect him to wink, but of course he doesn't. "Like I said, I'm on a roll and I don't want to lose my momentum."

He smiles. "Spoken like a true artist. Get to it then. I'm not going to be the one to stand in the way of a composer on a roll."

As I close the sound-room door behind me, I have to smile. A composer. It sounds so nice coming from him.

"Sleepover at my house tonight," Talia says as I take my usual spot on the steps at lunchtime. "Are you in, Allegra?"

"What's the occasion?" I ask, feigning intense interest in the list of ingredients in my yogurt.

"Just a girls' night. Pizza, pedicures, gossip, movies. You know, the usual."

No, I don't know, but for some reason this doesn't sound too bad. My house is suddenly way too empty in the evenings, and for the first time I can remember, I'm not freaking out when I'm with other kids.

"I guess that means I'm not invited," Spencer says, putting on a pouty face.

"That's right. So sorry," Talia says.

"I give good foot massages."

"Foot massages?" Molly asks. She turns to Talia. "Maybe we should reconsider the girls-only part of the party."

"Nope, sorry," Talia says.

"Can I take a rain check on the foot massage?" Molly asks Spencer.

"Sure," he says and grins.

Molly smiles, but she blushes too. Something in my stomach twists. I wasn't ready to kiss Spencer, but I don't like to see someone else flirting with him either, even if it is just Molly and even if I know it's only in fun.

"What time should I come over?" I ask Talia.

"Anytime after six." She pulls out her phone and texts me her address.

I take out my own phone and look at the message, but I don't recognize the street. I decide to Google it later instead of asking for directions. I know I should ask what to bring—sleeping bag, pillow?—but then it might be clear that I'm new at this. I just tuck my phone back into my backpack. "I didn't feel like taking dance class tonight anyway."

Talia just smiles.

The subject changes, my stomach relaxes, and I listen to the easy conversation of my friends.

Friends. I like the sound of that word.

Ten

"Wow!" Mom says.

Wow is right, I think, gawking out the window of the car. The houses in Talia's neighborhood are enormous. Ten houses the size of mine would fit on each of these properties. I've never been in a mansion before. A deep uneasiness settles over me.

Mom's agreed to drop me off at Talia's for the sleepover on her way to work. Part of me wants to ask why Marcus isn't driving her tonight, but part of me simply wants to keep my head buried in the sand and not even think about the two of them.

"Here it is," she says, gazing up at a house that's the size of a small hotel.

I glance down at the number on my phone and then up at the house. Yup. Same number.

The familiar apprehension returns. I had no idea Talia was from a wealthy family. Our house is dumpy in comparison. If I'd known she lived here, I'd never have invited her over. I want to turn around, to go home. This is so out of my league. Mom has pulled over, and her smile is encouraging as she waits for me to get out of the car. When I first told her about the sleepover she acted pleased for me, but I could tell she was also concerned; she knows how hard these things are for me. But right now, she seems totally confident. Maybe she thinks I'm finally becoming normal, whatever that is. Glancing at her, I know I can't back out now. I don't want to let her down.

I close my eyes and take a couple of deep breaths. Then I push open the car door and grab my bag from the backseat.

"Have fun!" Mom calls, pretending that all this is typical, that I go to sleepovers every weekend. Her smile is warm. I wave back, but I'm not feeling one bit comfortable. I watch miserably as she drives away.

Walking up the driveway, I remind myself that it's just Talia, Sophie and Molly. My friends. It's no big deal. We hang out every day at school. I can do this.

The front door is ajar and I knock, then push it open a little more and peer into the front hallway. I knock a little harder and call, "Hello." I hear voices upstairs, but no one responds.

Stepping into the tiled front hall, I glance around, hoping not to run into any of Talia's family members before I see Talia herself. The front foyer has vaulted ceilings and a spiral staircase leading to the second floor. A chandelier cascades down the center of the foyer, and the stairway carpeting is the plushest I've ever seen. I take another step into the house and peer down the hall, which opens into a massive kitchen. Straight ahead is a sunken living room, and through the windows I can see a kidney-shaped swimming pool surrounded by a deck and, beyond that, a lawn that looks like a golf course.

The doorbell chimes and I swing around to see a pizza-delivery guy standing in the doorway. He's weighted down by a stack of cardboard boxes.

"You order pizza?" he asks.

"Not me, I don't live here, but I'll see if I can find someone…"

"Don't worry about it," he says, thrusting the boxes toward me. "I'll just put the order on their account."

Their account? I put down my bag and take the boxes. "But…"

"No worries." He waves me off and is down the stairs and jogging to his car before I can say anything else.

Whoever heard of having an account with a takeout pizza company?

I look around, wondering where to place the stack of boxes. And who's going to eat six large pizzas anyway? How many people are in Talia's family? With a sigh, I realize I should have asked these things before agreeing to come over.

A figure emerges from a doorway at the top of the staircase. It's Talia. She starts to turn right to go down the hall but catches a glimpse of me and does a double take. She grins. "Allegra! What are you doing down there?"

"What does it look like?" I say, deeply relieved that she's the first person I've encountered. "Delivering pizza, obviously."

She laughs and calls to whoever else is in the room she's just left. "Pizza's here! Come and get it!"

My relief disappears in a flash as a stream of girls follows her out of the room and down the stairs. Strangers, all of them. My heart sinks completely. I'd thought it was just going to be the four of us tonight. That's the only reason I agreed to come.

Talia grabs the boxes from me and leads the way to the sprawling kitchen. "C'mon," she calls over her shoulder. "I'll introduce you to everyone in a sec."

I'm swept up in the noisy mob as the girls pass through the foyer and head down the hall. In the kitchen, there's a wide granite island with bar stools along one side. Talia places the pizza boxes in the center of the island, then reaches into a cupboard and pulls out a stack of plates, which she places beside the pizza.

Looking around, I see that the girls have carried bottles of vodka coolers, wine and an assortment of other drinks that I don't recognize down to the kitchen with them. Drinks are poured, slices of pizza are taken, and the fifteen or so girls perch on the bar stools and at the long kitchen table. The chatter is loud, and everyone appears to be talking at once. A wave of nausea overcomes me.

"Hey, Allegra!" Molly says, appearing for the first time. She rushes over and gives me a hug. Sophie also shows up, carrying a glass of wine. Her eyes have an odd shine to them.

"Hey," I answer back. I motion to the rest of the girls. "I didn't realize there was going to be so many of us."

"Yeah," Molly answers. "Par-tay!"

Sophie rolls her eyes but smiles too.

"Tally's parents are away for the weekend," Molly continues, "at her brother's soccer tournament, so she figured, why not? C'mon," she says. "I'm starving."

Sophie smiles like we're coconspirators or something and follows Molly to the counter. Loud laughter breaks out across the room. I'm feeling dizzy, and just like in my dream last night, my feet are stuck fast. I'm that ten-year-old girl at the birthday party again, and I simply can't do this.

For what seems an eternity, I stand frozen to the spot, just watching, and then my feet are released and I turn and scurry back to the front hallway. I grab my bag and slip outside, unnoticed.

I have to transfer buses three times to get back to my neighborhood. It takes most of that time for my heart to return to a regular beat and my breathing to go back to normal. Walking the last stretch, I look around at the familiar houses, noticing for the first time how tired-looking some of them are. All the yards are pathetically puny, and there are no swimming pools or expansive lawns. The gardens, even the ones that have been lovingly tended, would take up only a fraction of the space in the gardens in Talia's neighborhood.

It's too late to go to dance class. I consider doing homework or working on my music composition, but I'm just not in the mood. I flop down on the couch and stare out the window at the darkening evening. What is the matter with me? Why can't I just relax and enjoy parties like everyone else? I really like Talia, Sophie and Molly, and now I've blown it. How hard would it have been to stay, to pretend to have fun?

I sigh and sink deeper into the couch. It would have been impossible. The familiar symptoms would have gone from bad to worse. Excessive sweating would have been next, then shortness of breath. I might even have felt faint. It's impossible to hide these things and pretend to have fun, no matter how many slow, deep breaths I take.

I grab a cushion and chuck it, hard. It hits the wall and falls softly to the carpet. I throw a second one, a third. A growing rage fuels me. Jumping to my feet, I turn and kick the couch, over and over. "Stupid, stupid, stupid!"

One last kick, and my second toe connects with the wood base of the couch and bends back at an awkward angle. I flop back down in agony, massaging my aching toe.

The ringing of my cell phone snaps me back to the present. I check the caller ID. Molly. I just stare at it.

After a moment the phone beeps to tell me there is a voice message.

"Allegra? Are you there? We're worried about you." Molly's voice is soft. "You just up and disappeared. If you get this message, call us, okay?" Reaching for the TV remote, I click it on and begin channel surfing. I stare at the screen, but nothing really registers.

My phone rings again. Molly leaves another message, shorter this time. "Allegra, call Tally's house."

I flick through some more stations.

The house has grown completely dark. I wander through it, turning on the odd light. It's eleven o'clock. Mom will be home soon. What will I tell her?

I sigh, realizing I won't have to tell her anything. She'll know exactly what happened. I can already see the look of disappointment on her face.

The next time the phone rings, the caller doesn't leave a message.

Hands shake my shoulders. "Allegra, wake up."

My eyes blink open and I look up. Mom's leaning over me. She's still wearing her performance gown.

"I didn't know you were home," she says. "Spencer's at the door. He says no one could find you. That's why I checked your bedroom, and—"

"What time is it?"

"One o'clock."

"Why would Spencer be here? Is something wrong?"

"I'm assuming. Why else would he be here in the middle of the night?"

I pull on tights and a sweatshirt and run my fingers through my hair. In the hall, I pass the living room and notice candlelight. I jump, startled to see someone sitting in the semidarkness. Marcus. Two half-empty glasses of wine stand on the coffee table.

I glance back at Mom, who is following me down the hall.

"We're having a nightcap," she says quietly.

The truth of it hits me hard. She thought I was out for the entire night...that she had the house to herself. With lover boy.

Anger once again bubbles up, but I ignore it and continue to the back door, where Spencer is waiting.

"You *are* home," he says accusingly.

I hear my mom retreat to the living room and speak to Marcus in a soft voice.

"What's the matter?" I ask Spencer. I hear the irritation in my voice. It's not him I'm annoyed with, it's my mother, but he doesn't know that.

"That's what I came here to find out," he answers, sounding equally pissed off. "Talia says you left her party without saying goodbye or anything. They've been phoning you, but you didn't pick up. They asked me to come by to see if you're okay."

I think about this. "Why did they get you involved?"

"They'd been drinking. No one wanted to drive."

"So they phoned you in the middle of the night?"

"They were worried, Allegra."

I sigh, and some of the anger escapes with my breath. "I'm sorry. Please let them know I'm fine. And I'm sorry you had to get involved."

Spencer peers over my shoulder. "Can I come in for a few minutes?"

"No, my mom, she's got…company."

His eyebrows shoot up. "Musicians?" he asks hopefully.

Right then it hits me. An epiphany. My life is a total mess. This stuff with my parents, with my anxieties… Spencer would never get it. I step outside and shut the door behind me. I notice Marcus's car parked at the curb.

"There's stuff going on in my life right now," I tell him. "I need time. Alone."

"What are you talking about?" He looks genuinely puzzled.

I fold my arms across my chest. "You need to go. Please tell the girls I'm sorry."

He doesn't move. "Why don't you tell me what's going on?"

I shake my head. "I can't. It's not about you."

He just stares at me. I look down at my feet.

"We had such a good time that night at the rehearsal," he says softly. "What's changed since then?"

"You didn't do anything wrong, Spencer. It's other stuff." I hear myself sigh again. "I can't talk about it."

"Why not? That's what friends do."

"Not this stuff."

"Is it because of what happened...in the sound room?"

I notice he can't say the word *kiss*. "No, it's not about you. Honest." I look in his eyes again, willing him to believe me, but I can see only questions there. "I've got to go in." I push the door open with my shoulder.

"Allegra." There's a catch in his voice. I spin around and notice his creased brow and the clenching movement of his jaw. He shoves his hands in his pockets. His eyes narrow. "What is with you? I don't get it. I've seen you dance..."

"You have?" That surprises me.

"Yeah, I've watched a couple of your classes."

I think about the large glass window in the dance studio.

"I've never seen you."

"No, because you were totally into it, and you're like...amazing. And your music..." He shakes his head. "My god, it's so awesome, yet you..." He doesn't complete the sentence.

"Yet I what?"

He shuffles his feet and looks away. "You're distant. You put up a wall and don't let anyone in. It's like you're... you're protecting yourself from...from I don't know what. You're nothing like the girl who dances and writes music.

I just don't get it." He turns and starts walking down the driveway. As he passes the mailbox, he kicks the post, but he doesn't turn back.

In the house, Marcus has put on a jacket and is clearly getting ready to leave. I guess I've spoiled their fun. I try to slip down the hall without being noticed, but Mom calls out my name. With a sigh I return to the kitchen.

"Allegra, I don't think you've met Marcus."

"Hi, Allegra," he says. "That's a lovely name."

He looks totally uncomfortable. Good. I nod but can't find any words.

"Is everything okay with Spencer?" Mom asks.

"Yeah, just a…a misunderstanding. I'm going back to bed." I turn to leave.

"Nice to meet you, Allegra," Marcus says to my back. I don't reply.

"Teenagers," I hear my mom say apologetically. "You know how they are."

If Marcus responds, I don't hear it. A few minutes later, I hear his car pull away from the curb.

I lie in bed on Saturday morning thinking about what Spencer said. *You don't let anyone in.*

The counselor I went to as a kid had given me some suggestions for things to do when I was uncomfortable with other kids, but I'd always found it easier not to get into those situations in the first place. I still feel that way. Once again, I wonder how it is that I feel safe and confident performing, but put me in a social setting with kids my own age...

I should never have agreed to go to that sleepover.

When I finally get up, Mom is drinking coffee and reading the newspaper in the kitchen. I pull a loaf of bread out of the freezer and pop two slices into the toaster. I can feel her gaze on me as I rummage through the cupboard, looking for peanut butter. Finally she sighs, pulls off her reading glasses and pushes the paper aside. "Allegra, about last night..."

I don't let her finish the sentence and whirl about to face her. "You don't ask me about my evening, and I won't ask you why Marcus was here at one in the morning."

Her eyes flash and she looks away. "It's not what you think..."

"Right, Mom." I decide I'm not hungry after all. Stomping out of the kitchen, I head straight down to the studio. I pull all my old piano books out of the cupboard and play one piece after another. I force everything else out of my mind and just play.

When Dad calls, inviting me to have lunch with him, I tell him I'm not feeling well, which is only partly untrue. Being miserable counts as not feeling well, I figure. He suggests I invite my friends to that evening's rehearsal in our music studio. I tell him I'll think about it, which I do. In fact, I obsess over it; I want to call and apologize and invite them to the practice. But I'm afraid that they'll be too angry and will turn down my peace offering. Or, even worse, that they'll come and my anxiety will flare up again. Twice, I start to call them; twice, I don't follow through.

I spend the evening in my room, reading, while the band practices downstairs. I pretend to be asleep at the end of the session so that I don't have to watch my dad leave with the rest of the band.

I purposely arrive at my English class just as it's about to start. I slide into my desk beside Talia and open my books. I know she is staring at me, but I don't look at her. I can't.

When the teacher asks us to turn to page thirty in our textbooks, Talia takes the opportunity to toss a note onto my desk. I pick it up and unfold it in my lap. *What happened to you?*

I pick up my pen and scrawl an answer. *I wasn't feeling well. I'm sorry.* I wait until the teacher's attention is elsewhere and pass it back without looking at Talia. Moments later the note is tossed back to my desk. *Why didn't you just say so????*

I crumple up the paper and push it into my pocket. I can feel my face burning. There's no way I can explain. No one would get it. I pretend to focus on the lesson. At the end of the class, Talia collects her things and leaves without saying another word to me. It's easy to avoid each other in ballet; in music theory, I isolate myself in the sound room before Spencer arrives.

I eat my lunch in the portable and then spend the remainder of the time in the sound room. Other students are working on projects or practicing, so no one takes much notice of me.

The week continues the same way. On Tuesday I run into Sophie and Molly in the hall between classes. I say hi, try to smile, mumble something about being sorry about the other night, then keep going. They don't look mad so much as puzzled.

Things at home haven't changed much. Dad calls every day, but we're back to being self-conscious with one another. I don't have the energy or desire to dance, so I stop going to class. Angela calls, wondering why I'm not there, and I tell her I'm sick.

I stay in the sound room after music theory on Thursday, replaying my composition over and over. It's just a mindless kind of activity. I'm not inspired to change anything or add to it; I just keep clicking *Playback*. It's lunch hour, and I have nowhere else to go.

I hear the door open behind me, and I swing around. The four of them are standing there: Talia, Molly, Sophie and Spencer.

"I think you owe us an explanation," Talia says. She folds her arms across her chest.

"I told you, I wasn't feeling well. I'm really, really sorry."

"Right, but you haven't said why you didn't say something before you left."

Sweat breaks out on my palms. I feel like a cornered animal, trapped in the sound room.

"Well? Aren't you going to say something?"

I can only shrug and stare at my feet. A wave of dizziness passes over me.

"Is something the matter here?" I look up and see Mr. Rocchelli standing behind our small group. He's craning his neck to see into the room. Our eyes meet briefly before I look down again.

There's a long pause, and finally Spencer says, "No, nothing's wrong. We were just having a chat with Allegra."

"Let's go," Talia says.

I hear them move away, and then the door to the portable opens and closes.

My heart is beating fast now, and dizziness overwhelms me. I bend over and put my head between my knees.

"Allegra, what is it?" Mr. Rocchelli has put his hand on my back. I can only shake my head. He leaves, but moments later he's back in the room. "Here's some water."

I reach out and take the glass from him. My throat is dry, and I gulp the water down.

"Do you want more?" he asks.

Finally I can sit up again, but I don't look at him. I'm too embarrassed. "No, thanks."

He eases himself into the other chair in the cramped little room and leans toward me. "Want to talk about it?" he asks.

I shake my head again. I'm struggling to fight back tears. It's all so humiliating.

We sit in silence for another moment. Then his chair creaks as he gets to his feet. "I'm a good listener," he says. "Anytime you want to talk."

I nod, still staring at my feet.

He stands there. His foot taps the floor a couple of times and then he leaves the sound room. A realization washes over me: it has taken me less than a month to totally screw up my fresh start at a new school. Combine that with the situation at home and my anxiety flaring up, and, well, things couldn't get much worse.

I get up, shut the door and then click *Playback* on the computer. For the remainder of the lunch hour, I listen to my composition over and over again.

Eleven

"C'mon, Allegra, watch your turnout. How many times have we talked about that? And stretch your feet."

I stretch them.

"Harder!"

Ms. Dekker's been hollering corrections at me for the full hour of ballet. I don't know why she's decided to pick on me today. There must be somebody else who's less than perfect.

Finally the hour is up, and I tug sweatpants on over my ballet tights. I can't wait to get out of this room. Out of this school.

"Allegra, could you stay behind for a moment, please?"

I glance over at her, puzzled. She's sitting in a chair, making some notes in a book and not looking at me. This is not a good sign.

Pulling on my hoodie, I slide into street shoes and grab my dance bag. She keeps writing in her book. One by one all the other dancers leave. I slump against the wall. Finally she looks up at me. Her expression is kinder than I expected, given the way she spoke to me in class.

"Have a seat," she says, motioning to a chair beside hers.

I feel her studying me as I sit down.

"Is everything okay, Allegra?"

The question startles me. What's she getting at? What does she know?

"Yeah, fine. Why?"

She tilts her head and stares at me for another moment, as if trying to come to a decision. I hold her gaze, even though it's an effort. "When you first began taking my dance classes in the fall, I could see something in your dancing. An energy, a spark. Something rare and, well, yes, exceptional."

I almost fall off my chair. "Are you serious? All I remember is you telling me about all the bad habits I'd picked up at Turning Pointe."

"Well, yes, you did. And you still have them."

"So…I don't get it. I have bad technique but you like the way I dance?"

She smiles. "Yes. Something like that." Crossing her legs, she continues. "Allegra, a dance teacher can teach just about anybody good dance technique, and most people can learn it. But the rare student, like you, has an intrinsic gift.

You don't just perform the dance, you feel it. It comes from inside. Think of Karen Kain, or Michael Jackson, for that matter. They were more than just good technique and great choreography. They *became* the dance."

I wait, stunned that she's putting me in the same league as two of my favorite dancers.

"But something has changed in the past week." My heart sinks, and I look down at my feet. "Your energy and spark have evaporated. You're going through the motions, but that's about it. Now all I can see are the bad habits."

I don't know how to respond, so I just continue staring at my feet.

There is a long silence, and then she speaks again. "Maybe *evaporated* is too strong a word. But for some reason, your talent seems to have gone into hibernation for a while. I know it's still there. That's why I think something must be going on."

I just shrug, still trying to digest the fact that she thinks I have natural talent. Until two minutes ago, I was sure she thought I was a hopeless case.

"There are counselors available at the school if you need someone to talk to."

I glance at her, relieved that she hasn't asked me to spill my guts to her. She's studying my face. "Okay, I am dealing with some stuff, but I'll be all right," I lie.

The truth is, I don't know if I'll be all right. I'm feeling numb inside. No, worse than numb. Dead. No wonder she picked up on it.

"I'm sorry to hear that you've got problems, Allegra, but here's the thing. You say you want to dance professionally after you graduate. Professional dancers have problems too, but they dance through them. You'll be out of work in a New York minute if you allow your personal life to affect your dancing."

I nod but don't tell her that it's not that simple. I've danced through problems before. In fact, dance was the perfect stress-buster, but not this time. The dancer me feels likes she's gone.

"You need to come to class and put everything else out of your mind," she continues. "Try to arrive early and sit in stillness for a bit. Let all your worries float away. Then, when we start warm-up, you'll be able to set that dance spirit of yours free."

She's dead, I want to tell her but don't.

Ms. Dekker pushes her chair back and stands up. I guess our meeting is over. "I'll see you tomorrow, Allegra. And I hope it's the professional dancer who shows up to class."

"I'll try."

"That's a start."

Mom has a night off on Monday, and she suggests we do something together.

"Like what?" I ask. I'm lying on my bed, staring at the ceiling.

"Well, anything. See a movie, go for a swim." Her eyes light up. "How about a pedicure?"

I recall how the girls were going to give each other pedicures at Talia's sleepover. "I have a lot of homework."

She tilts her head. "You don't look too busy to me."

"I'm just taking a break."

She stands in my doorway, staring at me. Finally she speaks again. "Your dad called earlier."

I don't respond. What is there to say?

"He says you haven't been attending your dance classes. He's been showing up to watch, but you haven't been there."

"I haven't felt like going."

"Are you sick?"

"No."

"Well," she says gently, "if you're not sick, what's going on? It's not like you to miss the opportunity to dance."

I flip over, putting my back to her. "It's none of your business."

How can I possibly tell her that her behavior is a big part of my problem?

I can't see her, but I can hear—loud and clear—the change in her tone. "I'm paying for those classes, Allegra. If you're not going to attend, then I'd like to know so I can quit writing the checks."

I don't answer. I really don't know if I'll be going back.

"You sure you don't want to do something tonight?" she asks, her tone softening. "I'd really like to get out."

"Go ahead. I'll be fine." I expect she'll end up doing something with Marcus, but I don't say anything.

I hear the car pulling out of the driveway a short time later. I try to do some homework, but I just can't concentrate. Same thing in the studio, working on my composition. The ever-present numbness keeps any creativity from sparking in my brain. As well, the studio reminds me too much of my dad, and when I think about why he's not here, it just makes me sadder. And madder. Eventually I turn on the TV and scroll through the channels.

I must have nodded off, because the next thing I know, Dad is sitting on the couch beside me. "Good show?" he asks, nodding toward the TV.

"Where did you come from?" I ask, sitting up.

"Through the front door." He picks up the remote and turns the TV off. "I went to the dance studio again, but you weren't there. Obviously. You'd think I'd learn."

"Sorry. I should have told you." But then I would have had to explain why I wasn't going to dance, and I'm not sure that I can.

"Is everything okay?" he asks.

"Yeah, I just haven't felt like dancing."

"That's not like you." I can feel him studying me, but I can't look at him.

"Just going through a bit of a slump, I guess." Major understatement.

"I wanted to see you because I'm leaving next week, and you and I haven't connected in the past two weeks."

"You're going back on tour already?"

"Actually, it's just me going next week. I've lined up a few solo gigs to pay my way. The band is going to follow me two weeks after that. I need to get away on my own for a bit, to sort stuff out. Kind of like a holiday but not really."

Something about this ticks me off. I get up and go into the kitchen. He follows me. I take the milk out of the fridge and pour myself a glass. "Are you sure you're not just running away from your problems?"

Now he reaches for the milk too, and pours himself a glass. He stares at it before answering. "Maybe I am, Allegra. But my living situation is not ideal. I feel like I've overstayed my welcome at Steve's, and your mom doesn't want me here."

Even though I know this, hearing him say it out loud causes a huge pang in my stomach. I slump into a chair and rest my arms and head on the table. Dad comes up behind me and gently begins massaging my neck and shoulders. He often gave me back massages at bedtime when I was little. It seemed like he was home a lot more then, but maybe I'm remembering wrong.

I sit for a long time and simply enjoy the feeling of his warm, strong hands kneading my shoulders, but eventually my brain clicks in again. "If you stayed near here—somewhere, anywhere—at least you and I could get together sometimes."

His hands leave my shoulders, and he moves to sit across from me. "I thought of that, Legs, but it felt like you've been avoiding me the last little while, so I wasn't sure if there was any point in staying in town." He pauses. "And I think a change of scenery will do me good."

My heart sinks even deeper as I consider this. Have I been avoiding him? I hadn't thought of it that way, but I guess I have, in a sense. But now I desperately don't want him to leave.

He picks up a large envelope that is lying on the table and pulls out head shots of the band members. "These are for Spencer," he says. "They're all signed. Tell him I'd still like to see his collection someday. Maybe when I get back."

Like that's going to happen.

"So, can we plan to do something together before I leave?"

I let out a sigh. I don't want to *do* things with either my mom or my dad. I just want everything to go back to the way it used to be, when he'd come home and we'd have meals together, and the band would rehearse downstairs, and he'd be here when I got home from school.

"Hey," he says, sitting up taller. "I haven't heard your composition for a while. Could I take a listen?"

I remember the night I wanted so badly to share it with him and he wasn't around. Now I'm totally not in the mood.

"C'mon, Legs," he says, getting up and walking over to the door that leads down to the studio. He flicks on the lights that illuminate the stairs.

I grab my backpack from the floor by the front door. Passing him in the doorway, I point to his upper lip. "Nice milk mustache, Dad."

He laughs. The sound of it lightens my heart.

Downstairs, I turn on the computer and plug in the flash drive. Dad sits on the stool at the keyboard, and I settle onto the old couch. The familiar phrases play through the small speakers. I watch Dad's face as he listens to what I've written, but it doesn't give much away.

The music ends abruptly. "That's it," I say.

Dad turns to look at me, his eyebrows arched. Finally, he speaks. "That was truly beautiful." His voice is soft and sincere. There is an odd glow in his eyes. "I am really impressed."

Something inside of me awakens at his words, but I simply shrug.

"Did you get much help on this?" he asks.

"Only the help you gave me a few weeks ago."

"Really?" He shakes his head. "You've really got something special here," he says. "I can't wait to hear the finished piece."

If I finish it, I think. But something about his response may have renewed my interest in it.

"Can we listen again?" he asks.

I nod, and the familiar music starts again. This time our eyes meet while the music plays and Dad smiles, nodding his head.

I continue to spend my lunch hours in the music portable, but I've given up the pretense of being there to write music. I usually do homework or read. I get left alone, even by Mr. Rocchelli. Talia and her gang seem to be avoiding me, and in music theory I make sure I'm safely tucked into the sound room before Spencer arrives in class.

Life feels flat. I try to give 100 percent in Ms. Dekker's dance classes, but I don't think I'm fooling her. I've resumed a few of my dance classes at Turning Pointe, but the dancer inside me hasn't been revived.

"Care for a coffee?" Dad asks. It's his last evening in town, and we're at the dance studio. He's just spent two hours watching my jazz and hip-hop classes.

"I don't think so. I'm too sweaty to go anywhere." I pluck a damp lock of hair off my cheek.

"What's a little sweat?" He smiles. "C'mon. We'll just go across the street. No one around here will know you anyway."

At the coffee shop, Dad steps aside to let me order first.

"A decaf, grande, soy, sugar-free, extra-hot caramel macchiato."

Dad turns to stare at me. "Huh? What the heck is that?"

"Should I hold the caramel syrup on top?" the cashier asks. "It's not sugar-free."

"Yeah. Please."

Dad just shakes his head. "Black coffee for me."

"Mild or dark roast?"

"Mild, I guess."

"For here or to go?"

"For here." He turns to look at me. "I long for the days when we simply ordered a cup of coffee."

Now it's my turn to shake my head.

"Do I know you from somewhere?" the cashier asks Dad as she hands him his change, her eyes scanning his face.

"I don't think so," Dad says politely.

The cashier calls my order to the barista and pours Dad his coffee. She's still studying his face. "You didn't teach at Bayview Secondary, did you?"

"Nope, I don't teach school," he says, accepting his coffee.

We find a table in a corner, and I wait for the barista to finish making my drink. The cashier has joined her behind the counter and they are conferring, sneaking glances at my dad. Eventually she calls out my drink order, and when I go to collect it, she says, "Is that Jerry Whitford from the Loose Ends?"

"Yep."

"Cool! Are you his date or…"

"I'm his daughter." Feeling slightly sickened by her assumption, I return to the table.

"She asked if I was your date," I tell Dad.

He tilts his head back and laughs.

"I didn't think it was funny."

"Well, I'm flattered."

"They figured out who you are."

"Oh."

"And they must think that Jerry Whitford would date girls my age."

"They're just being silly, Legs. Forget about it."

I can't just forget about it. I can't believe anyone would think my dad would date a teenager, even if he wasn't married.

We sip our drinks in silence. My body is finally cooling down, and I zip up my hoodie. I glance back at the cashier and see she is still staring at my dad.

"Does this happen to you everywhere you go?" I ask him, nodding to the cashier.

"Sometimes," he says. "No paparazzi though." He snaps his fingers in mock disappointment.

"So, Legs," he says, putting his cup down. "I'm gonna call you at least once a week. Hopefully you'll be home."

"You could get a cell phone, Dad. Then I could call you."

"I guess I could. Maybe it's time."

"It *is* time, Dad." I don't know why he resists having one. Is it because he doesn't want us calling him? I decide not to go there. "Are you still thinking this will be the last tour for you?"

His fingers tap his cup. "My thinking was that I wanted to spend more time at home, with you and your mom." He stops tapping and stares out the window for a moment. "Now I don't know if I'll be welcome at home."

I blink back tears. "How are you and Mom going to sort things out if you're away?"

"I don't know, Legs." He reaches over and places a hand on mine. "This is the stuff I need to sort out in the next couple of weeks. When I said I was going to quit touring, I guess it was because I sensed things weren't…weren't quite right here. But I guess I figured that out a little too late. I probably should have quit touring before the last one."

We sit in silence for a moment. I watch as the barista clears tables. She stops at one to chat with the customers. Suddenly, all their eyes turn to stare at us. I tug back my hand.

"I'm not giving up, Legs." He leans across the table. "When I get back, your mom and I will resume our counseling sessions."

"That's almost two months from now."

"I know. But it gives both your mom and me time to reflect on what we really want."

"And what about me? What about what I want?"

Dad stares into his empty mug, and I could be mistaken, but I think his eyes are glistening. "The sad truth is, Legs, we don't always get what we want."

I glance at the barista again. She quickly looks away.

A boy about my age approaches our table. He's holding a paper napkin and a pen. "Excuse me, Mr. Whitford, I was wondering if I could have your autograph?"

I'm about to tell him to get lost, but Dad sits up and takes the pen and napkin from the boy. He looks up, clears his throat and smiles warmly at him. "And what's your name?" he asks.

"Riley."

I watch Dad write on the napkin: *To Riley. With best wishes from Jerry Whitford.*

The boy thanks him and goes back to his table. I see him showing the napkin to his friends. I turn to look at Dad. How did he flip so easily from being a dad having a heart-to-heart talk with his daughter to being Mr. Cool Celebrity?

Dad must have read my thoughts. "It's just part of my job, honey." He shrugs. "Without fans, I'd have no income. I have to keep them happy."

I realize how rarely I'm out in public with him, and for the first time ever I get a glimpse into my dad's life on the road. "Do your fans swarm you after your performances?" I ask.

"Swarm is too strong a word, Legs. Sometimes they stick around for autographs."

I think about the barista, the cashier and the boy named Riley. I think about Spencer and the dance teachers and the moms at Turning Pointe. They all see someone else when they look at my dad. No doubt a lot of women are among those waiting around after performances for autographs. I don't like the images my mind is conjuring. Has he been a faithful husband all these years? I can't go there right now.

"So where were we?" he asks.

"I don't remember," I say, tilting my cup back and draining it. "But I think I should go. I have a lot of homework."

"I'm going to miss you, Legs." He's looking at me, hard. He reaches out and takes my chin between his fingers, forcing me to look back.

"I'm going to miss you too, Dad. Get that cell phone."

He lets me go and smiles. "I will," he says. "But you're the only one I'm giving the number to." He emphasizes the word *only*.

"Sounds good," I say.

A body slides into the chair across the table from where I'm working. I look up and find Mr. Rocchelli smiling at me. Looking around, I see that the music room is empty except for the two of us.

"Did I miss the bell or something?" I glance up at the wall clock.

"No, no, you're fine. The Battle of the Bands contest is going on during the lunch hour all week. There's been a lot of hype. I'm guessing everyone must be there."

I vaguely remember hearing something about that. "So how come you're not there?"

"I would be, Allegra, but I noticed you here and thought this would be a good opportunity to catch up on things."

"Catch up on things?" I don't like the sound of this.

"Yes, I'm afraid I've been neglecting you. We haven't had a chance to discuss your progress on the composition for a while. How's it going? Do you need any help?"

"No, everything's fine."

He nods. "That's good. Can I listen to what you've written?"

I glance at the sound room, suddenly remembering the last time I was alone in there with him and how anxious I was.

"I don't have it with me," I lie. "We don't have music theory today, so I left it at home."

He nods. "Tomorrow then. We'll make time in class when the rest of the students are working on something else."

I nod. That would definitely be better than now, alone.

"How are your dance classes going?"

I glance at him and notice how carefully he's examining my face. "They're fine." I feel my cheeks burn. Shit.

There's a long pause before he says, "That's not what Ms. Dekker tells me."

My head jerks up. "You were discussing *me* with *her*?"

"It's okay, Allegra." He puts up his hand in a kind of back-off gesture. I guess my reaction *was* a little strong. "Teachers often discuss their students, especially when one is struggling. Teachers need to know if they are also struggling in other classes."

"So what did you tell her?" Now I'm watching him carefully, looking for any signs of a cover-up.

"Well…that was when I realized I'd been neglecting you. I couldn't say for sure how you were doing."

"I'm doing fine. I played what I've written for my dad a few nights ago, and he thought it was great. So please tell Ms. Dekker not to worry." I can't mask the irritation in my voice.

"There's no need to get upset, Allegra. Ms. Dekker is just concerned about you. She says you're extremely talented, but something has been holding you back for a while."

"Maybe she's just imagining it," I say softly.

"I doubt that," Mr. Rocchelli says, just as quietly. I know he's studying me again, but I can't look at him.

"Now that I think of it, I've noticed a change in you too," he says.

"I'm fine." I begin to shove my books into my backpack.

"Did something happen with your friends?"

A surge of anger wells up inside me, and I fight back the urge to tell him to mind his own business. "No." I stand up and swing my backpack over my shoulder.

"Sit down, Allegra, please," Mr. Rocchelli says. I glance at his face. There's only kindness there. I take a deep breath and slump back into the chair.

"I'm sorry. I shouldn't pry. I'll try not to do it again. It's a bad habit of mine." He smiles, clearly trying to ease the tension. "But as I told you before, I'm a good listener. Anytime you—"

"I'll remember that."

"Good. Now, there's something else I've wanted to talk to you about. You mentioned your dad, and it jogged my memory. I like to invite guest speakers to class, to shake things up a bit. I was wondering if your dad would come to our class and talk about his music and the realities of playing in a band."

"He's away on tour."

"Oh." He tilts his head, looking surprised. I guess I blurted it out a bit fast.

"Then how about your mother? She could talk about life as a working musician. What do you think?"

I think it's a really stupid idea, but I need to find a tactful way to say that. "I always feel a bit...a bit uncomfortable when my parents get involved in my stuff."

Mr. Rocchelli looks baffled, so I elaborate. "With my dad...sometimes people treat him like a celebrity, and that's so weird for me." I think about the night in the coffee shop.

"Aren't you proud of him?"

"Yeah, I am, but...well, fame comes with a price, you know."

"What price is that?"

"Touring, for one. He's always away." What has gotten into me? Why am I telling him this?

"I guess you don't like that."

I give him a sharp look and stand up. "I think you're prying again."

He shakes his head, exasperated. "I guess I am. It's a fine line sometimes. No problem, Allegra. I'll find some other guest speakers."

"Thanks. So, are we caught up?" I pull my jacket on.

He nods, but he looks sad. "I guess we are. I'll see you tomorrow."

As I walk away, I realize I just did exactly what Spencer accused me of—I put up a wall. I don't know why I do it. Worse than that, I don't know how to stop.

Twelve

True to his word, Mr. Rocchelli assigns a written project for the students in his theory class. He knocks on the sound-room door before entering.

"Is this a good time?" he asks.

I nod. I've already put the flash drive into the computer and am jotting notes in my book.

When he's comfortably seated, I start the music. I try not to anticipate his reaction but find myself stealing glances at him. He just stares at the lines of music scrolling across the screen.

When the music ends, I wait for him to speak.

He swivels his chair slowly until he's facing me. He's frowning; he must hate what I've done with his tune but is too polite to say so. He hesitates, perhaps looking for the right words.

"Allegra," he says finally. His tone is serious, and he's staring at his hands. "When I gave you this assignment, I was curious about what you would do with it. I knew you understood your music theory, but I didn't know how well you'd be able to apply it."

He stops, obviously still searching for words. Now I know for sure he hates it.

"You have totally exceeded my expectations. I know it's not finished, but what you've done is complex and powerful. It is on its way to becoming a magnificent piece of music." He looks up, and now his expression is earnest.

A combination of relief and joy floods through me. "I'm glad you like it."

"I don't just like it. I'm moved by it, and I'm very impressed by your skill."

"Thank you." For the first time in more than a week, I feel the numbness begin to melt away.

We just stare at each other for a moment, neither of us knowing what else to say.

A knock at the door causes us both to start. We swing around and see Spencer standing behind the glass. Mr. Rocchelli waves him in.

"I'm sorry to interrupt," Spencer says.

Mr. Rocchelli doesn't give him chance to finish. "We were just listening to Allegra's music." He clicks the mouse to replay it. "Let's get an opinion from you."

I haven't made eye contact with Spencer, but I hear him close the door and lean against it. It's suddenly getting very warm in here.

The music plays again. When it's over, Mr. Rocchelli swings around. "So, what do you think, Spencer?"

"It's great," Spencer says. I still haven't looked at him.

"Great? That's it?" Mr. Rocchelli prods.

"No, it's way better than great. But I've told Allegra that already."

I remember that day, alone in this room with Spencer, when he claimed to be so moved by my music that he kissed me. My cheeks begin to burn.

"Oh." Mr. Rocchelli's eyebrows shoot up. He glances at me, then back to Spencer. "I didn't realize anyone else had heard it."

"It was awhile ago."

It was, and with an inward sigh I realize that nothing much has been added since then.

"Okay, so how can I help you, Spencer?"

"A bunch of us are having trouble with problem number three on the worksheet. We'd just like a little clarification of what you're really asking us to do."

I look through the glass and see the rest of the class watching us. Spencer must have volunteered to speak on their behalf.

"Oh yes, the one about harmony." Mr. Rocchelli stands up. "That one is a little ambiguous, isn't it? You keep at it,

Allegra," he says. "You're doing an amazing job." He passes Spencer in the doorway.

Spencer wheels about to follow him, but somehow I manage to find my voice.

"Spencer?"

He turns back to me. "Yes?" His eyes are guarded.

I reach into my backpack and pull out the envelope Dad gave me. I've been carrying it around for days, tucked between two textbooks to protect the photos. Spencer's here now, and I might as well get it over with. "This is for you. The signed head shots of the Loose Ends guys."

For the briefest of moments, as he pulls the photos out of the envelope, his eyes light up. A smile tugs at his mouth, then quickly disappears. "Tell your dad thanks. I really appreciate it."

"He's away right now, but I will when I talk to him."

He hesitates. I think he's about to say something else, but then we both hear Mr. Rocchelli speaking to the class, so with a last glance at me, Spencer steps back into the classroom.

"Back so soon?" Mr. Rocchelli notices me slipping into the sound room after school. His response to my piece of music has spurred me on.

"Yep."

He comes and leans against the doorjamb. "For a girl who came to this school to dance, you sure spend a lot of time in the music portable."

His comment feels like a challenge. I'm up for it. "I figure that once I get this project finished, I'll be excused from your class for the rest of the year. I'll be able to take another dance class in block seven." That thought had never occurred to me until this very moment, but I smile at him, feeling like I've suddenly one-upped him in our little battle.

His eyes widen in surprise, and then he throws back his head and laughs. "You're not going to escape my class so easily. Forget it."

I plug the flash drive into the computer and settle into the chair. Mr. Rocchelli is still standing at the door. I glance back at him.

"I'm wondering…could I make a couple of little suggestions about your piece?" He puts his hands up. "Feel free to say no. It's your composition, but there were some things I noticed when I was listening to it, especially the second time."

"Sure," I say, suddenly suspicious. Maybe he doesn't think it's so good after all.

He pulls the second chair closer to where I am. I start the music. After about fifteen seconds, he reaches out and stops it. "There. I think you need to repeat the melodic phrase at this point."

"Oh. How come?"

"Well, because one of the most important ingredients in music is repetition. People have an unconscious desire for it, and the repetition of the melodic phrase here would satisfy that need."

I nod. He's articulating something I know but haven't ever put into words.

He continues. "Repetition sets up a degree of predictability that's reassuring to a listener. With this solid base, you can then create surprises without taking the audience too far out of its comfort zone."

I start the piece again and realize that I do change the chord progression right at that point. Repeating the initial melodic phrase is a good idea.

"Perhaps you could feature another instrument, or add harmony in the repetition."

"Yeah, that's a good idea."

"The basis of writing music," he adds, "is building melodic ideas over an extended period of time, but you don't want to change the ideas too quickly."

Building melodic ideas over an extended period of time. That's a great way to sum it up. I look at Mr. Rocchelli with new respect. Maybe he can teach me something after all.

He clicks the mouse to continue the music. About a minute later he stops it again. "I think you're rushing it a little here."

"Really?" I go back just a little and play it again. He's exactly right. It does begin to speed up. I make a note in my book.

We listen to the remaining section, but he doesn't have any more suggestions. The room becomes still when the music finishes. I feel him turn to look at me. I return his gaze, noticing how dark his eyes are, how his lashes sweep his cheeks. There's stubble on his jaw, as if he forgot to shave this morning. The room suddenly shrinks, and I have to look away. "Do I dare ask you another question?" he asks quietly.

"You can ask," I mumble. "I might not answer."

"Fair enough." He studies me a little longer. I grow increasingly uneasy under his scrutiny. I glance through the window and wish someone would come into the classroom.

"If you have such a natural talent for music," he says, "why are you pursuing dance?"

The question is an easy one, and I relax a little. "I've been surrounded by music and musicians my whole life," I tell him. "My parents live and breathe it. Their friends are musicians too. All of them talk like nothing else in life really matters, and everyone assumed I'd follow in my parents' footsteps. When I was finally allowed to take dance classes, I felt...such a release. I discovered a whole new world. With music..." I pause, trying to find the words. "With music you can express a lot of emotion through an instrument, but with dance I *am* the instrument. It just feels...so good." I sigh, knowing how inadequately I'm expressing myself.

Mr. Rocchelli nods thoughtfully.

"And besides"—I meet his eyes again—"did you want to do exactly what your parents did? Or what they wanted you to do?"

He smiles. "Good point. Can you see me as a beekeeper?" He lowers his voice. "But you can't blame me, a music teacher, for being disappointed that one of my most talented students isn't as excited about her talents as I am."

I look away.

"And just think, if I hadn't been such a jerk and insisted that you take my class, I wouldn't have had this opportunity to see what you can do."

I know I should tell him that he's not a jerk—quite the opposite, in fact—but I can't make my mouth operate.

"So," he asks, "have you named the piece yet?"

"No. Any ideas?"

"Yeah. I think we should simply call it *Allegra*." He smiles.

"That's a dumb name."

"I don't think so." He stands and puts his hand on my shoulder. "You get back to it then. I've distracted you long enough." His fingers squeeze my shoulder before he leaves. I watch through the window as he walks through the empty classroom to his desk.

I try to work, but I'm too aware of Mr. Rocchelli's presence. He has no idea what a distraction he is. Finally I give up and put my things into my backpack. "Have a good night," I say as I cross the room toward the door.

He looks up from the paper he's reading. "You too, Allegra. You have a good night too."

Bending from the waist, I grab hold of the backs of my ankles and pull myself into a deep stretch. I've resumed my evening dance classes at Turning Pointe, and we're doing our usual warm-ups. I close my eyes and check in with my body. My mind settles on the same little ache that's been plaguing me for a while: not the discomfort of sore muscles, but the deep-inside ache I feel at messing things up with Talia, Molly, Sophie and Spencer. For years I went without any friends and thought I was perfectly content. Getting a taste of friendship has made me realize what I was missing all those years. And having a guy interested in me…well, I have to admit, I liked that feeling.

"Okay, girls," says Veronica, my ballet teacher. "Down on the floor. Twist to the right."

As I hold my twist, I remind myself that I didn't switch to Deer Lake to make friends but to dance. Fortunately, the dancer in me seems to be coming back to life. Even Ms. Dekker commented on it this afternoon.

"You nailed the pirouettes today," she said after class. "The old Allegra seems to be back."

Turning to stretch in the other direction, I think about my composition. It seems that the harder I work on it, the more alive I feel in the dance studio, and the harder I work in the dance studio, the more I can shake off everything else that is going on. Maybe the old Allegra really is back. The old Allegra with no friends or anxiety issues and—according to my teachers—lots of talent. I guess you can't have everything.

Moving into a right-legged split, my mind settles on my composition. It's really coming along. I think about Mr. Rocchelli, and immediately my face gets warm. I switch to a left-legged split. When he comes into the sound room to check on my progress, I get really nervous, but when he's not there, I wish he was. I even found myself seeking him out today to ask a question—a question I already knew the answer to. What is wrong with me? This is the same guy who totally ticked me off six weeks ago. And besides, he's a teacher.

I catch a glimpse of Angela in the mirror. She's watching me with a funny smile on her face. "What?" I mouth to her reflection.

She just shakes her head and rolls her eyes, but the smug little smile stays on her face as she continues to stretch. I refuse to look at her for the remainder of the class.

Angela plunks herself down on the bench beside me in the change room. "So, are you back for good?" she asks, pulling off her ballet slippers. "It was lonely around here while you were on your little sabbatical."

"I didn't miss that many classes."

"Allegra, you don't usually miss *any* classes."

"Well, I'm back."

"Good. I missed you."

I smile at her. It's good to have at least one friend, even if we never see each other outside of the dance school.

"What was that look you gave me in the warm-up?" I ask her.

"You should have seen your face," she laughs. "You were, like, totally in la-la land. What were you thinking about?"

I feel my cheeks burn when I remember. She tilts her head. "Maybe I should ask *who* you were thinking about," she says.

I swat her arm with my ballet slipper. "I wasn't thinking about anything or anyone. I was concentrating on my splits and wondering why I can't get the left one as low as the right one."

"Sure you were," Angela says. "And I'm thinking about how much fun tomorrow's math test is going to be."

I shake my head but wonder at how easily she was able to read me. I'll have to work on that. What if Mr. Rocchelli can read me as easily as that? My skin burns even hotter at the thought.

True to his word, Dad gets himself a cell phone and checks in regularly. We don't have much to say when he calls, but I like to hear his voice anyway. Besides, I like to know that he's thinking of me. He made me swear not to give out his number to anyone else. I wonder if he's afraid of getting inundated with calls from crazed fans.

"How's your mom?" he asks me one afternoon.

"She's fine." What else is there to say?

"Still getting rides to work with Marcus?" he asks.

I'm startled that he mentioned Marcus's name. "I don't know." I actually don't. I make a point of not being around when Mom leaves for the theater. On the other hand, I'm back to taking the car to dance classes, so unless she's found someone else to ride with…

"You could buy me a car," I suggest. "And then Mom wouldn't need a ride."

"Ha!" he laughs. "You should be so lucky."

"How's the tour going?"

"Oh, about the same as all the others. What about you? How's dance?"

"Good."

"How about the composition?"

"Good. Mr. Rocchelli thinks I have talent." I don't know why, but it feels good to mention that.

"We already knew that."

I smile. "When are you coming home?"

"About a week before Christmas."

I wonder how that will go. Will he be here with Mom and me?

"I've got to run, Legs. Sound-check time. I miss you."

"I miss you too, Dad."

"Love you." The phone goes dead.

For some reason, tears spring to my eyes. I know it was my idea for him to get a cell phone and call me, but now hearing his voice makes me miss him even more.

~

During the next couple of weeks, I book the sound room as often as I can without appearing greedy. With the positive feedback I've received from both Dad and Mr. Rocchelli, I want to immerse myself in the project, get it finished.

I've become hyperaware of Mr. Rocchelli's presence. More and more, I'm distracted by him, my eyes following him as he moves about the room, assisting students or conducting various band and choral practices. He moves gracefully, as though he, too, were a dancer. I sigh, watching his fingers run along a keyboard as he demonstrates something for another student. She giggles as she tries to copy his lead, clearly enjoying the one-on-one attention. Occasionally he seems to sense my gaze on him, and when he looks at me I quickly avert my eyes, making me look as guilty as I feel, I'm sure. But hard as I try not to go back to staring at him, I inevitably find myself doing just that.

~

It's a Friday afternoon in early November. Once again I'm in the sound room, working. Mr. Rocchelli is tutoring some students in the larger room. I think vaguely about the weekend ahead. How I am going to fill the long days? Perhaps enough time has passed that I can call Talia or Spencer, apologize for my stupidity and suggest we go to a movie or something. But just thinking about this scenario makes my palms sweat, and I have to push the thoughts away.

After about an hour of struggling with a transition, I slump back in my chair. Looking around, I see that the music room has emptied. Mr. Rocchelli is the only person remaining, and he's wandering about the classroom, straightening chairs, collecting sheets of music and just generally tidying up from the week. I feel myself tense as he passes the sound-room door, which I've left open.

"Any big weekend plans, Allegra?" He leans against the doorjamb, smiling at me.

I shake my head and feign total concentration on what I'm doing.

"Anything I can help you with here?" he asks.

"Well, actually..." I look at him, trying to determine whether he really wants to help or is just being teacher-like. I decide he's sincere, and I really *am* stuck. "I'm having trouble with the transition from the second section to the third section." I sigh. "Any suggestions?"

He comes all the way into the room and sits down. "Play what you have, the part you're struggling with."

I play just the last section that I've completed, which he hasn't heard yet. He listens, his head cocked.

"What I can't figure out," I say once he's heard it, "is how to tie it into this section." I play the third section of the composition. I haven't progressed very far, so I stop it after a few bars.

"Transitions can be hard, can't they?" he comments. He thinks for a moment, then seems to come to a decision. "What I often do when faced with this kind of problem is go to the masters and listen to what they've done."

"Which masters?"

"Bach, Schubert, Handel." He steps out of the sound room and I watch as he takes a set of keys from his desk drawer. He unlocks a cabinet, which I see is filled with CDs. He selects a few and brings them to me. "Take these home for the weekend and listen to them, concentrating on the transitions. That might help."

My mom has tons of CDs, but I take them from him anyway. "You want me to copy what these guys have done?" I smile. He's so easy to tease. "Isn't that plagiarism?"

"Very funny, Allegra. No, you'll put your own spin on it, but there's a lot to be learned from studying these old guys."

"Too bad there are no famous female composers."

"It is a shame, isn't it? I'm sure the women of the day would have had a lot to offer these guys if they'd been consulted."

"Consulted? Imagine if they'd been free to compose their own music!"

"You're right. What was I thinking?"

We stand there smiling at one another. I feel totally relaxed.

"Allegra, there's something I want to ask you."

"What is it?"

"I'm wondering if you would allow me to work with you a bit on this composition."

His suggestion startles me, and my reaction must show on my face.

"I know, I know," he says. "You've worked hard on it, and it's not really right for me to suddenly want to add my two bits, but I'm just so impressed with what you're doing, and a creative project is often enhanced with additional minds working on it."

He looks at me. I'm too shocked to say anything.

"Never mind," he says, shaking his head. "I'm totally out of line here. Forget I said anything."

"No, no." Now I shake my head. "It was your piece of music to start with. I wouldn't have come this far without the melody you gave me. I'm totally fine with it. In fact, I'd really like some help."

His face breaks into a wide grin. "That's great!" He nods. "On Monday maybe we can draw up a schedule of times we can work together."

"Yeah, okay." This sudden turn of events has caught me totally off guard. We're still standing, facing one another, and he's still grinning widely. Suddenly, the easiness of our conversation evaporates. I swear I can feel his body heat radiating toward me. I wrack my brain, trying to find a way to return to the easy banter of just a moment ago, but my mind has gone blank.

He must feel the sudden awkwardness too. "Is there anything else I can help you with right now, Allegra?"

I shake my head and look down at the CDs he's handed me. I'm aware of my own body heat now, and I recognize the familiar physical symptoms of anxiety. I shuffle my feet and mumble something about listening to the CDs, but his presence is filling the room, and now I'm beginning to feel dizzy. I slump into a chair.

"You're sure you're okay?' he asks gently. His hand touches my shoulder.

"Yeah." Deep breaths.

"Okay..." I can hear the uncertainty in his voice. "If you don't need anything else, then..."

I just shake my head, still staring at the CDs in my hands.

"Then I think I'll call it a day." He glances at his watch. "And I do have a date. Shall I leave you the keys to lock up, or are you heading home too?"

I don't trust my wobbly legs to carry me out of the room right now. "I'd like to stay a bit longer, if that's okay."

"Sure," he says. "I know I can trust you to lock up when you leave." He unhooks a key from the set in his hand and tosses it to me. "Just return it on Monday. I have another one."

I nod.

"Have a good weekend. And Allegra, I'm really looking forward to working on this together." With a last look at me, he grabs his jacket off the back of his desk chair and leaves the room.

I'm left wondering what just happened.

Thirteen

I'm already in the sound room when Mr. Rocchelli arrives on Monday morning.

"Did you even go home this weekend?" he asks, smiling. He's standing in the doorway, looking in at me.

I just nod and pretend to be busy playing a pattern of notes on the keyboard. I watch as he walks over to his desk and shuffles papers around. He looks up and catches me staring at him. I quickly return to my work, but I sense him walking back toward the sound room. My heart flip-flops.

"Seriously, I hope you took some time off this weekend, Allegra," he says, standing in the doorway again.

"Of course I did." I roll my eyes, relieved that he'll never know how much time I actually spent pacing around the house, fretting over the plan to collaborate on the piece. "I just wanted to make sure you weren't locked out this morning," I say, pulling the key out of my pocket. "Here."

He takes the key and smiles. "Thanks. You must have me figured out already. I can be a bit scattered, and it wouldn't have been the first time I'd forgotten my spare set." I go back to the keyboard, but he stays where he is. The familiar scent of his aftershave wafts through the tiny space. "So," he says, "shall we map out some blocks of time when we can work together?"

"Sure." I pull my phone out of my pack. *Stay calm.*

"You still okay with that?" he asks, his voice full of doubt.

"Oh yeah, totally," I assure him. "I can really use some help." I look up, feeling a sudden surge of panic that he might change his mind. I've been thinking of nothing but working with him all weekend.

"Good," he says, nodding.

I scroll through the weeks on my calendar. "What afternoons are good for you?"

"Actually," he says, frowning, "I have rehearsals every afternoon this week."

"Oh." I try not to sound too disappointed.

"I often have students come back to school in the evening for small group rehearsals. Would evenings work for you?"

I glance at him, surprised. "Hmm. I dance most evenings. Tuesday through Friday anyway."

"Oh. Then how about mornings, before school?"

"Yeah, I guess that would work."

"And you're free tonight? Shall we start then?"

I nod.

"Good. We'll work tonight and carry on tomorrow morning. Then we'll decide when to meet again."

I shut off my phone. He turns to leave, then steps back into the room. "Will your parents be okay with this?" He looks a little embarrassed.

"Yeah, of course. They know all about squeezing in rehearsals between other things."

"All right!" He grins. "Let's meet about seven."

I spend the rest of the morning trying not to think about working with him that evening, but it's all I can think of.

Before lunch I'm back in the sound room for music-theory class. There's a tap on the glass, and I look up. Spencer is standing there, his head cocked. I nod toward the door, inviting him in.

"Hey," he says.

"Hey."

"How have you been?"

"Okay." I don't understand the sudden friendliness. "How 'bout you?"

"I'm fine." He looks at his feet. "But I miss hanging out with you. I can hardly remember what happened or what went wrong."

I do, but I don't want to remind him. Looking at him now, I'm wondering what I ever even saw in him. He looks so…young. And awkward.

"Mr. Rocchelli sent me to ask you if you'd help some of us with our four-part-harmony work. A lot of us are having trouble with it."

I look out through the glass and see a class full of heads bowed over sheets of paper. Mr. Rocchelli is at one table, working out a problem for the group seated there. "Sure." So this wasn't just a social call after all. I get up from my chair, but Spencer blocks the doorway.

"Maybe we could hang out one of these days."

"Yeah, okay," my mouth says. My head says that will never happen.

"Why don't you join us for lunch tomorrow?" he asks.

I study his face, wondering if this is some kind of trick. "How would the girls feel about that?"

"They'd be fine." He shrugs. "We all overreacted. It's no big deal."

I feel my heart swell at the peace offering. "Okay. Usual place?"

He grins. "Yeah."

As I follow him through the door, he turns and says very quietly, "Thanks."

"Thanks?"

"For making that so easy."

As I look at him, I remember how I felt that day the two of us were in this room alone and he kissed me. I feel my face burn. I give him a little push, steering him into the classroom. "Whatever," is all I can think of to say.

I tell my mom that I need the car so I can go to the library to work on a group project. If she's surprised, she doesn't say anything, and she doesn't object.

At exactly 7:00 PM, I pull into the school driveway. Somehow, I've managed to keep myself calm. It's almost dark, but there are enough exterior lights on around the school to find my way to the music portable. I can see the lights on inside.

Feeling shy, I tap lightly on the door before stepping into the classroom. He looks up from his desk, where he's marking papers.

"Hi, Allegra," he says. His smile is warm.

"Hey." I glance about, surprised to see that there is no one else here.

He reads my thoughts. "The jazz combo that often meets on Monday nights cancelled. Apparently, there's a big Geography 10 exam tomorrow."

"Oh."

"Ready to get to work?" He stands and watches as I cross the room.

"Yeah."

He flicks off the classroom lights as he follows me into the brightly lit sound room. "Might as well conserve energy," he says.

I sit down and push the flash drive into the computer. It's just me, him and the music in our bright little bubble. "Where shall we start?" I ask.

He sits in the other chair. "How about at the beginning?"

I nod and start the music. We listen in silence. I glance at him once and see that his eyes are closed. When we get to the end of the piece—or as far as I've written—I wait for his comments. His eyes open slowly.

"Well?" I ask.

He sits quietly for a moment, then says, "Have you had that experience where you hear a piece of music… and it…it resonates with you—somewhere deep?"

I can hardly breathe as I realize where he is going with this. I simply nod.

"This piece…it does that for me."

"Oh." I nod some more. "I'm glad." What else can I say? What else is there to say?

He sits still for another long moment, as if savoring what he has just heard. Finally he shakes his head, pulling himself back into the present. "If it's okay with you," he says, "I don't want to change anything you have here, just add another layer."

"Another layer?" I'm intrigued, and I feel myself relax a little.

"Yeah, I think we could overlay another whole voice on what is here." Using his heels, he wheels his chair a little closer. I wheel mine away from the computer, allowing him to take the mouse. "How about this?"

He starts the piece from the beginning, pointing the cursor to an icon that adds a track of stringed instruments to the mix. He listens. "No, that's not right." He goes back to the beginning, this time choosing woodwinds. He continues this way for a while, adding one new instrument sound after another and listening to the mix. He quickly loses himself in the work. I think he's even forgotten that I'm there. I roll my chair even farther away and simply watch him. Without looking up, he rolls his chair a little closer to the computer and continues experimenting.

"Hey, that's it!" I say, sitting up taller. Finally I get what he's trying to do.

"You think?" he says, looking over at me. He looks a little dazed, like he's forgotten where he is.

"Yeah. Play that again, with the flute."

He does, and we watch each other while the section plays through with the flute track blending in.

I find myself smiling, excited. The piece now has a whole new resonance. "I like it," I say, nodding.

"Are you sure?" he asks. "I don't want to impose."

"No, seriously, that's exactly what was missing."

"Good." He fiddles with the score for a few more minutes, making tiny changes. Eventually, he sits back. "Well, that was fun," he says. He looks at me and laughs.

"It wasn't exactly teamwork, though, was it? Sorry about that. I just kind of took over."

"Works for me," I tell him.

He laughs again.

"Besides, I've done all the work so far. If this is going to be a collaboration, you have some catching up to do."

He smiles, then scans my face, as if seeing something there for the first time. It makes me uncomfortable. "Shall we keep working?" I ask, turning to the screen. Our bright little bubble suddenly feels claustrophobic.

He stretches and runs his fingers through his hair. "All that concentrating…I'm exhausted!" He laughs at himself. It's a nice laugh, warm and contagious. "How about a tea break?" he asks. "Can I make you a cup?"

I nod. "Sure," I say, but truthfully I'm sorry to stop working on the music. I'm in my comfort zone with that. I'm not comfortable with drinking tea together.

He leaves the sound room, flicks on the classroom lights and returns to his desk, plugging in the kettle that sits on a counter behind it.

I get up, stretch and follow him toward his desk. He's pulling various kinds of tea out of a cupboard. "Peppermint?" he asks. "Green? Black currant?"

"Whatever you're having."

He scans the boxes. "Chamomile," he says. "Does that work for you?"

"Sure." I have no idea what chamomile is. I watch as he pulls a couple of mugs out of the cupboard and drops a tea bag into each of them. He pours boiling water into the mugs, then pushes at the tea bags with a spoon. He seems lost in thought as he swirls the tea bags around. When he decides the tea is ready, he holds a mug out to me. I watch as he brings his cup up to his face and inhales. His eyes close briefly.

"Chamomile always reminds me of my mom," he says. "It was her favorite."

I inhale too. The fragrance doesn't remind me of anything.

"I miss her," he says, taking a sip.

"Where is she?"

"She passed away a year ago." A sad expression crosses his face. "Almost to the day." He pulls up the sleeve of his T-shirt so I can see his entire tattoo. I can't help but notice the long muscles. "These are the dates of her life."

"Oh. I'm sorry."

"Thanks." He lets the sleeve drop. "She really supported my ambition to be a musician. Unlike my father."

"What did he think you should do?"

"Anything that provides a steady paycheck."

I think about my parents. They've encouraged me to be a musician even though they know the income isn't always steady.

"So is that why you became a music teacher?"

He nods. "It really wasn't a compromise though. I belong to a small jazz ensemble and we perform a couple of times a month, and landing a job at a fine-arts school, well, it all worked out." He smiles at me and takes a big gulp of tea.

"How about you?" he asks. "Do your parents support your ambition to be a dancer?"

I think about that and then smile. "Not really," I say. "Ironically, they want me to be a musician, like them."

He smiles at that too.

"They worry that I won't be able to support myself with dance."

"I guess all parents are the same that way."

"Except your mom," I remind him.

"Yeah." He nods, staring into his mug. "She was special."

The room is still as Mr. Rocchelli regards his tea. Finally he gives his head a little shake and looks up. "Sorry," he says. "I didn't mean to go there. It was the tea…"

"No worries."

He smiles. "Tell me a little about yourself, Allegra," he says, leaning back against the counter.

I sit on the edge of a table. "There's not much to tell," I say. "I dance, go to school…" My mind goes completely blank. "And that's about it."

"You have interesting parents."

"Maybe to you." I smile.

He smiles back. "Good point. How about your friends?"

I don't want to tell him that I don't "do" friends very well. "I have a friend at my dance school. Angela. She's great."

He nods, waiting for me to go on.

"But that's about it."

He cocks his head. "I was under the impression that you were friends with Spencer."

"Was."

"Oh?" His eyebrows arch: a question.

I take a long sip of my tea, then sigh. "I blew it with him."

I can't believe I've just admitted that. It must be because he shared with me about his mother. "But he invited me to have lunch with him and his friends tomorrow," I add.

Mr. Rocchelli is still studying me. "That sounds positive."

I shrug. "Who knows? I've never been very good at keeping friends."

"I'm surprised to hear that," he says gently.

"I never really got kids my age," I tell him. "All the drama and the things they talked about...well, none of it interested me. So I removed myself, I guess, and then it got so I didn't even know how to act with them."

Mr. Rocchelli doesn't respond and I don't look at him, but I know he's listening intently.

"So I figure it's best just to stick to myself. Less difficult that way."

"Maybe you had the advantage of releasing all that adolescent drama and angst in your music and dance."

"Maybe."

"Will you have lunch with Spencer and the others tomorrow?"

Now it's my turn to gaze into my mug. "Yeah, I guess."

"You know, Allegra,"—Mr. Rocchelli's voice is very soft and kind—"you'll find that once you're finished school and are out in the world, dancing professionally, you'll connect with people more like yourself, people who are passionate about what they're doing, and you'll suddenly find that you fit in."

"I thought that was what I was going to find at this school; it's why I transferred."

"You *are* different from most girls your age," he adds.

Our eyes meet and hold a moment too long. I nod and look away. There's a current running between us, something so strong it feels almost tangible.

"In a good way," he adds, breaking the serious mood with a laugh. I feel the current snap. I don't know whether I'm relieved or disappointed.

"There's nothing wrong with the other girls!" he adds quickly. He rotates his mug, watching the tea slosh around the bottom. "They're just more...more social than you. And this is still a high school, no matter what they call it."

I have nothing to say to that, so I gulp down the remainder of my tea. He does too. "Let's get back to work shall we?" he suggests.

As I follow him back to the sound room, I know something in our relationship has shifted. Something important.

As I make my way through the crowded hallway toward the multipurpose room where I'm meeting Spencer and the girls, I think about Mr. Rocchelli's last words to me this morning: *Just relax at lunch, Allegra. It will be fine.*

My parents have been saying the same thing to me all my life, but it never is fine. Somehow, though, coming from him the advice doesn't sound hollow. I believe him, and I was touched this morning that he'd even remembered what I told him last night about having lunch with Spencer and the girls today.

This morning's music-writing session went just as well as last night's. In only two sessions, he's pushed me to think outside the box and come up with musical ideas I never would have had without his encouragement. His own ideas of adding subtle layers to the music have made it that much richer.

"Mr. Rocchelli," I'd said today, pointing to a place on the rough score, "why did you change these quarter notes to eighth notes?"

He'd looked at me then, clearly trying to come to some kind of decision. Then, instead of answering my question, he'd said, "Allegra, when we're working like this, could you please just call me Noel? Mr. Rocchelli sounds way too formal in this kind of setting. It makes me uncomfortable. You can go back to Mr. Rocchelli when we're in class."

I'd nodded, and realized that I'd been right. Something really has shifted between us.

I'd far sooner be having lunch in the music room, near Noel, than in the multipurpose room with Spencer and the girls.

I spot them sitting in their usual places. Spencer sees me coming and waves. The girls' heads turn, in unison, to watch me approach.

Spencer shuffles over to make room for me beside him. I squeeze in between him and Talia.

"Good to see you, Allegra," Molly says. Sophie nods in agreement.

"Good to see you too," I answer. I open my lunch bag. "I'm sorry about…about everything." There. I'd said it, and it was easy.

"We don't even remember what went wrong," Talia says. "It was so stupid."

There are nods of agreement all around.

"So what's new?" Molly asks, unwrapping some cookies. She offers one to me.

I shake my head. "Not much, really."

"Your dad's on tour?" Spencer asks.

"Uh-huh."

"That was so much fun, the night we sat in on the rehearsal," says Sophie.

"It was amazing," Spencer agrees, biting into the cookie he's taken from Molly.

I unwrap my sandwich and find my thoughts are already back to Mr. Rocchelli, wondering if he's made any time for his own lunch.

"Still dancing lots?" Talia asks.

"Yeah, the usual." I smile at her. "And I'm still working really hard on my music-theory project." Her eyebrows arch. I look away. "I want to get it done. Free up some more time to dance." Even as I say it, I know it isn't true.

Fortunately, the subject changes, and I relax and listen to the chatter around me. It feels good to be included again, and I'm relieved that it all happened so easily, yet I'm aware that something has changed in me since the last time I sat here with the four of them. When I think about who I was then, and even though it's only been a few weeks, it's like I've become a different person. That other Allegra was anxious about being liked by these four and trying not to say or do anything stupid. But now… now that doesn't seem important. I still like the four of them. I'm glad to have lunch with them, but my thoughts are still in the music room with Mr. Rocchelli. Noel.

Fourteen

I feel like I'm floating through my days. Nothing really matters except my time in the sound room with Mr. Rocchelli. Working on the composition has become my entire life. I still show up for my dance classes and meet Spencer and the girls for lunch, but my mind is always on the next music-writing session. Spencer keeps urging me to hang out with him after school, but so far I've been able to put him off. Even the problems my parents are having seem less important. Mom and I have occasional meals together, but we don't talk much.

The bell rings, ending my jazz class with Ms. Dekker. "Allegra," she says. I'm mopping myself off with my towel, as there's no time for a shower between classes. "Could you remain behind for a moment?"

I look at her, surprised. She hasn't been on my case for several weeks now. What could she want? Come to think of it, I *have* been distracted, not really able to focus on anything. Maybe it's showing in my dance. I brace myself for the inevitable lecture and wait by her desk until everyone else has left. She comes over and perches on the corner of it. She's smiling, for a change.

"You're dancing like you're in love or something, Allegra," she says.

I feel my eyes widen, and she tilts her head back and laughs. "I'm sorry," she says, reaching out and lightly touching my shoulder. "I'm teasing. It's just that your dancing has taken on a whole new, very expressive dimension. You've not only returned from the funk you were in, but you're really tapped into your musicality. You're dancing like you're inside the music."

Inside the music. That's huge praise coming from her.

"Anyway," she says, still smiling, "I just wanted to welcome you back and tell you to keep doing whatever it is that's making you so happy. It suits you."

I walk off down the hall, thinking I'm heading toward my English class, then realize I'm going in the wrong direction. I turn around and pick up my pace, arriving just as Mr. Clement is shutting the door.

"Glad you could join us, Allegra," he says, smiling, but he's watching me carefully. Can he also see a change in me?

I flop into my chair and drop my dance bag on the floor beside me. I glance over at Talia, only to find that she, too, is watching me.

"What?" I mouth, keeping half an eye on Mr. Clement.

She just smiles and shakes her head. "Nothing," she mouths back.

I open up my notebook and try to concentrate on what Mr. Clement is saying, but my mind keeps floating back to Ms. Dekker's comment. *You're dancing like you're in love*. Why would she say that? And who does she think I'm in love with?

The truth settles over me like a soft blanket. Mr. Rocchelli. Noel. He's all I ever think about. I've never been in love before, so I didn't recognize what was going on with me. My whole body goes numb as it sinks in. I glance over at Talia again. She's still watching me, a soft smile on her face. I turn away, pretending to be completely focused on the lesson, but butterfly wings flutter in my stomach. Can Talia possibly know what is going on with me?

Talia hangs back after class, waiting. I take my time, collecting my things slowly and hoping she'll leave without me. She hovers by my desk. There's something about the way she's been watching me that's unnerving, like she knew what was going on with me even before I did.

"I think I'm going to skip lunch and take a shower instead," I tell her. "Jazz class was tough. I can't stand the smell of myself."

"You smell fine to me," she says, leaning over and inhaling deeply.

"Just wait another hour."

"Are you sure you don't want to go somewhere and talk?" she asks.

"No." I feign puzzlement. "Is everything okay?" I ask, trying to bounce the conversation into her court.

"You look like a lovesick puppy," she says.

I give her my best what-are-you-talking-about expression.

"And I know it's not Spencer," she says. "So that leaves only one person that I can think of."

I grab my things, stand and push past her toward the door. "I don't know what you're talking about."

"From what I can tell," she says to my back, "you're spending an awful lot of time in Mr. Rocchelli's portable."

I swing around. "You know perfectly well that I'm composing a piece for my project in music theory."

She just stares at me, a smug little smile on her face. "He's hot, Allegra. Every girl in the school thinks so. And he's not that old."

The room is empty. I can hear students in the hall, lockers banging shut, everyone heading to their lunch-hour haunts, but we are totally alone in this room, facing one another. I feel a fury building up inside me. I am not like every other girl. Mr. Rocchelli and I have something special going on, but she would never understand that.

"Did you ever think that I might have friends outside of this school, maybe even a boyfriend?" I ask, the lie coming easily to my lips.

I see a moment of doubt cross her face, but the smugness returns almost immediately. "I'm sure you do. But I don't know when you'd find time to see him, with your dance and school schedule. And especially with all the time you spend in the music portable."

"I don't know why we're having this conversation," I say and step toward the door.

She steps in front of me, blocking the doorway. "Because I like you, Allegra. And I've been watching you. You've changed a lot since September. Spencer is crazy about you, and I think you should give him another chance."

"I'm not sure when my business became your business."

"That's what friends do. We take care of each other."

I meet her gaze, startled by her words. I've never thought of friendship quite that way before, and yet…is that really what is happening here? "This feels more like some kind of weird accusation."

She shrugs. "I'm sorry it feels that way." She hesitates, and in that moment the smugness leaves her face. "I thought maybe you could use a friend who looks out for you."

I am surprised to see the kindness in her eyes. "I don't need you to look out for me," I tell her. "But I do need to take a shower." I shove past her and through the door.

"Make it a cold one, Allegra," she says to my back.

I'm ultrasensitive to Noel's presence as I walk across the portable toward the sound room. Without even glancing at him, I know he's watching me.

Clamping the headphones over my ears, I fire up the computer and attempt to look like I'm working, but really I just want to be left alone. Alone to think. Alone to make sense of this strange new understanding.

I close my eyes and breathe deeply. When I open them again, I sneak a glance at him. He is standing beside a girl, showing her something on a keyboard. He plays a chord, looks at her to see if she's grasped the concept and plays another one. He moves aside, allowing her to step in front of the keys. She places her hands down, and I watch as he reaches over and rests his hands lightly over hers, then slides her hands slightly to the left. She plays the chord and together their hands slide to the right and play another one. Her face lights up. He takes his hands off hers and they smile at each other. A pang of jealousy rips through me. Is it true? Does every girl here really think Noel is hot? I look down at my own keyboard, willing myself to get back to work, but I'm staggered by the weight of this newfound realization. I'd always thought love would feel light, free, liberating. Why, then, do I feel so paralyzed?

I tinker with the composition for a while but quickly realize that when the two of us are working together, the music feels like it's writing itself. We go into another zone, as though the musical ideas are being channeled through us from some greater force. Noel will play a musical phrase that gives me an idea, and my idea appears to infuse him with increased creativity. We heap musical ideas on top of musical ideas, and they come faster and faster once we're warmed up. The process works so well that it's impossible to go back to writing alone.

The bell sounds, indicating the end of the lunch hour. Pulling off the headphones, I sign out of the program, grab my bag and turn to leave the room, but Noel is leaning on the doorjamb, gazing down at me. I can't believe I didn't sense him standing there. My heart skips a beat. I can't look at him.

"Did you make any changes I should know about?" he asks. His voice is light, teasing. It tugs me out of my mood.

"Actually, I deleted the whole thing. It was garbage."

"You better not have!" He laughs, and I feel myself relax. "Or you'll be back taking my class again next year!"

Another realization hits me, hard: when we're working together, he just has to laugh or tease me, and I tease back, and the anxiety evaporates.

"I'm looking forward to tonight," he tells me as I pass him in the doorway. "We're almost done."

I nod, then feel my mood dip again. *Almost done.* I don't ever want to finish, because then our time together will be over too.

I spend the afternoon, pretending to concentrate in class but thinking only of Noel, wondering how he feels about me. I pull out a blank page in my notebook and make a list of things I know for sure.

1. *He likes the music I write.*
2. *He knows that the music we write together is so much. better than what either of us could write alone.*
3. *He understands why I can't relate to people my own age.*
4. *When he looks at me, he really sees me.*
5. *He shares personal stories with me.*

I study the list, then add one more entry.

6. *Is he in love with me too?*

I crumple up the page and shove it into my backpack.

I have to skip my dance class tonight to meet with Noel, but I don't care. Dance has become second to my interest in the composition. If I had my way, we'd spend every evening on the piece, smoothing out the rough patches, slowly, steadily working on the crescendo, reaching for that final, stirring cadence.

My windshield wipers slap at high speed as I pull up to the school. I fish around in the backseat, looking for an umbrella. Nothing. It won't matter how fast I run. I'll be soaked before I reach the portable. I peer out into the night, wondering if the rain will let up if I wait a few minutes.

Headlights flash in my rearview mirror, and a car pulls into the stall beside mine. Immediately I recognize it as Noel's. I get my bag and pull my hood up over my head, but before I can even open the car door, I see him standing there, holding an umbrella. He opens my door for me and peers in.

"Wanna share my umbrella?" he asks, grinning.

"Sure," I say, sliding out of the driver's seat and moving in close to him.

He pushes my door shut with his free hand and effortlessly pulls my left arm around his right one, the one that's holding the umbrella. The rain is bouncing off the pavement. "C'mon," he says. "Let's get inside."

Linked at the arms, we jog around the school toward the music portable. The wind is blowing the rain straight at us, threatening to suck the umbrella inside out. Mr. Rocchelli struggles to hang on to it. Our shoulders bang into each other as we run. I laugh at the craziness of it. In the pitch-dark I can't see the ground beneath my feet, but I do feel how water-soaked my shoes have become.

Suddenly my ankle rolls, and my foot slides into a water-filled hole with a *splosh*. "Ow!"

Mr. Rocchelli tightens his grip on my arm to keep me upright. "Are you okay?"

"Yeah." I put my weight on my soggy foot, but a searing pain shoots up my leg. "Oh no." I begin to limp. Our strides are no longer in unison.

"Allegra?" Mr. Rocchelli is frowning down at me.

"I just twisted my ankle a bit. Let's keep going."

Like a dancer leading his partner into a graceful transition, Mr. Rocchelli switches the umbrella to his other hand and manages to wrap his right arm around my waist, allowing my left arm to go across his shoulder for support. We hobble over to the portable. Despite the pain shooting up my leg, I relish the moment, feeling his hand squeezing my waist. Disappointment washes over me as he releases his grip to fish the key out of his pocket and unlock the door. Pushing it open with his shoulder, he deftly puts down the umbrella and helps me into the room. I fall into the nearest chair while he flicks on some lights.

He rushes back to me and squats down, gently lifting my foot. I pull it away, embarrassed. "I'll be fine in a minute. It happens all the time in dance class."

We both stare at my waterlogged shoe. My jeans are soaked all the way to my knees.

I reach down and carefully unlace my shoe. Tugging at the heel makes me flinch again. I let it go with a sigh. Mr. Rocchelli, settled in a chair facing mine, leans toward me, obviously anxious about my ankle. I look up, and our eyes meet. His brow is knit with concern, and I try to smile to reassure him. Despite the ache in my ankle, I don't want this little crisis to ruin our evening.

A drip of water slides from a lock of his hair and lands on the bridge of his nose. Without a thought, I reach out and blot it with my thumb before it can run down the entire length of his nose.

I pause there, my face only inches from his, my ankle forgotten. Our eyes hold for a split second and then he abruptly sits back.

"I'm sorry, I just..." I can't finish the sentence, too mortified that I've crossed some invisible line.

"That's okay." He smiles, but his face flushes and his gaze returns to my foot. He uses his hand to slick back his wet hair. "I guess we're going to have to call tonight off. You need to get your foot checked out. Shall we call one of your parents to come and get you? You shouldn't be driving."

The businesslike tone of his voice disturbs me. All the usual warmth is gone. I feel panicky, not wanting to lose the close bond we've established. "I'll be fine, really." I rotate my ankle, ignoring the stabs of pain. I lean over and massage it a little, then gently remove my shoe and massage it some more. I ignore the swelling I feel around my anklebone. A chill runs though me, and I feel myself shake involuntarily.

"You're soaked, Allegra," Mr. Rocchelli says, more gently now. "I'm sorry, but I don't think it was meant to be tonight."

"I have some sweatpants in my locker that I could change into." I know I'm sounding too anxious.

Our eyes meet again before he looks back down at my foot. His gaze moves to the window, and he looks out into the night as he considers. "You need to call your parents, Allegra."

"No. I want to work." I shudder as another chill washes through me.

He sighs, stands up and moves away from me. "I've been foolish, Allegra. This is wrong."

"Wrong?" I ask the question, but I don't really want to know the answer.

"It's inappropriate for me to be working with you here alone at night. I don't know what I was thinking." His gaze goes back to the window again. "I allowed myself to get so caught up in what we were doing, what we were creating, that I forgot to use common sense. We need to reschedule our sessions to daytime slots."

I just stare at him, not wanting to comprehend.

"Unless there are other groups here," he says, shoving his hands into his pockets. "Allegra," he says, turning to look at me again, "I believe we have created something pretty spectacular together. Seriously. I try not to think about it too much, but..." He lets out another sigh.

"But what?" The room is still except for the drumming of the rain on the metal roof.

"I think we could get it published. Hear it performed."

I stare at him. He's talking about the music. For some reason, I thought he was talking about us.

He smiles, just a little. "And because I'm so excited about the music, I've allowed myself to become too close to you, my student. We need to step back a little, Allegra, keep this professional—teacher and student. You're completing an assignment, and I'm coaching you. That's all."

He looks so sad as he speaks, trying to convince himself—and me—that this is just a case of a student completing an assignment, that I know, suddenly, the truth of this situation. He loves me too.

The rain continues to pummel the roof of the portable. Mr. Rocchelli has gone back to staring out the window. His profile is beautiful. The surge of my heart is greater than the throbbing in my ankle.

"I love you."

It was not planned. I didn't even know the words were going to come out of my mouth. They hang in the air between us for a moment. Mr. Rocchelli's eyes widen as he stares at me.

Suddenly, he strides across the room and goes behind his desk. "Phone your parents, Allegra. Have one of them come and get you. Now!"

I feel the blood drain from my face, and then, just as suddenly, a rage courses through me. I stand and face him, ignoring my throbbing ankle. "Neither of them are home."

"Where are they?"

"My dad's on a road trip with his band, and my mom's performing tonight."

"But she knows you're here, right?"

I hesitate, wondering if I should lie, and in that moment his expression changes.

"Allegra, you did tell your parents that you've been coming here to work with me, right?"

I meet his gaze. "No. It was none of their business. Besides, they wouldn't care."

He stares at me. I stare back. I can't believe he's reacting like this.

He flips open his laptop and types something.

I jam my foot back into my soaking-wet shoe, hardly noticing the pain. Mr. Rochelli is still across the room, and I assume he's looking up the phone number for a cab company. I grab my bag and hobble to the door. Then I reach into my bag and pull out the flash drive that contains our piece of music. Slamming it onto a desk, I look back at him. "It's all yours. And as of this moment, I am no longer enrolled in music theory." I see his brow crease, but I just pull open the door and head back out into the rain.

I'm almost at my car when I hear his footsteps behind me. He grabs my arm and tries to pull me around to face him. I yank my arm away and try to press the Open button on my key fob, but my hand is shaking so hard that I keep missing it.

His hand closes over mine, and he tugs away the keys. I don't resist, just slump against my car, the rain coming down even harder now, if that's possible. I feel tears sliding down my face, warm on my skin where the raindrops are cold.

Noel pulls me around to face him. His hands rest on my shoulders. I feel his hand slip under my chin, forcing me to look up at him. "I'm sorry, Allegra. I handled that badly."

I can't look at him and gaze instead over his shoulder, into the parking lot. The glow from the lone streetlight barely reaches this corner. My breathing is ragged as I struggle to hold back more tears.

"This is all my fault," he says. "I've acted like a complete fool. No wonder you were confused."

I feel myself flinch. Confused? I don't think so.

"I like you a lot, Allegra," he says, his voice shaky. "You know that. You're also one of my most gifted students, and I want to push you to make the most of your talent." His hands squeeze my shoulders. I look up, wondering if he'll kiss me. His hair is plastered against his head, his eyelashes clumped together with moisture. "But Allegra, I am your teacher, and you are my student, and that's it." His eyes bore into mine, and then he drops his hands, turns and unlocks his car. He opens the passenger door for me. "I'll drive you home," he says, his voice cracking. "Get in."

"My mom…she'll need her car tomorrow."

"How did she get to the theater tonight?"

"A friend drove her." I frown, thinking of Marcus.

"Then I'm sure she can find a friend to drop her off here tomorrow."

I'm too cold to argue, so I slump into the passenger seat. He shuts the door and walks around to the driver's side. After starting the engine, he turns the heat on full blast and backs out of the stall. Except for me giving him the odd direction, neither of us says a thing until we arrive at my house. As I reach for the door handle, I feel his hand on my arm.

"Are we okay, Allegra?"

I can't look at him, but I shrug. I have yet to process what has happened tonight.

"We will finish the project though," he says. "It's important."

"I'll think about it."

"No, don't think about it. Commit to it. Tomorrow in class, we'll map out some new times."

I close my eyes and sigh.

"It's easy to get confused, Allegra."

I just shrug again. He's wrong, but I can't tell him that.

"Is your ankle okay?"

I rotate it. "It'll mend. It's not the first time I've twisted it." I reach for the door handle again. This time he doesn't try to stop me.

"Good night, Allegra," he says softly as I get out of the car. I don't answer and start to limp up the driveway.

His car pulls away.

Fifteen

I slide down into the warm, sudsy water, allowing the fragrant bubbles to cover me. The anger has melted away, and now I simply feel numb. Resting my head on the back of the tub, I close my eyes and allow my thoughts to run free.

When, exactly, did everything go sideways tonight? Sharing the umbrella, running together through the rain, laughing at the craziness of it...we were in complete sync, just like when we're writing music.

I open my eyes and watch as bubbles burst open, releasing their fragrance. Twisting my ankle...that's when things went wrong. If that hadn't happened, we'd still be at the school right now, working on the piece. The musical ideas would be dancing around us, and we would pull them in and enter them into the score. The music would become more and more powerful and the realization of that would be like a drug, drawing us closer and closer. Our musical dance would be a flawless performance.

I run a washcloth up and down my arms, then let my hand drop back into the water with a splash. The truth hits me, and the numbness is replaced with complete and utter shame. I should never have told him that I love him. That was when things really went sideways. If I could only rewind the clock, go back to those few seconds before I turned my ankle. We'd skirt around that hole in the pavement, tumble into the classroom, arms still linked, passionate about creating music together…

I watch a steady drip of water falling from the faucet head. My eyes close, heavy, but then flutter open; I sit up. I slam my hand into the water and watch as it splashes up the tile wall. Somehow I need to fix this mess I've created. I can't turn the clock back, and I can't take the words back either. Can we find that magic place again or have I spoiled it forever?

I hum the first few bars of the piece. It relaxes me. I hum a little more.

I turn on the tap and swirl more hot water into my bath. Perhaps we can get back on track. Noel let it slip that he wants to see our piece get published and performed. Was he serious? If he was, our names would be forever linked together, as composers.

Shutting off the water, I notice that the bubbles have mostly disappeared, and I lift my foot to inspect my ankle. It is swollen and starting to change color. I'll have to miss a few dance classes, but it's not too bad. I've had worse.

Lying back, I allow the entire piece of music to run through my head. I can see the notes on the page and feel how they blend to create various moods. I take a long, head-clearing breath and sigh. I like it. Maybe it is as good as he thinks. It's hard to tell. I'm too close to it; I know it too intimately. It's like it is with dance: all I can do is perform and hope the audience connects with me. I can't see what they are seeing, I can't tell how "good" it is, I can just hope they feel something.

Will people respond to our music?

I pull the plug and watch as the water swirls down the drain. Perhaps not all is lost. I step out of the tub and wrap a towel around me. Using a hand towel, I clear a circle in the mirror. I stare into large gray eyes. Coils of hair have escaped from where I'd gathered them into a knot at the top of my head.

I graduate from school in less than a year. He won't have to obey those teacher-student rules once I'm no longer his student. I smile at the face in the mirror. The face smiles back, confidently. I may have found a way to fix this mess after all. All I need is patience.

The phone rings as I'm stepping into flannel pajamas. It's Dad.

"I'll be home for Christmas," he says, "but only for a couple of days. We have a gig on the twenty-eighth, but then there's only a couple more weeks after that and we're finished."

My heart flips at the word *Christmas*. I hadn't even thought about what that would be like this year, with my parents separated.

"Legs, are you still there?" he asks.

"Yeah yeah, sorry. My mind just wandered."

"I've been talking to your mom. We figure we'll drive up to Dave's on Christmas Eve."

Dave is my mom's brother, and most years her whole family descends on his home, as he has the most space and his wife, Sandra, loves to put on a big Christmas dinner.

"We're still a family," he says, "and we'll spend Christmas together as usual. The rest of the family doesn't know about our new arrangement, and this doesn't seem the time to tell them."

"Whatever," I say. Christmas seems so unimportant right now. I just want to think about the music, and Mr. Rocchelli. Noel.

There's a long pause. "How's the composing going?" he asks, as if reading my thoughts.

"Really well," I tell him, feeling myself brighten. "Mr. Rocchelli thinks we may be able to get the piece published when we're finished."

"When *we're* finished?" Dad asks.

"We've been working together on it," I tell him, somewhat sheepishly. I'm glad he can't see my face, as I know my expression would give too much away. When he doesn't respond, I add softly, "You bailed on me, remember?"

"I didn't bail, Legs. There's nothing I'd like more than to be working on that piece with you."

"But you chose to go on tour."

"I had to get out of town, honey, but it wasn't an easy choice. I'd much rather be there with you, but that didn't seem like an option."

I don't respond. The way I see it, if he *chose* to leave, he had options. It's as simple as that.

"I look forward to hearing it when I get back. Is it almost done?"

"It's close, but we keep going back and polishing and improving what we've already completed. It's been an amazing process." I know I've said too much, and with too much enthusiasm, but it just spilled out.

"That's great, Legs. I'm really happy that you're writing music. Maybe you and I will write some together someday too."

"Maybe," I tell him, but deep in my heart I want it to be Mr. Rocchelli—*Noel*—and me writing music together in the future.

"And how's dance going?" he asks. "Are you ready to take on the world stage next year?"

"Actually, I've slowed down a little. I twisted my ankle, so I have to take some time off." I don't mention that the injury only occurred tonight. "Besides, the writing is taking up most of my time right now."

"Really? It's hard to imagine that anything could keep my girl from dancing. How bad is your ankle?"

"Not bad." I rotate it and flinch in pain.

"Well, I hope it heals up quickly so you don't lose too much time."

His words make me think. It's amazing how fast I've lost interest in dance. Right now, I couldn't care less about taking a week or two off.

"Anyway," he says, "I'd better get some sleep. We have five nights in a row of shows coming up." He sighs. "I think I'm getting too old for this."

Ms. Dekker takes one look at my ankle and excuses me from ballet class. "Take the week off from all your dance classes," she says, "and then we'll reassess the situation."

I limp down to the library, determined to start on my English essay, which I've put off for far too long—something that never would have happened in the past. I slide into a chair and pull my English binder and textbook from my backpack. I'm just starting to write when I sense someone sliding into the chair across the table from me.

"Hi, Allegra," Spencer says, pulling me out of the world of Alice Munro's short stories.

"Hey."

"Are you skipping dance class?" he asks.

"No," I tell him, noting that he seems to know my schedule. "I have an injury. What are you skipping?"

"I have a spare." He reaches into his pack and also pulls out a binder. "Is your dad back from his road trip yet?"

"No, not until Christmas. And then he's just taking a few days off."

He nods and begins flipping through the pages. "I really appreciated getting all those autographed photos. I hope you told him."

"I did." I return to my textbook, but now I have trouble concentrating on the words. Talia told me that Spencer likes me. I glance at him, then go back to my textbook. It seems more like it's my dad and his band that he likes, and I'm just the person who can keep him posted on their activities.

We work in comfortable silence for a while, but I'm not getting anywhere with my assignment. I grab my pen and notebook. "I'm going to use a computer," I tell him, standing up. "Watch my stuff?"

He nods, and I turn and begin to limp away.

"Allegra?"

I turn to see what he wants. He's scribbling on a pad, but his pen appears to be out of ink. "Have you got a pen I can borrow?"

"Maybe. Try the bottom of my backpack."

"Thanks."

I see him reach for my bag before I turn around.

I spend the rest of the period researching information for my project and trying to put thoughts of Noel out of my mind, but not very successfully. When the bell rings, I head back to the table.

Spencer has packed up his things; he hands me a pen. “This is yours,” he says. “Thanks.” I take it from him and note that he doesn’t look at me.

“See ya later,” he mumbles before turning and practically dashing out of the library.

I wonder, briefly, what has come over him. He usually hovers around, and with my sore ankle I thought he might even offer to carry my backpack for me, but I shrug it off. He must have something on his mind. I toss my pack onto my shoulder and limp off to my history class.

When the lunch bell rings, I suck up all my courage and head toward the music portable, but at the door of the main building, I feel that familiar shortness of breath, and sweat breaks out in my armpits. My chest feels tight. I turn and start walking toward the multipurpose room instead. My breathing returns to normal and my skin dries quickly. I wonder how I’ll ever be able to enter the music portable again.

It’s slow going through the crowded hallways. Every time I get jostled in the crowd, I put too much weight on my ankle and pain shoots up my leg. Eventually,

I take cover at the end of a bank of lockers and wait for the crowd to disperse. Once the traffic becomes lighter, I continue toward the multipurpose room.

I see the girls and Spencer in their usual places. They're huddled together, reading something that Spencer has in his lap. Talia looks up and spots me walking toward them. I see her lips move, and suddenly all their heads jerk to look in my direction. Spencer tucks the sheet of paper he was holding into his pack.

"What's up with you guys?" I ask, sitting down beside Talia and taking an orange and a tub of yogurt from my lunch bag.

She looks directly at me, but the others suddenly become very interested in their own lunches.

I look more carefully at each of them, but they continue to avoid my eyes.

Spencer suddenly grabs his pack and stands up. "I have to be somewhere," he says.

I watch as he leaves. "What's with him?" I feel a sinking sensation in my stomach. I've just been accepted back into their circle, but something is wrong already. "He started acting all weird in the library too," I add, but mostly to myself.

None of them answer my question, but I see Sophie look past me, and her eyes widen.

I turn just as Mr. Rocchelli sits down on the step right below me.

"Hi, girls," he says brightly, looking into each of our faces.

"Hi," we all say in unison. I can feel Talia staring at me, so I focus on peeling my orange and hope my face doesn't give me away.

"Allegra, I've been looking for you all morning," he says. "I wanted to return this." He hands me my flash drive.

I take it hesitantly.

"And to see how your ankle is."

"I'll live," I mumble.

"I guess Allegra told you she had a little accident in the parking lot yesterday," he tells the others.

"No, actually, she didn't," Talia says, still staring at me. I won't meet her eyes.

"Did you get a doctor to check it out?" he asks, ignoring Talia.

I can't look at him. "No, it'll be fine." I hate that my face is crimson, like I have something to be ashamed of. "I have to take a week off from dance, but I'm sure I'll be good to go after that," I say.

"It occurred to me this morning," he continues, "that accidents on the school grounds need to be reported. I'll grab the paperwork from the office and you can fill it in during music theory this afternoon."

I just shrug. As if I'm going to do that. And besides, why would he want it reported that I was here alone at night with him?

"As well, Allegra," he says, "we need to schedule some new sessions in the sound room. Let's not forget to do that this afternoon."

I finally get up the nerve to look at him and find his eyes searching mine, looking for…what?

"Okay," I say.

"Good." His eyes are still glued to mine, as if he's trying to size me up or perhaps tell me more through his gaze. Finally he gets up. "Have a good afternoon, girls," he says and, without looking back, walks away.

My heart thumps. I don't know why he would track me down at lunchtime unless he really wanted to see me. He could just as easily have waited until this afternoon to talk about those things. I peel off a segment of orange and slide it into my mouth.

"When did you have this little accident?" Talia asks.

"Last night." I bite into the orange and enjoy the burst of tangy juice.

"You were here last night? With Mr. Rocchelli?"

"Yeah." I look directly into her eyes. "What's wrong with that? We were supposed to work, but then I twisted my ankle on the way to the portable so I went home instead."

She stares at me. "Have you being doing this a lot? Meeting Mr. Rocchelli at night?"

I don't like the accusatory tone in her voice. "A few times. Our schedules are full. It's the only time we can get together. He often has students come back to work in the evening."

Talia glances at the other girls, but they remain focused on their lunches.

"Were there other students last night?"

"No." *Stay cool*, I tell myself.

"Do you really think it's a good idea, being here alone with him at night?"

I shove my lunch bag back into my pack and stand up. "Look, Talia, I don't like what you're implying, now or yesterday after English."

Her eyes narrow, but she doesn't answer.

With as much dignity as I can muster, I swing my backpack over my shoulder and limp away. I feel all their eyes on my back.

I step into the library and immediately see Spencer, slumped over some books at the same table we were at earlier. Not wanting to return to the multipurpose room or sit alone in the cafeteria, I'm left with no choice. I head outside and cross the short driveway to the music portable. My next class is here anyway. I don't go to the sound room but to a table. There are other students scattered around the room. I sense Noel's presence at his desk, but I don't look at him. Instead, I pull my history textbook out of my pack and turn to chapter 12, "The Reformation." My eyes scan the words, but nothing sinks in. I think about Talia and what she has implied. It ticks me off that she's figured it out, that she knows what I'm feeling.

Well, she may *know*, but she doesn't *understand*. All the girls may think Mr. Rocchelli is hot, but they haven't created music with him like I have. They don't have the chemistry with him that I do. He doesn't relate to them the way he relates to me. We simply have to take it slow, finish the music, get through the remainder of the year and then, once I graduate…I smile to myself, thinking about it.

"What happened to your friends?"

Noel is standing across the table from me, looking down. I squirm, remembering what happened in here last night. His face, however, shows nothing but open friendliness.

"I need to get some reading done, and the library was full." The lies just get easier and easier.

He nods. "I meant to ask, will your mom be able to collect her car?"

"Yeah, no problem." Actually, I have no idea. I'd told her the truth about why I left it at school last night, except that I led her to believe I was meeting a whole group of students here. She said she'd find a way to get over to pick it up. I'd like to think she'll take the bus, but somehow I doubt that.

"I don't want to keep you from your homework," he says, "but now might be a good time for us to compare schedules."

"Sure." I check the calendar on my phone, even though I don't need to. Without dance classes or a social life, my time is wide open.

He grabs a daytimer from his desk. "So," he says, flipping through the pages. "Does Thursday morning before school work for you? And then"—he flips the page—"Friday afternoon, right after school?"

I feel like saying something flippant about the risk of his being alone with me before school, when it's still dark, but I don't. I just enter the times into my calendar. As if I'd forget.

He glances around the room, checking on the other students. "Allegra, I'm really sorry about your ankle." He pauses. "And everything else. I'm glad you're willing to get the project finished."

I meet his eyes for a brief moment, but this time he looks away first. For some reason that pleases me.

"I can use a break from dance."

"Feel free to use the sound room whenever it's available," he says. "And that reminds me, I've got the accident form on my desk." He spins around and strides back across the room. I watch, noting how neatly his plaid shirt tucks into his faded jeans, jeans that look like they were designed specifically for him. His shoulders are broad—the shoulders of a grown man, not a kid. His hips are narrow. My eyes dart away when he turns back in my direction.

Sliding the sheet onto the table in front of me, he says, "I've filled in the parts I can. The rest are personal details that you need to fill in."

I glance at the form and see that he's been completely honest, not giving any more information than is asked for, but not leaving anything out either.

Detailed description of accident: Student at school for an evening music theory meeting. She twisted her ankle in pothole in driveway. Assisted into music portable, then driven home.

Mr. Rocchelli is watching me, head tilted. "Okay?" he asks.

I just nod. The bell rings, and lunch is over.

Sixteen

My fingers slide along the keys on Dad's keyboard, but I don't play the notes. I'm lost in thoughts of Noel and wishing tomorrow would hurry up and get here. I can no longer compose anything without his input. We are so close to taking the piece to its musical peak; after that, there's just the resolution to write.

"Allegra?" Mom calls down the stairs. "Dinner is ready."

As I sit down to a bowl of steaming soup, I realize it's been a few days since we've had the chance to eat together. "So what's new with you?" I ask, blowing on my soup to cool it down.

She smiles, just a little. "Oh, you know, same old. Students in the mornings, work at night. But it's all good."

It's all good? Her marriage is crumbling. Shouldn't she be feeling a little less-than-good about that? I'd love to ask her about Marcus, but I don't dare.

"How about you?" she asks. "How's your ankle?"

"It's not so bad. Black and blue, but I can get around."

"You must be missing your dance classes."

I shrug. "Maybe I needed a little break."

I feel rather than see her glance at me.

"I haven't seen your friends around...not since that night they all came for dinner."

"I have lunch with them, but we're all busy the rest of the time."

She simply nods and then concentrates on her food.

We eat in silence for a few minutes. My thoughts return to Noel. I wonder who he eats dinner with. I remember him saying a few weeks ago that he had a date. It didn't sink in at the time, but now I wonder if he's seeing someone. That thought never occurred to me. I'd just assumed a date meant he was meeting someone or had a rehearsal. Picturing him with a woman...well... I put down my spoon, alarmed, and look up. Mom is studying me.

"A penny for your thoughts," she says, dipping a piece of focaccia bread into some balsamic vinegar and olive oil.

"Nothing, really," I say, but I've suddenly lost my appetite. Maybe being patient and waiting until I graduate to pursue a relationship with him is not such a good idea after all. Anything could happen between now and then.

Mom is still staring at me, so I pick up my spoon and change the subject. "Dad says we're all going to Uncle Dave's for Christmas?"

She looks back down at her food, and her expression changes. "Yeah, I guess," she says, without much enthusiasm.

"Where will Dad stay when he comes home?"

"We haven't talked about that yet."

She doesn't offer anything more, so I decide to drop the subject. We go back to our own thoughts, my mind taking me to all kinds of unpleasant places featuring Noel and beautiful women.

"I'll take the car tonight if you're not using it," Mom says, breaking the long silence. She begins clearing the dishes.

"That's fine; I'm not going anywhere." I wonder some more about Marcus as I carry my dishes to the counter. I haven't seen him or his sports car in a few weeks. "I'll be down in the studio if you need me."

"How's the composition going?" she asks, brightening at the change in subject.

"Not bad."

"Do you need any help?"

"No, no, I'm fine." I feel almost panicky at the thought of her getting involved. This is my project, mine and Noel's. I smile inwardly at his name. I'm getting more used to using Noel rather than Mr. Rocchelli. I hope I don't accidentally slip up at school, although I doubt he'd mind that much. A lot of the kids are actually calling him Rocky.

"Okay." She sounds disappointed.

"I'll let you listen in a few days. We're almost at the end."

"We?"

I realize with a start that I've let it slip again, the fact that I'm not working on it alone. "I've had some help... so we're all good."

"I didn't know this was a group project."

"It's not, but...like I said, I don't need any help."

She just regards me for a moment, then continues filling the dishwasher. I limp down the stairs to the music studio.

I'm pulled out of my daydreams a few hours later by the sound of the doorbell ringing upstairs. I know it's probably just someone canvassing for a charity, but it always unsettles me when someone arrives uninvited at night.

I limp up the stairs and peek out the window. There are no cars parked at the curb. Opening the door just a crack, I find Talia standing there. My heart sinks.

"Hey," I say, opening the door fully. "What's up?"

"Can I come in?" she asks.

"Yeah, I guess." I step aside to let her pass.

She peers down the hall. "Is anyone home?"

"No." I remember what her house looks like and suddenly feel embarrassed at the state of my little home.

"Good." She walks into the kitchen and plants herself in a chair. I lean against the kitchen counter and wait.

"Aren't you going to join me?" she asks, motioning toward another chair.

"It depends."

"On what?"

"On why you're here."

She sighs and looks down at her hands, but she doesn't say anything.

"So, why *are* you here?" I reiterate.

She stays quiet for another moment, then looks up. "That's not very friendly, Allegra."

"Really? Well, the last few conversations I've had with you haven't been very friendly either. Is it my fault if I figure this is going to be another lecture?"

"I haven't lectured you," she says quietly.

"Then why are you here?" I ask again. "You've never dropped in before."

"Because of this." She pulls a crumpled sheet of paper out of the pocket of her jacket. She unfolds it and begins flattening it out on the table. I recognize my own handwriting and then, with a pang, I realize what it is: my list of things I know about Noel. I lurch over and try to snatch it away, but she's faster than me. She grabs it and holds it behind her back. I slump into a chair, realizing the futility of struggling with her to get it. Besides, she's obviously read it already.

"How did you get that?" My heart is slamming against my ribs.

"Spencer found it in your backpack. He was looking for a pen or something."

I remember now how the three girls and Spencer were reading something when I joined them for lunch earlier, and how the paper was quickly tucked away when they saw me approaching. "He shouldn't have snooped. And it's none of your business either." The acute embarrassment of the situation is causing me to snarl, but I can't help myself.

"It is if we're friends."

I glare at her.

"But then again, maybe we're not." She holds up the paper. "Point number three," she says. "*He understands why I can't relate to people my own age*." She looks at me. "Why is that, Allegra? Do you think you're better than the rest of us?"

My face burns, but I don't respond.

She continues reading. "Point number four. *When he looks at me, he really sees me*." She draws out the word *really*. I realize how silly it sounds read this way. "You don't think I see you, Allegra?"

I know she is studying my face, but I look out the window, too mortified to say anything. What else did I write on that stupid page?

"Have you found the answer to your question, Allegra?"

"What question?"

"Point number six. *Is he in love with me too*?"

My mortification turns to fury. Now I do snatch the crumpled sheet away. She doesn't try to hang on to it.

"Well, is he?"

"It's none of your business."

"What *were* you guys doing in that portable, alone, at night?"

I refuse to dignify her question with an answer.

"You've been screwing the hot teacher, haven't you, Allegra?" Her voice is soft, steady.

I'm so mad I decide to let her think what she wants. How would she ever understand the kind of relationship Noel and I have? "If you're about done, Talia, I have homework to do."

Surprise flickers across her face. It wasn't the response she was expecting. "You could get him fired, Allegra. Is that any way to treat someone you supposedly love?"

I walk to the front door and open it. As she passes me in the hallway, she puts her face right up to mine and says, very quietly, "What you're doing—both of you— is wrong."

I just glare at her.

She leaves without another word. I shut the door behind her and slide the deadbolt firmly into place.

In order to get to my early-morning composition session on time, Mom allows me to take the car. She thinks it's another group project that I'm working on, though I didn't actually come right out and say that.

Noel's car is in the lot when I arrive. I pull in beside it, turn off the ignition and just sit. I tossed and turned all night, rehashing the conversation with Talia. It makes me nauseous that the whole group has read that stupid list I made. My heart speeds up again just thinking about it. How am I ever going to face them? When I wasn't rehashing what happened with Talia, I fretted about how this session with Noel will go. I've been so excited to be with him again, but will he want to talk about what happened the other night? I slump into my seat, unable to decide which situation is more embarrassing. Taking a deep breath, I close my eyes and sigh loudly. When I open them again, I see that the sky is starting to get light in the east. I climb out of the car and grab my backpack.

When I enter the portable, Noel is already at work in the sound room. He has the headphones on and his back to the door, so he doesn't hear me approach. I stand in the doorway for a moment, just watching him deep in concentration. There is something intensely beautiful about a person who is totally involved in work that he loves.

Eventually he senses my presence and swivels around to face me. He pulls the headphones off and smiles widely. "Hey. Good morning, Allegra. Ready to get to work?"

The warmth of his smile relaxes me, and the nausea eases. I roll the other chair alongside his and stare into the computer screen. "What are you working on?"

"Listen to this." He clicks the mouse, and the familiar music fills the small room. I listen to a few bars, then smile. He shuts off the music.

"That's perfect, using the string instruments to tie those two passages together. I don't know why we didn't think of that before."

He laughs. "I know. Something so simple...sometimes it eludes us. So, I was thinking, shall we go back to the beginning this morning and try to smooth out the other rough patches?"

"Okay, but I'd say you're actually avoiding the really big problem," I tease.

"Which is?" He cocks his head.

"The ending. Neither of us knows how to tackle that."

"Yeah, I know." He chuckles. "It's easier to edit than compose, especially an ending, which is so important, and so complicated. But how about this for a plan? Our time is limited right now...the other students will be arriving in just over an hour. If we get on a creative roll this morning, we won't want to stop. Let's save the ending for tomorrow's session, after school, when we're not as pressed for time." He frowns. "Or maybe you are? Sorry, I shouldn't assume."

"No, that's a good plan."

For the next hour we concentrate fully on the project. A suggestion from me releases some new idea from him, which, in turn, helps me think of something even better. I get lost in a vortex of creative energy, and everything but the music is forgotten.

Eventually Mr. Rocchelli sits back in his chair and sighs, breaking the spell. He glances through the glass partition to the wall clock in the classroom. "Wow." He takes a deep breath and sighs again. "We accomplished a lot in that one hour."

I glance at the clock, surprised that a full hour has passed. "Yeah, we did."

His eyes scan my face. "So we're all okay then? No bad feelings about the other night?"

"We're okay." I mean it, yet for the first time this morning, I can't meet his eyes.

"You know, Allegra, this process has been really rewarding for me. Usually I write alone, but I find that two brains are not just two times more creative than one but about ten times more creative. It's wonderful how it works."

"Yeah, I know what you mean." Our eyes meet and I feel that deep emotional connection again.

"I'm looking forward to working on the ending tomorrow afternoon."

"Me too." I smile.

With sudden abruptness, he reaches for his flash drive and saves the work. I pull my own out of my backpack.

"Any plans for the weekend?" he asks as I save the work to my drive.

"No, not really," I answer. "What about you?" I think again of the date he referred to once.

"Not much. I have a gig booked this Saturday, which will be fun."

"What's the gig?"

He rolls his chair back, stands, stretches. I follow him out of the sound room. "It's at the legion. Some old guy's birthday party. Not very glamorous, but we get to play music and that's what counts. Now, what your dad does, that sounds glamorous. I have all the Loose Ends' CDs." He turns and smiles at me as he tosses his flash drive into the top drawer of his desk.

"Glamorous? I don't know about that. Dad sounded pretty burned-out last time I talked to him. He thinks he may retire from touring for a while."

"Really?"

A few students have entered the portable. I slip into my jacket. "Yeah...he thinks it's time to spend more time with his family, but I'm afraid it may be too late for that. See you this afternoon, in class."

All day I manage to avoid any contact with Talia and Co., as I've come to think of them, but my luck changes just before I head home. As I walk across the parking lot to my car, I see them waiting there for me.

"Hi," I say, without much warmth. I look from Sophie's face to Molly's, but they both continue to stare at their feet.

"Look," I say quietly, glancing around to make sure no one else is within earshot. "I don't know what Talia has told you, but I'm not doing anything wrong. I meet with Mr. Rocchelli to compose music. That's it."

Talia rolls her eyes. "Yeah, right. That wasn't your story yesterday."

"I never said anything else, Talia. You implied that I was doing something inappropriate, and I didn't deny it because I was so mad, but this is the truth. I haven't done anything wrong."

I turn to Spencer. He looks away. "Spencer, you believe me, don't you?"

He just shrugs.

I grab his arm. "So you're going to believe her over me? I'm telling the truth here."

He jerks his arm free. "I'm the one who found the note in your backpack."

"That was just stupid. I don't know why I wrote those things down." Spencer has shoved his hands into his pockets. "Spencer…you have to believe me."

He looks up and our eyes meet for a moment. Then he looks to Talia, Sophie and Molly. His eyes move back to mine. "I'd like to believe you, Allegra. I really would, but, like, you *have* been avoiding me for some reason. And I've known Talia a lot longer than I've known you."

I just stare at him.

"And you implied that you're in love with him. A teacher."

I want to disappear.

"And we don't like what you're doing, Allegra." Talia practically spits the words out. "There's a waiting list of kids who want to attend this school—talented kids, not sluts who take advantage of young teachers."

A fury is building inside of me. "I am not taking advantage of anyone, Talia! If Mr. Rocchelli likes to spend time with me, it's because we have something in common. We are creating something together. All you guys are creating is another stupid high-school drama over a situation that doesn't even exist. Can you blame me for wanting to spend time with someone more mature?"

Talia's brow springs up and her cheeks color, but she just turns and stomps away. The other three hesitate; Spencer gives me one more glance, and then, without a word, they turn in unison and follow her. Part of me knows I've just blown it, big-time, but the other part of me doesn't care. I have Noel.

Friday is unbearably long as I wait for our after-school music-writing session. I think about how connected we were at yesterday's session…and my imagination starts to create stories about what could happen. Romantic stories. I smile, thinking about them, but then push them out of my head, remembering Talia's accusations. I can't go there. My ankle is already feeling much better, and I decide to speak to Ms. Dekker about at least doing the warm-ups in my dance classes next week. I duck into the office at lunchtime, hoping to find her there. I don't, but I do see Spencer going into Ms. Jennings's office. As Ms. Jennings reaches to close the door behind him, she notices me, and I see a kind of surprised recognition in her face, but I turn and leave without acknowledging her. I haven't had to deal with her since the first week of school, and that suits me just fine.

There are still students lingering in the music portable when I arrive at the end of the day. Noel greets me and suggests I get started in the sound room while he finishes up with them. I pretend to read over my notes while I wait for him, but I am so excited I simply can't concentrate.

Finally he comes in and drops into the other chair. "I thought I'd never get rid of them all," he says with a laugh. I return his smile. I know just what he means.

"So, where are we?" He glances at my notes.

I shut my notebook. "We're going to work on the ending," I remind him.

"Ah yes. The ending. Have you roughed anything out yet?"

"Not really, though I know it has to echo the beginning in some way."

"That's right—echo it, but with a slight variation. A winding-down of all the emotion. Let's listen to the initial bars again and see what we have." He rolls his chair closer to the computer. His arm is only millimeters from mine, and I feel the heat of his skin radiating through his shirt.

Noel takes over the writing process. I'm too aware of him—his scent, the curls of hair at the nape of his neck, the eyetooth that is slightly crooked—to fully concentrate. Occasionally he asks for my opinion and I try to sound intelligent, but I realize I'm not offering much; we're not creating in unison the way we were yesterday. It's more him creating and me watching, absorbing him.

After a long period where I haven't offered anything, he pushes away from the computer. "Let's take a bit of a break," he says. "We could both use a cup of tea, I'm sure."

I follow him into the main classroom and wait while he plugs in the kettle. He sits on the edge of his desk, waiting for the water to boil. I lean against a table, suddenly feeling shy.

"So," he says. "Yesterday morning you made a comment that left me curious."

"I did?"

"Yeah. I know I promised not to pry, but I've been wondering what you meant."

"What did I say?"

"You were referring to your dad, and how he wanted to spend more time with his family. You said you thought it was too late for that."

"Oh, that."

"No need to explain if you don't want to." He drops tea bags into mugs and pours the boiling water over them. Chamomile again.

"No biggie," I explain. "It's just that I'm seventeen, almost eighteen, and I'll be graduating at the end of this year. Who knows where I'll be next year? If he wanted to spend more time with me, he should have done it before now."

Noel passes me a mug. I blow across the top.

"It must have been hard to have your father on the road so much when you were growing up," he says. He blows across his mug too.

I shrug. "I didn't know any different. It was always great when he came home, but I was never used to having him around much, so I didn't expect it. Him being away was my normal."

He nods thoughtfully. "Do you think it was hard for your mom to be a single parent for long stretches?"

"I doubt it. I was a pretty easy kid." I smile.

"I'm sure you were." He smiles back. "But maybe she was lonely for him?"

I feel a sudden rush of understanding. I had never thought about what it was like for her to have him away so much. Maybe that's why things started up with Marcus, not that that is any excuse for having an affair. I slide down into a chair, taken aback by the realization.

"Are you okay?" he asks.

"Yeah." I see the look of concern on his face. "It's just that..." I can't finish the sentence.

I'm trying to regain my sense of balance, but suddenly the room is swirling around me. "My parents...have separated."

Unexpected tears have sprung to my eyes. I don't know where this rush of emotion has come from, and I will it away. This was going to be such a special afternoon. I don't want to ruin it with some stupid outburst.

Noel approaches me and rests his hand on my shoulder. "Hey, I had no idea. I'm so sorry."

The tears have spilled over now. I can feel them running down my cheeks. I shake my head. "No, no. *I'm* sorry. I have no idea why I suddenly got so emotional." I use my palm to wipe the tears away.

Noel goes over to his desk and returns with a box of tissue. I pull a couple out and blow my nose, then wipe my eyes. "Wow. That was bizarre. I was fine about it until now."

He doesn't say anything, just stands there, watching me.

"Maybe it was the music," I say. "It must have triggered something."

"Music has a way of doing that."

I glance at him, wondering if he is implying something else, but he's looking out the window.

We sip our tea and I struggle to compose myself.

"Are you back to dance yet?" Noel asks gently, changing the subject.

"Just a bit. Mostly stretching."

"I'm glad to hear it. And what about your friends? Have you sorted that all out?"

The mention of my friends makes the tears well up again. I think about my last encounter with them. I shrug and clear my throat, struggling to remain composed. "Not so much."

The room becomes quiet. I think I hear the scraping of shoes on the gravel outside, but when I look out the window, no one is there.

"Are you sure you're okay?" he asks, taking my mug from me. "We should get back to work."

"Yeah yeah. I'll be fine," I say, but my voice wobbles.

He hesitates, then places both mugs on the table and pulls me into a hug. "I'm sorry about your parents, Allegra." After a moment he releases me, but his hands remain on my shoulders and he looks into my face. "Friends, right?"

I smile, feeling better and knowing it's much more than that, but I'll go along with it for now. "Right."

A sudden rap on the door makes us both jump. It swings open and Ms. Jennings steps into the portable. "Mr. Rocchelli," she says. "You're wanted in the principal's office. Now. Allegra, collect your things and go home. Immediately."

Noel and I glance at each other. "What's up?" he asks, frowning. He doesn't move.

"We'll discuss that in the office."

"Allegra and I are working on a project. Can we schedule this meeting for another time?"

"No."

A look of annoyance crosses Noel's face. "Okay. Allegra, let's save our work, and we'll reschedule for next week. Feel free to work on it over the weekend."

We return to the sound room. I collect my bag and jacket while he saves our work to both of our flash drives. Tension radiates through his stiff shoulders, but I only feel a huge sense of disappointment. When we come out of the sound room, Ms. Jennings is still standing at the door, arms crossed, a scowl on her face.

"Have a good weekend," I say to Noel as I pass her in the doorway. I don't say anything to her.

Seventeen

Music theory is my first class on Monday morning. I arrive early, hoping to ask Noel what happened after I left on Friday afternoon. I'd emailed him—all the teachers' email addresses are posted on the school website—but he hadn't responded.

When I enter the portable, I find the principal, Mr. Carter, and a stranger talking quietly beside Noel's desk.

"Hi," I say, heading to the sound room.

They both regard me seriously. "Are you Allegra Whitford?" Mr. Carter asks.

"Yeah." I turn to face the two of them. Something is clearly wrong. Has Noel been in an accident?

"This is Mr. Rae," the principal says, nodding toward the stranger. "He's a teacher on call, and he will be replacing Mr. Rocchelli."

I feel like I've been kicked in the gut. "What happened to No…Mr. Rocchelli? Is he okay?"

Mr. Carter gives me a sharp look, and I know he's registered the fact that I almost called Mr. Rocchelli by his first name. "You and I will discuss that in a few minutes," he says. "Right now I just want to stay and introduce Mr. Rae to the rest of the class."

He and I will discuss it? Something bad must have happened. I feel the blood drain from my face and I take a chair, feeling numb. Has Noel asked Mr. Carter to break the news to me himself, maybe because he knows how much I'll worry? The possibilities are frightening.

The other students trickle in. I see Spencer come into the room, but he doesn't acknowledge me. When everyone has arrived and is seated, Mr. Carter clears his throat and begins. "Mr. Rocchelli will not be returning to teach for an undetermined amount of time." There is a rumble of voices as the news settles over the class. "I cannot discuss the situation," Mr. Carter continues, "but I do want you to welcome Mr. Rae and treat him with the same courtesy and respect that we give all our teachers at Deer Lake. I know it will take some time for him to get up to speed on where you are at in your studies, but I ask that you be patient and help him get to know you and what you are working on. It's not easy to step into a classroom, especially at our school, in the middle of a semester."

Julia raises her hand. "Why can't you discuss what happened to Mr. Rocchelli?"

"It's a personal situation, Julia. Any other questions?"

The class sits in stunned silence. Mr. Rocchelli is well liked by all his students, and everyone will be worried about him until they get some answers.

"Okay then," he says. "I'll leave and let Mr. Rae get started. Allegra, would you come with me, please?"

In that instant, I see Spencer's head swivel around to look at me. His eyes are flat. I can't read his expression.

I grab my bag and follow Mr. Carter out of the portable and across the pavement to the school. He holds the door open for me, then leads the way down the hall to the school office. When we enter the room, Ms. Jennings gets up from her chair. She follows us into the principal's office. Clearly, she was invited to this meeting and was just waiting for us. He shuts the door and asks me take a seat. Ms. Jennings sits as well.

I glance at Ms. Jennings, but she doesn't acknowledge me.

"Allegra, I will get right to the point. Another student has reported to Ms. Jennings that you are involved in an inappropriate relationship with Mr. Rocchelli. A second student has confirmed the allegation."

For the second time in just minutes, the blood drains from my face.

"This is a very serious allegation," he continues. "What do you have to say about it?"

Shock is turning to anger. "I am NOT having an inappropriate relationship with anyone," I tell them.

"Mr. Rocchelli and I are writing some music together. That's it."

"I was told that you confessed to having a relationship."

"I did not confess anything!" Damn Talia anyway. "Talia accused me of it, and I was so mad she'd even think such a thing that I didn't answer her. That was all."

He regards me for a moment. My palms are sweating, but I won't allow myself to fall apart right now. Noel is counting on me to set the record straight. "Ms. Jennings saw Mr. Rocchelli embracing you in the portable on Friday afternoon."

I turn to look at her. "Through the window," she says quietly.

"That was not an *embrace*," I say, spitting out the words. "It was a hug. I'd just shared some sad news with him and he was giving me a friendly hug. Is that not allowed?"

"No, Allegra, it's not. It's too easy for a hug to be misconstrued as something else. Mr. Rocchelli knows the rules."

I just roll my eyes.

"As well, it has come to my attention that you have been meeting him in the portable at night. Were there any other students with you at these sessions?"

Talia and her big mouth. "No," I say quietly. "Because no one else was writing the music with us. It was my project."

"You can't see how this is inappropriate behavior, Allegra? For a young male teacher to be meeting his student, alone, at night?"

"No, I can't see how it's inappropriate. He teaches all day and I have a busy dance schedule. We meet whenever we can squeeze in the time."

"Are you sure you're not just denying these allegations to protect Mr. Rocchelli, Allegra?" Ms. Jennings's voice is low.

"No, I am not." Tears spring to my eyes.

"That looked like a pretty intimate hug to me."

"It was a friendly hug, nothing more."

"What was the news that you shared with him?"

"It's none of your business."

"I think it is. This is a very serious situation, and we need to gather all relevant information."

I stare at her, wondering again why such an insensitive woman is working at a school where the students are supposed to dig deep to create their art. She has no idea about passion.

"Allegra?" Mr. Carter says. "It's important that you tell us everything."

I look first at him, then her. "My parents have separated."

A momentary look of concern crosses her face before she goes back to looking cranky. "We'll be calling your parents, Allegra. They will be asked to verify this information."

"You don't believe me about that either?"

"That's not what I'm saying."

"That's exactly what you're saying."

"Allegra," Mr. Carter says, breaking in like a referee. "I'm sorry. This is clearly very difficult for everyone. But here are the facts. A student came to us with some information about you and Mr. Rocchelli. Another student confirmed that information with evidence that supposedly came directly from you. Ms. Jennings saw the two of you hugging when there was no one else in the room. I have no choice but to launch an investigation into this matter. If there is enough evidence, then charges will be laid against Mr. Rocchelli. I would hope that we will have your total cooperation."

Charges will be laid. The words repeat themselves over and over in my head as the enormity of the situation begins to sink in.

"In the meantime, Mr. Rocchelli has been suspended until the investigation is complete."

My heart slams. I breathe deeply, trying to fight the nausea and dizziness, but it's too late. Black spots appear in the air around me.

"Allegra?"

I hear Mr. Carter's voice, but I can no longer see him across the desk. The last thing I remember is noticing how cool the floor is as my cheek makes contact with it.

Mom picks me up from school and we drive home in silence. My cheek is bruised, but the only other injury from my fainting was to my dignity. Ms. Jennings had helped me to the medical room, where I lay on the cot until Mom arrived. I have no idea what they told her.

At home, I head straight to my room and bury myself under my blankets. A short time later, I hear my mom enter my room, and I can smell the tea she places on my desk.

"We need to talk, Allegra," she says from the foot of my bed.

"I didn't do anything wrong!" I say, my voice muffled by the blankets that are pulled over my head.

I feel her tug at the blankets. "Okay, then that's what we'll talk about."

I don't respond; instead, I begin to think of ways I could end this agony. Running away, maybe joining Dad on tour, seems like the only option.

Mom sits down on the end of my bed. "Did Mr. Rocchelli behave inappropriately with you?"

"No!" I sit up with a lurch and smack the bed with my fist.

"Okay, okay," she says. "I believe you." She places a hand on my knee. "So why, then, does the school think something happened?" she asks gently.

That whole misunderstanding with Talia and the hug that Ms. Jennings witnessed...it all feels way too complicated to explain. "I don't know!" It comes out in a kind of wail.

"You must have an idea, Allegra. These kinds of allegations don't come out of nowhere."

We sit in silence for a long moment. Then she says, "They asked me if your dad and I had separated. What does that have to do with this situation?"

"What did you tell them?" I freeze, knowing her answer is crucial to my credibility.

She sighs. "I told them yes, for now we are living separately, but that we are trying to sort things out."

A trace of relief runs through me. At least they'll know I wasn't lying about that.

After a few more minutes, I'm finally ready to explain; I know I'm going to have to get this over with some-time. Taking a deep breath, I let it out. "Noel and I were composing a piece of music together. We often worked alone in the music portable, but nothing inappropriate ever happened." There.

Feeling slightly better, I pick up the mug of tea she's brought, thinking of the chamomile tea that I drank with Noel.

"Noel? You call him by his first name?"

"He asked me to call him that because we were more like collaborators than student and teacher when we were writing."

Her eyes widen. "Are you serious?"

"Yes! What's wrong with that?" Anger surges through me again.

"This is the music-theory assignment we talked about."

"Uh-huh."

She thinks about it. "Okay. I believe you, of course. But why don't the others?"

I'm not sure that she really does believe me, but I explain about the night I twisted my ankle, about how Talia accused me of having sex with Noel and how I was too pissed off at her to even deny it. I told her about the hug in the portable and how innocent it was. What I don't tell her about are my feelings for Noel and how I think maybe he feels the same for me. I don't need to, because the thing is, we didn't do anything wrong.

We didn't, I suddenly think, lying back on my pillow. But *I* did. I didn't deny Talia's accusations. If I'd only told her the truth from the start, this would never have happened, Noel would still be teaching, and the two of us would still be writing music together.

Dad arrives on Wednesday afternoon and knocks on the door to my room, which I haven't left since Monday afternoon except to use the bathroom. After getting the call from the school, Mom had contacted him, and he immediately arranged to come home for a few days. "Hey, Legs," he says as he steps inside, a sad smile on his face. "I hear there's been some trouble."

Obviously Mom has filled him in. Despite my best intentions, I feel yet another onslaught of tears threatening to overcome me.

"Oh, honey," he says, picking up one of my hands. "We'll sort this all out."

I don't know what to say, so I simply melt into his shoulder. "It's all my fault," I sob. "I should have told Talia the truth, and none of this would have happened."

After some time, Dad sighs and clears his throat. I pull myself away. "It's funny," he says, wiping a tear off my cheek. "I feel like it's all *my* fault. If I'd been here to work on the composition with you, maybe none of this would have happened. And your mom feels like it's all her fault, that she should have been paying closer attention to what was going on in your life."

"And Noel probably feels like it's all his fault, for being so enthusiastic about our music," I add.

Dad lifts my chin and looks into my eyes. "Maybe we are all a little bit to blame, or maybe none of us are." He shrugs. "But whatever," he adds. "Like I said, we're going to sort it all out."

The weeks pass slowly. I don't return to school, and no one seems to expect me to. I can't bring myself to dance or play the piano. Dad has left the tour and moved back in; he sleeps on the couch in the music studio. I hear him and Mom talking late at night. Mom continues to work, and Dad stays home with me. He tries to give me space by spending a lot of time in the studio, but I know he's also keeping a close eye on me.

I spend my days reading, stretching and watching mindless TV. I did chat online with Angela, but when she told me that the situation between me and Noel was all over Facebook, I decided to stay completely away from the computer, too.

A police officer came to question me one night, but I haven't heard anything else about the investigation. Mom and Dad have hired a lawyer, just in case I need one, who spent an evening asking me questions, but he didn't give us any indication of what will happen next. I could tell by his questions that he thought it was inappropriate for Noel to be spending time alone with me.

Mom only made one more attempt to talk to me about it. We were alone, making dinner together. Out of the blue, she said, "It never occurred to you, honey, that it might have been wrong for Mr. Rocchelli to work alone with you, especially at night?"

I just narrowed my eyes and replied, "You never thought it might have been wrong for Marcus to be here, alone with you, in the middle of the night?"

That shut her up.

Living in limbo, not knowing what's going to happen next, is killing me, and not an hour goes by that I don't think of Noel and wonder how he is doing. Does he hate me for what has happened?

Christmas comes. Dad, Mom and I end up staying home. Mom makes a turkey dinner; they both give me some gifts, but the day is anything but festive. I sleep a lot. When I'm not sleeping, I'm thinking about Noel.

These are the darkest, shortest days of the year. It's harder and harder to get out of bed. I've never felt so helpless.

At the start of January, we receive a letter asking us to appear at an information-gathering meeting at the police station on January 10. Suddenly I go from constantly sleeping to not sleeping at all. I toss and turn at night, wondering what will happen at this meeting. I try to mentally prepare myself. It's imperative that I remain calm. For Noel's sake, I have to convince the authorities that nothing inappropriate ever happened.

Eighteen

Finally the day arrives. We gather around a table in a small room at the police station: my parents, my lawyer, Mr. Carter, Noel, his lawyer and Officer O'Neil.

"So." Officer O'Neil takes a moment to look at each of us. "This was to be an information-gathering meeting only," he says, "but I now understand that Mr. Noel Rocchelli has a statement to make that may change how we proceed. Mr. Rocchelli, what is it you wish to say?"

Everyone's focus turns to Noel. His gaze is on the table. I notice how pale he is, and how there are now dark circles under his eyes. He takes a deep breath and lets it out slowly. "As you all know, Allegra and I were writing a piece of music together. It started out as an assignment for her, but I very quickly discovered the talent she had for composing, and despite myself, I found I couldn't resist working on it with her."

Breathe, Allegra, breathe…

"Because I became so caught up in the composition," he continues, "and even had hopes of getting it published and performed, I admit I lost my objectivity regarding my relationship with a student."

He pauses here, and I feel everyone lean forward, myself included, anxious to hear where he is going with this. Is he going to admit his feelings for me in front of these people?

"As both of us have said, there was no inappropriate behavior between us, except for one hug, the kind of hug you give a friend when you can see the friend needs one. However, upon reflection, I now understand that I should have remained in my role as teacher, not friend, with Allegra. It was a grave error in my own judgment."

A grave error? How could he help his feelings for me? I slump back in my chair.

Noel glances at me before he continues. "The reason I am a music teacher," he says, "is because of my great passion for music, and for composing music in particular. Allegra has a rare talent for composition. When we worked together, I would forget she was a seventeen-year-old high-school student. In some ways, working with her was like working with a colleague, a fellow musician. That is probably why I lost perspective in my relationship with her."

I feel everyone's gaze turn to me. I just stare at the table.

At this point Mr. Rocchelli leans back in his chair and takes a deep breath. The room is completely still. It is clear that he has not finished what he wants to say. I hold my breath.

He continues, and his voice becomes wobbly. "I have cherished my work as teacher at Deer Lake High, but as you all know, the outpouring of rumors, speculation and outright lies that has been humming on the social network sites since mid-November has been overwhelming." He pauses to rub his face with his hands. "Even if I am cleared of any wrongdoing," he continues, "it would be very hard, if not impossible, to resume teaching under that cloud."

The truth of what he is saying hits me like a punch to the stomach.

"Allegra," he says, "you have done nothing to cause this situation. You need to know that. I was the one who should have been more professional. I do not in any way hold you responsible for what I have to do."

I look up and meet his eyes. There is only sorrow there. I brush away tears.

"Even though it may look like an admission of guilt," he continues, "I have submitted my notice of resignation from the Lakeview School District, effective immediately."

The room remains completely still. Shock has paralyzed me. He is dead wrong. This is completely my fault.

All I had to do was tell Talia that she was wrong, that nothing had happened between us, and we wouldn't be here.

Officer O'Neil taps his pencil on his pad of paper. He turns to Mr. Carter. "Well," he says, sighing. "Here's what I recommend then. Given that Mr. Rocchelli has resigned from teaching, and given that there isn't any conclusive evidence that anything truly inappropriate happened between Allegra and Mr. Rocchelli, I am going to recommend that we not proceed with the investigation."

Mr. Carter nods solemnly. "I'm terribly sorry that things ever got this far and that Deer Lake High is losing a fine teacher, but I have to agree with Mr. Rocchelli: it would be impossible for him to return to his teaching duties. As far as any charges are concerned, I agree that they should be dropped."

Dad slides his arm around my shoulders and pulls me toward him. I don't look up, but I hear the legs on Mr. Rocchelli's chair scrape the floor as he rises. A moment later I sense him standing behind us.

"Mr. and Mrs. Whitford," he says, his voice thick with emotion. I don't move, but my parents turn to look up at him. "I apologize for any pain I have caused you and Allegra."

Neither of them responds.

"You have an extraordinarily talented daughter. I wish her well in the future."

Our eyes meet for a brief moment, but there's a universe of unspoken words in that moment.

Mr. Rocchelli turns and leaves the room.

An impossible heaviness floods through my body as the truth of what just happened sinks in. I have single-handedly destroyed the man's career. The man I love.

I wish I were dead.

Without Noel, without the music, there is no reason to get out of bed. Dancing is pointless; it's hard enough to get up to go to the bathroom, which I don't have to do often because swallowing food or water has become almost impossible.

I'm aware of my parents tiptoeing into my room, bringing herbal tea and my favorite foods, but I can't bring myself to eat. I'm also aware of them sitting on my bed, stroking my hair, talking gently, but I don't hear what they say. I just want them to go away so I can fall back to sleep, that blissful place where I don't have to feel anything.

Days pass, possibly weeks; I have no idea.

"Enough's enough already, Allegra."

I'm jolted from the fog by a flash of sunlight. Mom is pulling open my blinds and pushing open the window.

A blast of cold air swooshes through the room. I note, numbly, that it must be morning, given the direction of the sun. How many mornings have passed since that awful day at the police station? As another wave of remorse washes over me, I pull my covers back over my head, blocking out the sunlight. Instantly they're yanked off.

"You've got to get out of bed and have a shower," Mom says firmly. "We've given you your space, but now it's time to get on with life."

Get on with life? Right. How do I do that when I've ruined Noel's? For the hundredth time, I wonder what he is doing. Is he missing me the way I'm missing him?

Dad is standing in the doorway. He looks sad. "Your mom's right, Legs," he says quietly. "It is time to get going again."

A surge of annoyance rises up in me, but I decide it would require more effort to fight with them than to get up. Slowly, stiffly, I pull myself out of bed and walk across the hall to the bathroom. Glancing in the mirror, I note the long coils of greasy hair that fall over my shoulders. My skin, usually clear, is covered in angry-looking pimples. I shrug, and my housecoat falls to the floor, revealing a much skinnier version of the old me. Stepping into the shower, I let the water pummel my head, hoping to clear the fog, but nothing changes. I go through the motions of washing my hair and my body, but the effort of it exhausts me, and when I'm done it's all I can do to get back into my robe, stumble across the hall and climb back under the covers. Dad is the first to appear at the door. I open my eyes long enough to see him standing there, but sleep quickly returns to spare me from any conversation.

More days and nights pass. Once a day Mom airs out my room and bullies me into the shower, but that's as far as she can get me to go. A family friend, a doctor, pays me a visit, and I answer her questions to the best of my ability, but all I want is for her, too, to leave me alone. She mumbles something about the hospital, but I don't understand what she is saying. I notice that Mom is putting some pills on my tongue and waiting to see that I swallow them before she leaves me with my meals, which I barely touch. Each time I drift off, I hope to stay asleep, forever.

I awake slowly, vaguely aware of piano music floating up from the studio below. I waft between sleep and wakefulness until I notice that the fog feels like it has lifted somewhat. I lounge under the quilt, surprised at the tingling sensation in my limbs, wondering at the sudden urge to climb out of bed, to stretch.

With a jolt I sit up, fully awake, as I realize what the music is. The sudden change in position brings a wave of dizziness, but as soon as it passes I pull on my housecoat and stumble down the hall. I pull open the door to the basement studio. Dad is at the keyboard, and he turns sharply when he hears me there.

"Legs!" He jumps up and grabs my arm, helping me down the stairs. He gently guides me over to the couch, and I sit down. He settles in beside me.

"What were you just playing?" I whisper.

His cheeks redden as he looks down at his hands, folded in his lap. "I'm sorry, Allegra. I know I shouldn't have snooped, but I found your flash drive in your backpack and I listened to your composition."

My whole body clenches. "You shouldn't have listened to it." I hear my own voice, thick and raw. I don't know why I'm so angry, but I am. Maybe because it's all I have left of Noel…the music, so intimate, so private.

"I know it was wrong." Dad looks mortified. "But I listened to it over and over again. I've been so worried about you. I wanted to figure out how to help. The music…it is…" He stops, unable to find the words. "It is…simply breathtaking," he says finally. Now he looks directly at me. "I think I understand…" His voice trails off.

"Understand what?" I whisper. Can it be? Could he possibly understand? I feel the first trace of hope I've experienced in days.

"I…I think I understand the power that this music has had over you, because it is so…so intense. I can imagine the rush you would have experienced while composing it, and how…well, how it would bring you very close to the person you are writing it with."

Something snaps inside my chest, possibly my heart. Relief floods through me. To know that, on some level, he gets it…it is exactly what I needed to hear. It is a flicker of light at the end of a very long, completely dark tunnel. I throw my arms around him and sob into his shoulder. It feels like a whole ocean of tears pours out of me, but the release feels overwhelmingly good.

"I ruined his career," I sniffle. "His life."

"No, honey. That's not what happened."

"Then what did happen?"

He just holds me close. After a long while he lets out a deep sigh, but he doesn't say anything.

Eventually I pull away. "You were playing it on the keyboard."

"Yes." He wipes a tear off my cheek. "I've listened to it so many times now that I know it by heart. When I sat down at the keys…well, it just started playing itself."

We sit in silence for a while as a new realization begins to dawn. Part of me wants to climb back up those stairs, bury myself in my blankets and escape the pain, but a new part of me wants to stay right here, in this moment, with my dad, who understands. The pain is not so bad when someone else gets it. Part of me even wants to embrace the pain and remember those magical moments of composing, when the surge of music swept through us, intangible until the notes were on the page and then brought to life through the combination of instruments.

"Do you think you're ready to listen to it?" Dad asks gently.

I nod.

He gets up and inserts the flash drive into the computer. Then he sinks back down onto the couch and takes my hand. The beginning notes of the music fill the room, and I close my eyes and simply let it sweep me away.

For six full minutes, the numbness of the past few weeks completely disappears as I soar with the music, feeling intensely all the moods it evokes. Feeling something other than remorse and shame. Feeling alive.

And then it ends, abruptly, and my eyes snap open as I remember. We never finished the music.

Dad's gaze is already on me as I turn to look at him. I'm getting choked up again. "It is beautiful, isn't it?" I say.

He pulls me into a hug. "Yes, Legs, it is."

"It really is," says a voice at the top of the stairs.

I look up. Mom is sitting on the top step. Her eyes are glassy with tears too. "Allegra, you've created an extraordinary piece of music."

"Not just me." I feel a wail coming on. "Noel and I created it together." Another onslaught of tears overcomes me, but in that moment I know what I have to do: I have to complete the music and hear it performed.

Dad holds me close. Behind me, I feel my mom lower herself onto the couch and she, too, wraps her arms around me, enveloping me between them. I cry for a long time, but we sit in a quiet embrace for a much longer time.

Nineteen

"No, not a trumpet. Try the French horn," Mom suggests.

Dad finds the icon for the French horn, and we listen to the new track.

"That's perfect!" Mom says.

Dad and I look at each other. "Well?" he asks.

"I think so too," I say. "Play it back again."

We sit together and listen to the section. "Good call, Cindy," Dad says enthusiastically. "Clearly Allegra inherited her talent for composing from you." He saves the new track.

"Don't be silly," Mom says modestly, but I notice the look they exchange before Mom smiles, almost shyly, and looks away.

It's become a family project: Mom, Dad and me finishing *Allegra*, which is now the composition's official name, despite my objections. We don't have too many hours in a week to work on it because I'm finishing grade twelve through online education, Mom has her students and her performances, and Dad's picking up a lot of gigs in town as a solo artist. But when we can, we meet in the studio and create. Unexpectedly, I've discovered that creative energy is unleashed when I'm working with my parents, just as it was when I wrote with Noel. Mom has her classical training to offer, Dad his beautiful songwriting experience, and I have the passion and commitment to see this thing through. It can be unwieldy with three of us brainstorming, but for the most part it works.

Working on it is also a constant reminder of Noel, though I don't need any help remembering him. But on the flip side, working on the music seems to be just the therapy my parents needed. Dad has moved from the studio back into the bedroom with Mom. It could be because the studio is a busy place these days and his makeshift bed is in the way, but whatever it is, I'm feeling hopeful for them. They've also purchased a second car, so there always seems to be one available for each of us when we need it.

The expectations of online courses seem twice as high as regular school, and completing the assignments fills my days. I'm also back at Turning Pointe and putting in more hours there than ever. I take workshops from guest teachers who come from all over: New York, Los Angeles and even London, England. Like Ms. Dekker from Deer Lake High, these teachers push me to my edge. A well-known dancer/instructor from Seattle has suggested that I contact her when I finish high school. She thinks her own agent may be willing to represent me. That gives me the incentive to dance until I think I'll literally drop. Physical pain seems to ease the mental pain I live with daily—the guilt of causing Noel to lose his job—although there are still days when it's almost impossible to get out of bed, thinking about my role in that. And God, how I miss him.

It's not quite summer, but the weather is stifling hot. I can't sleep, so I'm in the studio, tinkering with the music. We've finished it, but I'm still finding the odd rough patch. Mom has offered to get the score copyrighted, and she also has a meeting with the conductor of the Deer Lake Symphony Orchestra to see if he'd be willing to have the orchestra perform it sometime soon.

The upstairs door creaks opens and Dad comes down the stairs.

"You're up late, Legs," he says.

"Too hot to sleep. How was your gig tonight?"

"Fun, actually."

I look up at him. There's an expression on his face that I can't read. "That's good."

He picks up a guitar, settles himself on the couch and plays a little tune. "I was playing at the legion, for an event."

"*You* were playing at the legion?" I remember Noel telling me he played for a function there. I can't believe Dad agreed to it. He was a member of the Loose Ends, after all. He can do a lot better than that.

"It was work. And very little stress. I enjoyed it."

"Huh." What else can I say?

He plays a few more bars of a song. "I ran into a friend of yours tonight," he says.

A friend? I only have Angela. "I thought you had to be of legal drinking age to hang out at the legion."

"This friend is legal," he says. "And a fine musician."

I go completely still as I comprehend what he is telling me. Dad waits for my reaction. I can only stare at him, dumbfounded.

"I didn't actually run into him," he says. "I played with his band. I was filling in for an absent bass player."

I just continue to stare.

"I didn't know he was in the band when I accepted the gig," he adds quietly.

I still can't think of anything to say.

"He's a nice guy, honey. I can see why you got on so well."

Got on. That's an interesting way of putting it. "Is he okay?" I hear the quiver in my voice.

"He seems fine." He strums the guitar, and I wonder if he's telling the truth. "He asked me for permission to contact you."

"What did you say?" Although I've wanted nothing more than to see him and speak with him, this makes me feel panicky.

"I asked him what he wanted, why he wanted to get in touch with you."

"And?"

"He said he just wanted you to know he was doing well, that leaving teaching was a blessing in disguise because writing and performing music was always his passion, but he didn't have much time for it when he was going to university and then teaching. Now he's managing to scrape by as a working musician, and he also has time to write."

I think about that. He's finally following his dream. "Did you believe him?"

"Absolutely. He looks very happy, and he's an excellent musician."

"He was an excellent teacher too," I tell him.

Dad glances at me but doesn't respond. I watch his face. He plays another riff on his guitar. I can tell he's not finished telling me about Noel.

"I told him I would pass on the message. I also told him that we finished the composition, you, me and your mom."

"You did?"

"Yeah." He nods. "You should have seen his face."

"Was he mad?"

"No, not mad. Surprised, and maybe a little sad."

"Oh." I'm struggling to process this turn of events.

"I actually began to feel badly, because he should be given credit for his part in the writing. Mom didn't put his name on it when she applied for the copyright."

"Can we change that?"

"I think we should."

I continue thinking about all this.

"His band has asked me to play with them again, and I think I will. I also think Noel should sit in with the Loose Ends the next time they're in town. They could use some young blood, and he has the talent to fill in if necessary."

Now I see what Dad is up to. He's trying to set things right. I feel an overwhelming rush of gratitude. I get up and sit beside him on the couch. "Thank you, Dad."

"Oh, Legs, there's nothing to thank me for. Just one musician helping out another."

"He's not just *any* musician."

He thinks about that. "No, he's the musician who helped my daughter discover her talent for composing music."

I rest my head on his arm. "I think I'm retiring from the music-writing business. I feel like it sucked the soul right out of me."

I can feel him nodding. "You certainly did put a lot of yourself into it, and perhaps lost yourself in it too, I'll give you that. And being good at something doesn't necessarily mean that it's the thing you should be doing. We should each choose the career that we want to pursue."

I think about Noel. He may be a good teacher, but he's also a great musician, and writing and performing is what he really wanted to do. In a bizarre kind of way, I helped him realize that dream.

"And the great thing is, Legs, the human spirit, or soul, as you called it, has a wonderful way of regenerating itself."

I smile, realizing how right he is. I close my eyes and listen to him play the opening notes of *Allegra* on his guitar.

It makes me want to dance.

Acknowledgments

Once again I am grateful for the wise feedback from my "first readers" and cheering committee, Diane Tullson and Kim Denman. Huge thanks and hugs to my daughter Cara Lee Hrdlitschka for sharing her passion for dance, musician extraordinaire Geoffrey Kelly for advice on music composition, and my sister Heather Verrier for her continued enthusiasm and support. Finally, a special thank-you to all the wonderful people at Orca Book Publishers for keeping me in the pod.

Shelley Hrdlitschka discovered her love for children's literature as a teacher. This gave her the idea to try writing her own books, and she is now the author of nine novels for teens, all published by Orca Book Publishers. Shelley lives in North Vancouver, British Columbia. When she's not writing she can be found hiking, snowshoeing, practicing yoga, Zumba dancing or volunteering at the Grouse Mountain Refuge for Endangered Wildlife.